Erik Erikson and the American Psyche

PSYCHOLOGICAL ISSUES

Series Editor: Morris N. Eagle

Psychological Issues is a monograph series that was begun by G. S. Klein in the 1950s. The first manuscript was published in 1959. The editors since Klein's death have been Herbert Schlesinger, Stuart Hauser, and currently Morris Eagle.

The mission of Psychological Issues is to publish intellectually challenging and significant manuscripts that are of interest to the psychoanalytic community as well as psychologists, psychiatrists, social workers, students, and interested lay people. Since its inception, a large number of distinguished authors have published their work under the imprimatur of Psychological Issues. These authors include, among many others, Erik Erikson, Merton Gill, Robert Holt, Phillip Holzman, David Rapaport, and Benjamin Rubinstein. Psychological Issues is fortunate in having an equally distinguished Editorial Board consisting of leaders in their field.

Erik Erikson and the American Psyche

Ego, Ethics, and Evolution

Daniel Burston

JASON ARONSON

Lanham • Boulder • New York • Toronto • Plymouth, UK

Published in the United States of America
by Jason Aronson
An imprint of Rowman & Littlefield Publishers, Inc.

A wholly owned subsidiary of
The Rowman & Littlefield Publishing Group, Inc.
4501 Forbes Boulevard, Suite 200, Lanham, Maryland 20706
www.rowmanlittlefield.com

Estover Road
Plymouth PL6 7PY
United Kingdom

British Library Cataloguing in Publication Information Available

Library of Congress Cataloging-in-Publication Data

Burston, Daniel, 1954–
   Erik Erikson and the American psyche : Ego, ethics, and evolution / Daniel Burston.
   p. cm. — (Psychological issues)
   Includes bibliographical references and index.
   ISBN-13: 978-0-7657-0494-8 (cloth : alk. paper)
   ISBN-10: 0-7657-0494-3 (cloth : alk. paper)
   ISBN-13: 978-0-7657-0495-5 (pbk. : alk. paper)
   ISBN-10: 0-7657-0495-1 (pbk. : alk. paper)
   1. Erikson, Erik H. (Erik Homburger), 1902–1994. 2. Psychoanalysis. I. Title.

  BF109.E7B87 2007
  150.19'5092—dc22
  [B]   2006031976

Printed in the United States of America

♾™ The paper used in this publication meets the minimum requirements of American
National Standard for Information Sciences—Permanence of Paper for Printed Library
Materials, ANSI/NISO Z39.48-1992.

For
Adam, Gavriela, and their children's children's children

[W]e mortals cannot help playing a kind of card game with the lives of our famous men. We all have before us a by now standard series of biographic data. . . . We can only put these data on cards, shuffle them, and spread them out before us to see whether we can discern an order for the particular game we think we know how to play.

Erik Erikson, "On Einstein's Centennary," 1982

Contents

Preface

Though doubtless an odd preoccupation for a nonpractitioner, the fact remains that I have been studying the history of psychoanalysis my entire adult life. I encountered Erik Erikson for the first time in 1975, when I was but twenty years old and debating which university to attend. At the time, I was coming to the end of a turbulent psychosocial moratorium, gearing up for a more adult existence, and Erikson's concept of the adolescent identity crisis had enormous resonance for me. Though keen to commence my studies, I was also what Erikson called an "old soul"—wary, weary, and deeply disenchanted with the hypocrisy of both the "establishment" and the rapidly waning "counterculture," searching for an identity and work role either between or somehow outside them both. Being inclined toward pessimism at the time, I was deeply moved by the spirit of sympathy, tolerance, and hopefulness in his work, and the expressive artistry of his style. At a time when so many popular writers and intellectuals oozed with anger and despair, Erikson gave me hope about my prospects for developing a viable identity in the not-too-distant future: for "growing up" without "selling out." Here, I thought, is a member of the establishment who understands; a real mensch.

At the same time, as it happens, I was also deeply immersed in the work of Erich Fromm and R. D. Laing, and I became intrigued with the relationship of psychoanalysis to social and political theory. I therefore majored in political science at York University near Toronto, where I studied with Paul Roazen, whose book *Freud and His Followers* influenced me deeply (Roazen 1971). Then, as now, I was ambivalent about ego psychology, with which Erikson is still intimately associated in most people's minds. So, much as I admired him, I put Erikson aside to focus on Freud, Jung, Fromm, and Laing, who were the subjects of most of my first three books (Burston 1991, 1996, 2000) .

Nevertheless, one way or another Erikson kept popping up, seemingly demanding more sustained reflection. For example, in 1990, while preparing my dissertation for publication, I appended a brief mention of Erikson's theory of generativity and intergenerational identification to *The Legacy of Erich Fromm* (Burston 1991, p. 128). I thought—and indeed still think—that Erikson's epigenetic perspective and his critique of contemporary culture account well for our collective obsession with and simultaneous neglect of youth. And as my book on Fromm went to press, my wife began researching psychoanalytic theories of gender, lingering at length on Erikson's notion of "inner space" and the harsh feminist critique it elicited. Though her thoughtful reflections on this score were, sadly, not published, they rekindled my interest in Erikson's work.

Later that same year, Roazen kindly invited me to his home in Toronto, where I met Lawrence Friedman and learned about his monumental work-in-progress, which eventually appeared as *Identity's Architect: A Biography of Erik Erikson* (Friedman 1999). Shortly after that, I left Toronto to teach at Duquesne University in Pittsburgh, where I currently live and work. My research priorities at the time still precluded taking Erikson on in a serious or systematic fashion, but he was never far from my thoughts. In conversation with graduate students at Duquesne, for example, it dawned on me that Laing, like Erikson, was much taken with the "inner space," though Laing did not think of it in specifically feminine terms. For a variety of reasons, these reflections were not included in *The Wing of Madness: The Life and Work of R. D. Laing* (Burston 1996), though I did devote two pages to contrasting the discussion of intergenerational factors in psychosis in Erikson and Laing (pp. 217–218), to demonstrate how a theorist's upbringing and formative life experience influences his (or her) theories of development and psychopathology.

Of course, emphasizing the formative impact of childhood experience is nothing new in analytic circles, and one of Erikson's outstanding accomplishments is that he stretched our psychosocial perspectives well beyond childhood, and to underscore the impact of intergenerational identification (and its absence) in fostering or eroding our mental health at *all* points in the human life cycle (Erikson 1964b). So despite Erikson's tendency to exaggerate his fidelity to Freud and to obscure his debts to others who left the fold (Roazen 1976, 2000c), I found that as I delved into his life and work, I was intrigued by and in some ways sympathetic to his steadfast determination to keep faith with Freud and to avoid creating yet another schism in the psychoanalytic movement. Moreover, and perhaps more importantly, after a year of research and reflection, during my second stint as an Erikson Fellow at Austen Riggs in 2000, it finally dawned on me that contrary to popular misconception, Erikson was *not* an atypical ego psychologist, as some of his critics and expositors have claimed. Despite his warm praise for Heinz Hartmann, David Rapaport, and Robert White, Erikson really *wasn't an ego psychologist at all*. In fact, in probing his work deeply one finds that Erikson is impossible to pigeonhole. For that very reason I am quite severe with him at times, but I never lose sight of his humanity and good intentions, and I hope that fact registers clearly throughout.

Acknowledgments

This book took many years to write, and many people gave me material, intellectual, technical, and emotional support that contributed to its eventual completion. In thanking them, however, I hasten to add that many of them disagree with some of the opinions expressed here—some quite emphatically—so that ultimate responsibility for this monograph is entirely my own.

First, my deep thanks to the late Dr. Paul Roazen, who taught me so much about the history of psychoanalysis, and invited me into his home to meet Erikson's biographer, Lawrence Friedman, in Toronto in the summer of 1990. Next, warm thanks to Dr. Edward Shapiro, Dr. John Muller and Dr. Gerrard Fromm of the Erik Erikson Institute at the Austen Riggs Center in Stockbridge, Massachusetts, who granted me two Erik Erikson Fellowships, in the summers of 1999 and 2000, enabling me to use their wonderful library, interview many of their staff, and "test run" my evolving ideas about *Young Man Luther* and some of the striking convergences between Erikson's and Charles Rycroft's ideas on intergenerational issues.

Warm thanks are also due to Dr. James Lennox, former director of the Center for Philosophy of Science at the University of Pittsburgh, who taught me a thing or two about evolutionary theory, gave me a comfy office and secretarial support during my sabbatical in 2000, and provided ample opportunity for me to share my work in progress with congenial scholars from a multitude of countries and disciplines. Among the scholars at the Center for Philosophy of Science are Professor Adolf Grünbaum and Professor Peter Machamer, who responded vigorously to my talks and presentations there, and read earlier drafts of this monograph.

Next I wish to thank Dr. George Makari, director of the Institute for the History of Psychiatry at Cornell University Medical Center for reading and commenting on the manuscript, and Dr. Nathan Kravis, Dr. Doris Nagel-Baker, Professor Louis Sass, Dr. Joseph Reppen and Mr. Peter Swales for their generous reception of my "work-in-progress" seminar there in 2002. Also, sincere thanks to Dr. Stanton Marlan and Dr. Brian Skea of the C. G. Jung Analyst Training Program of Pittsburgh, who let me instruct (and learn from) their analytic candidates in connection with Erikson and Joseph Wheelwright, and to Dr. Marta Bachino for her help as my research assistant in 2001.

Thanks also to Dr. John Murray and the late Dr. Michael Weber of Duquesne University, who awarded me a Presidential Writing Grant to see this project to completion. And thanks to Father Michael Slusser, chair of the Theology Department of Duquesne University, for reading a preliminary draft of the psychohistory chapter, and for his illuminating remarks about Martin Luther.

During frequent visits to Toronto in the late 1990s, I had several stimulating conversations with Ruth Columbo about Erikson's approach to ethics; these conversations prompted me to delve deeper into this aspect of his work. While an Erikson Fellow at Austen Riggs, I had the pleasure of speaking with Professor John and Dr. Virginia Demos, whose long-standing friendships with Erikson gave me a unique perspective on him and his work, and with Dr. Paul Lippman, who had the unique privilege of having been supervised by Erik Erikson and Erich Fromm. All these conversations provided a powerful stimulus to thought, so to all of them, my heartfelt thanks. Thanks also to the many people who read and commented on various chapters from a distance, including my old friend and teacher Dr. Morris Eagle; historian Ronald Schechter of the College of William and Mary; Professor C. K. Raju, an Editorial Fellow on the Project of History of Indian Science, Philosophy and Culture at the Centre for Studies in Civilizations in Delhi; Professor Stuart Shanker and Dr. Stanley Greenspan, founders of the Council for Human Development; and authors of countless books and papers about children's mental health. Thanks also to my wife, Dr. Sharna Olfman, whose many efforts on behalf of children and teens in recent years increasingly inform my own work.

1

In Hitler's Shadow

SAGES, PSYCHOANALYSTS, AND THE PUBLIC SPHERE

We live in curious times. Before William James, Sigmund Freud, and Carl Jung, no educated person regarded a specialist in mental disorders as a preceptor to humanity at large. A saint, a sage, a prophet, a great artist, or philosopher might have aspired to that elevated role, and to that kind of hold on posterity—but a psychiatrist or psychologist? The very idea was faintly ridiculous. They might be worthy and dedicated healers, but of what possible relevance could their insights be to *us*?

As the nineteenth century drew to a close, however, it slowly dawned on some people that the malaise experienced by mad and acutely neurotic individuals is different in degree, rather than in kind, from the suffering of relatively normal people who struggle daily with the manifold constraints and injustices of civilized life. Philosophy, art, literature, and drama all contributed to this emergent cultural awareness. Through their palpable fascination with the unconscious, they created the climate of opinion that enabled Freud and Jung to become cultural icons, and for the discourse of the mental health professions to be assimilated into the language and thought patterns of ordinary people, albeit in distorted and oversimplified form. Still, the die was cast, as many people acknowledged that lessons gleaned from the study of acute mental disorder might be applicable to all of us, to some degree. Even to experts in the field, the boundaries between normal people and the mentally ill seemed fluid and at times quite obscure.

Many objected strenuously to this fashionable new trend. Many still do. Some were rigidly old-fashioned, clinging to old moral codes or to an outdated rationalism that attempted to expunge irrationality in all its forms from our

1

concept of the human. Others were empirically oriented scientists who dismissed the idea of the unconscious as trivial or misleading, and who insisted that the boundaries between "us" and "them" are not permeable, as the avant garde suggested, but distinct and intelligible to any clear-headed individual.

Because people like these were—and in some circles still are—quite numerous and powerful, Freud and Jung addressed themselves to a very broad and diverse audience, hoping to strike a responsive chord. In the process they discovered and refined a powerful strategy for engaging the educated public. Though they leaned heavily on philosophy and literature, they legitimated their theoretical and therapeutic efforts by invoking the prestige of the natural sciences, which enjoyed unparalleled growth and popularity in the nineteenth century.

Though they presented themselves as medical men, however, Freud and Jung were really inveterate boundary transgressors who were more concerned with the meanings of irrational behavior than its neurobiological causes. Accordingly, they could not help but address issues that are traditionally the domain of the humanities, the social sciences, comparative religion, and theology.

In any case, the appearance of Freud and Jung at the dawn of the twentieth century marked the creation of a whole new cultural form: the alienist or "head shrinker" as public intellectual. This new cultural trend abated somewhat during World War II but made a vigorous comeback during the fifties and sixties, when the psychoanalyst as public intellectual became a cultural commonplace in America once again. Bruno Bettelheim, Erik Erikson, Erich Fromm, and R. D. Laing were the preeminent examples of this phenomenon in the Cold War era.

Unlike Erikson, the subject of this book, Fromm and Laing were ambivalent admirers of Freud who were trained by reputable Freudians but became deeply disenchanted with the International Psychoanalytic Association (IPA). To remedy their isolation within the psychoanalytic movement, they started their own training institutes, in which traditional analytic training was supplemented with instruction in philosophy and spiritual disciplines from both the East and the West (Burston 1991, 1996). Despite their large public followings, however, Fromm and Laing remained marginal figures in the psychoanalytic mainstream. By contrast, Erikson was a movement insider, albeit one whose relationship with the IPA's leadership and training procedures was fraught with ambivalence (Burston 2002a). Indeed, one of the points of this study is that Erikson wrestled with the analytic vocation far more than his friends and critics generally realize.

Another important difference between Erikson and the others was that unlike Fromm, Erikson was not a systematic thinker, nor yet an *antisystematic* thinker, as Laing was (Burston 2000). But like Laing, Erikson was far more concerned with conveying "a way of seeing things"—in his case a very playful, *gentle* vision—than with achieving perfect clarity or consistency. Indeed, achieving greater clarity or consistency might have worked against Erikson, or rather, against his contradictory project of attempting to defend his Freudian pedigree while introducing new (and old) ways of thinking about mental disturbance (and life in general) into analytic discourse—a point we return to frequently in the pages that follow.

What is Erikson's legacy to the twenty-first century, and what impact will he have on the future of psychoanalysis? It is too early to answer these questions definitively, but much depends on whether psychoanalysis itself has a future. And that is open to doubt, at least in North America. Unless we change course in the not-too-distant future, the phenomenon of the psychoanalyst as public intellectual, which contributed so much to intellectual and cultural life of the twentieth century, will *remain* a twentieth-century phenomenon, which future historians will ponder with detached curiosity in centuries to come. On the whole, psychoanalysts have done little to rescue themselves from their imminent irrelevance in the digital age, in which the mental health field is dominated by Big Pharma and HMOs that are hostile or indifferent to their methods and perspectives. One way they could help themselves, and society at large, is by heeding some of the cultural and historical concepts embedded in Erikson's work—things clinicians, with their narrow focus on treatment issues, generally overlook. The concept of *intergenerational identification* is the single most important concept Erikson offers us along these lines, as it enables us to develop a kind of cultural critique that raises awareness of our responsibility to future generations without succumbing to the sterile and ideologically polarized rhetoric of the Left or the Right.

That being so, my reading of Erikson emphasizes three phases of his epigenetic sequence, and, therefore, three phases or aspects of human development that are central to Erikson's concept of generational interconnectedness—infancy, adolescence, and middle age. My emphasis on these three stages and their corresponding "virtues"—basic trust and hope, identity and fidelity, generativity and conscience—is not entirely original, of course. But the way I approach them is, and by revisiting them all from a fresh, biographical perspective, I hope to give them renewed currency among psychoanalysts, who would profit from revisiting them in their clinical and cultural work as well.

CHILDHOOD AND ADOLESCENCE

Viewed through the prism of Erikson's theories about human development, one can conclude only that his early years were fraught with difficulty. According to Lawrence Friedman, whose thorough and engrossing biography I rely on extensively in the first three chapters (Friedman 1999), he was born in 1902 in Frankfurt, Germany, to Karla Abrahamsen (1877–1960), a beautiful, spirited, well-educated young woman of Jewish-Danish origin. In 1898, at age twenty-one, she married the son of a family friend, a young stockbroker named Valdemar Isidor Salmonsen. Soon thereafter the marriage disintegrated, and Salmonsen, who had some shadowy underworld connections, disappeared. Though her feelings toward him were probably quite negative on balance, Karla retained Salmonsen's name for legal purposes. When she became pregnant (in unknown circumstances) four years later, she was on holiday in northern Germany and, at her family's request, stayed there under the watchful eye of three spinster aunts.

In those days, of course, single motherhood entailed enormous stigma, so to spare her family, herself, and her child needless hardship, Karla listed Valdemar Salmonsen as young Erik's father. Fortunately for her, perhaps, four months later, evidence surfaced that Salmonsen had died in mysterious circumstances abroad. One can only imagine that Karla must have greeted this news with a considerable sense of relief. After all, though they had been separated for four years, she had never divorced her feckless husband. She was now a widow and therefore able to remarry if she wished.

At any rate, Karla soon left Frankfurt for the nearby town of Buehl, where she worked as nurse. In her spare time she read Kierkegaard, Brandes, and Emerson, or wandered around the Bohemian side of town, where she made many friends among the artists and artisans who ostensibly gave young Erik his first "male imprinting." In "'Identity Crisis' in Autobiographical Perspective" (1975), Erikson recalled that during his infancy, his mother was often very sad, but that she remained dignified, and tender in her ministrations. Unfortunately, however, young Erik's recurrent gastric distress prompted consultations with Theodor Homberger, a gentle, reserved pediatrician from nearby Karlsruhe, who became quite enamored with his young patient's mother. Homberger was nine years older than Karla, a man of regular habits and an impeccable reputation. To the great relief of the Abrahamsen clan in Copenhagen, he was also prosperous and observant, and promised to erase the scandal of Erik's illegitimacy. The only condition he insisted on to secure that future for Karla's infant son was that Erik be told that he, Theodor, was his biological father.

Karla agreed, and married Theodor Homberger on July 15, 1905, which was also Erik's third birthday. However, as Friedman perceptively points out, the adoption process that ensued thereafter was lengthy and fraught with complications. Despite Karla and Theodor's shared desire to present themselves as a normal family, Erik's certificate of naturalization as a German citizen dated 1909, gives his name as Erik Salmonsen, and, based on other information in Friedman's biography, it appears that the adoption and guardian-ship procedure was not complete until 1911—almost seven years after the ini-tial engagement—and took fully two years longer than was strictly necessary. Even more astonishing is the fact that Homberger did not actually acknowl-edge Erik as his son in so many words in a legal document until he drew up his will in 1942, when Erik was forty.

Evidently, Friedman concludes, Homberger harbored a profound ambiva-lence toward his illegitimate stepson. And as Erikson himself noted many years later, children have an uncanny ability to sense an adult's real feelings and attitudes, even when they are at variance with the individual's conscious attitudes or surface behavior. No doubt Homberger's ambivalence toward Erik was reciprocated in full, and the fears and resentments young Erik ex-pressed as he lost his monopoly on his mother's affections reinforced the un-dercurrent of rejection in Homberger's overall posture toward his gifted but insecure stepson. Homberger's passionate pursuit of middle-class re-spectability, which was supposed to shield and support young Erik, was part of the problem, too. After all, unlike his short, dark mother and his recently acquired stepfather, who was also short of stature, young Erik was blond, blue-eyed, and, in due course, "flagrantly tall," as he jokingly put it. Perhaps Homberger feared that people would note this striking incongruity and intuit the embarrassing truth that lay behind the well-cultivated facade of domestic propriety. They did, of course, and the whispering and gossip occasioned by Karla and Theodor's transparent charade caused Erik much doubt, confusion, and anguish as he grew up. Judging from Friedman's account, Karla also did little to diminish Theodor's reservations about his patient-turned-stepson. In-deed, she complicated the dynamics between them; reluctant to acknowledge Theodor's parental rights, she needed to maintain a special relationship with her first child after his half-sisters were born.

While she might have denied it, of course, one reason Karla remarried was to give her son a real chance in life. So while she probably loved and re-spected Homberger in her fashion, this was also a marriage of convenience— at least initially. Nevertheless, in the ensuing years, Karla bore Theodor three daughters, two of whom, Ruth and Ellen, survived. In deference to her hus-band's wishes, this formerly adventurous and unconventional Jewish-Danish beauty kept a strictly kosher house and spoke only German with her three children. Moreover, it is instructive to note that Theodor Homberger was on the governing council of the local Reform temple for thirteen years and its president for another five. During this lengthy period of time, Karla also worked diligently and wholeheartedly in charity and relief efforts for impov-erished Jews in the Karlsruhe district, winning the deep gratitude and admi-ration of many of them.

But while Karla poured herself into charity work and, like any traditional Jewish housewife, balanced the books, planned the family's social calendar, and so on, she also clung vigorously to vestiges of her former self. Though she never spoke Danish to her children, she evidently read a Danish newspaper every day and made frequent border crossings to visit her family and friends. Moreover, while Theodor was sedulous in the observance of Jewish dietary laws (kashruth), she ate shrimp and other impure foods (*traif*) with gusto—in her own children's presence—on her native soil, and maintained numerous friendships with local artists in Karlsruhe, most of whom were Gentile. And above all, perhaps, Karla frequently reminded her son that in days gone by, the Abrahamsen clan had boasted a chief rabbi in Stockholm *and* a prominent church historian in their midst, hinting broadly at the existence of conversions and mixed marriages in her family background.

Finally, and in addition to the preceding anomalies, it is instructive to note that like the Austrian neurologist Sigmund Freud, who was beginning to make a name for himself at the time, Karla was an admirer of Georg Brandes (Erikson 1975), a Danish literary critic who befriended Friedrich Nietzsche and who argued outspokenly for the abolition of marriage (Santaniello 1994). She also admired Søren Kierkegaard, a devout (if unconventional) Lutheran who felt that a solitary, celibate life was vital to the unfolding of his spiritual vocation (Friedman 1994). Different as they were in their attitudes toward faith, Brandes and Kierkegaard converged impressively on one point—their contempt for convention and for "bourgeois" marriage.

On the face of it, perhaps, Karla's many inconsistencies were merely the expression of a powerful, protean personality, which occasionally liked to throw off conventional constraints and revisit earlier periods of her life. But while he could not have said so in so many words, of course, a boy as sensitive as Erik probably sensed that Karla's idiosyncratic tastes hinted at the secret recesses of her soul. They declared, in effect, that there was more to her than meets the eye—that in her heart of hearts she valued sensual pleasures and spiritual horizons that were strictly off-limits to respectable middle-class Jews.

And as if all this were not enough to digest, Karla engaged the preadolescent Erik in earnest conversation about Kierkegaard, urging him to take the existential core of Christianity to heart, but without losing sight of his own Jewishness—and this *before* his bar mitzvah. Admittedly, a famous Jewish contemporary of Karla's—Martin Buber—was deeply influenced by Kierkegaard as a young adult (Buber 1988). But Buber was a young man at the time, and never subject to the barrage of mixed messages young Erik was receiving from his mother. Moreover, it is instructive to note that Karla never addressed her daughters in this way. The fact that Erik was singled out for this kind of treatment suggests that Karla had a hidden agenda. In effect, if not in so many words, Karla was trying to convey the following message: *Honor thy (biological) father (whose existence we may not discuss) by not closing your mind to his religious perspective; but meanwhile, honor your (step)father as if he were your true father, by not inquiring too deeply about your relationship to him.*

Though she never formulated or stated this injunction in straightforward terms, it is easy to see how a youth like Erik might respond to this powerful meta-communication. Being deeply attuned to unverbalized aspects of human communication—as his work with children would prove later—Erik probably became deeply identified with the publicly repudiated parts of his mother's personality, which were at variance with prevailing cultural expectations of who he was and what he should become. And his burgeoning neurosis was intensified by the fact that he could never imagine Theodor Homberger as his biological father, whom he conjured in fantasy from oblique intimations he received regarding the dissociated fragments of his mother's past—Jewish but Christian, pious but artistic, endowed with rare honesty and a stubborn, elusive reticence; bold, broken, and prodigal, but able to rise above it all somehow. These mildly dissociated fragments of his mother's divided self—her *shadow*, in Jungian terminology—formed the nucleus of young Erik's *negative identity*, or those potential traits and ways of being he was taught to avoid, at least on the level of overt communication. (For more on the concept of negative identity, see section 5 of "The Problem of Ego Identity" [Erikson 1956a]).

Not all the oblique messages that unsettled Erik's mind originated with his mother and stepfather, however. As Friedman reports, the entire family network was abuzz with it. There were frequent whisperings among the Hombergers that were not consciously intended for Erik's sensitive ears, but which lodged fragments of furtive conversation in the remoter recesses of his mind, sowing seeds of doubt about his mother's truthfulness. In one instance, before he turned eight, Erik sat silently beneath a kitchen table while the adults above, oblivious to his presence, discussed his father as an artistic gentile. Erik received similar messages about his outsider status from his mother's family, too. The Abrahamsen clan did not stoop to gossip just within earshot, as the Hombergers did, but were decidedly cool and uncomfortable around him, with the notable exception of his beloved cousin Henrietta.

Finally, to dispel any shadow of doubt he cherished about his dubious outsider status, his stepfather's cronies at the local Reform temple referred to him derisively as "the goy" or "the Gentile," a fact that wounded him deeply. The glib cruelty behind this kind of banter should never be underestimated. As if this were not bad enough, it was an era of resurgent German nationalism, so many of his peers at school referred to him jeeringly as "the Jew" or "the Dane," hinting he would never belong in their midst, either. All this merely re-inforced the message he received elsewhere: *Don't delude yourself. No matter how hard you try, you will never really be one of us.* Is it any wonder, then, that Erik experienced his bar mitzvah as a hollow ritual performed solely for the sake of appearances, or that he held himself aloof from anything Jewish, as his rabbi, Hugo Schiff, complained? What other strategy, save religious fanaticism and overcompensation, could possibly have protected him from the bewilder-ing cacophony of mixed messages and meta-communications that were heaped on him from all sides?

No doubt the pervasive sense of ostracism Erik encountered contributed to his difficulties at school. From nursery onward, we are told that school is sup-posed to prepare us for the "real world" of adult roles and responsibilities, and young Erik was notified early that his prospects for belonging anywhere in that world were slim indeed. What is the point of trying to become accom-plished at anything if you are only going to be vilified and rejected in the end? Years later Virginia Demos, a friend and former student, observed that in terms of his own developmental schemata, Erikson's characteristic shyness, diffidence, and low self-esteem as an adult were consistent with the profile of a child caught in the conflict between industry and shame. Her assessment rings true. After all, by the middle of his childhood, Erikson had been exposed to enough cryptic and contradictory messages, oblique hints, and furtive sub-texts to cherish serious doubts about both his legitimacy and the honesty of his mother and stepfather. The resulting sense of shame must have interfered greatly with his school performance, and set the stage for his abnormally long adolescent identity crisis.

At the same time, other, specifically temperamental factors were probably in play as well. Quite apart from the vicissitudes of family life, the average middle and high school curriculum is really not designed for students with a shy and dreamy disposition, whose distinctive interests and learning styles are not accommodated or nurtured by their immediate surroundings (Erikson, 1982b: Levine 2002) Fortunately for posterity, like many Jewish mothers, Karla never doubted that her son was endowed with exceptional talent. But even with his mother's unwavering confidence in his talent to support him, the cumulative impact of his early childhood experience was what Erik later termed "a quiet sense of alienation from my entire childhood setting, German and Jewish." His childhood experience also kindled a deep attraction to the Christianity of the Gospels, reinforced by his mother's fascination with Kierkegaard. It is easy to see why. According to the New Testament, Jesus embraced all comers, Jewish and Gentile, and promised to banish forever dis-tinctions of class and ethnicity among his followers. Moreover, Joseph,

Mary's Jewish husband, was not his "true" father, and was largely incidental to the deeply triangulated drama between the mother, son, and the elusive but powerful Holy Spirit. Finally, we are told, after considerable torment Jesus accepted his suffering as being integral to his calling, his own unique destiny, and gave it a redemptive function in the cosmic scheme of things, which ultimately reunited him with his true Father, turning personal tragedy into collective triumph.

You don't have to be a psychoanalyst to discern the kind of solace and inspiration that a boy in young Erik's predicament would have drawn from this narrative. In fact, you have to be pretty heartless *not* to see it. For a sensitive lad bruised by the lingering stigma of illegitimacy, of parental duplicity and multiple intersecting ethnic prejudices, it is hard to imagine a myth that would be more attractive or serviceable. Unfortunately, however, Erik's sense of disconnection from all things German and Jewish frustrated his stepfather, whose main project in life — apart from being a pediatrician — was to combine the somewhat disparate identities that Erik took up halfheartedly at the best of times. As a result, perhaps, Theodor was slow to share his family name with Erik, and yet was still anxious to enmesh Erik in a world that told him repeatedly, in a faint but disconcerting chorus, that he did not belong.

As time passed, the relationship between Erik and his mother, which had been so close, also suffered. Sometime between the ages of eight and fourteen, as he later recalled, he was walking in the Black Forest near Karlsruhe when he encountered an old woman milking a cow. She asked him pointedly if he knew who his father was. He dashed home and confronted his mother, demanding to know the truth, and she finally disclosed that Theodor Homberger had adopted him. However, she then claimed that his real father was Valdemar Salmonsen, who abandoned her when she was pregnant, and begged Erik not to press her for further details. He desisted, even though his mother's account clashed with the widespread rumor that his father was Christian. In later life, Erik learned that Salmonsen was not his true father, either. He later made numerous attempts to determine his father's identity, all of them in vain. In old age he complained bitterly to Friedman that his mother had deceived him, and had given him many mixed messages about his father and her relationship to him (Friedman 1999).

Though the conflicts and contradictions that bedeviled his early life are fairly easy to reconstruct, it remains difficult to gauge the actual severity of the disturbance engendered by Karla and Theodor's collusive arrangement. Erikson said that his adolescent identity crisis brought him to the brink of psychosis (Erikson 1975), though Friedman thinks this statement was probably exaggerated for dramatic effect. Much as I respect Friedman's judgment on the whole, I see no reason to doubt its authenticity. While working at

Austen Riggs, Erikson displayed rare sympathy and skill working with adolescents in the throes of transient or borderline psychotic states, and his ability to put their characteristic conflicts, needs, and experiences into words may have stemmed from personal experience, much as Harry Stack Sullivan's expertise with schizophrenics was rooted in his own adolescent psychosis. And even if Erikson was not clinically psychotic at some point, he probably coped with the fears and fantasies typical of young people who are teetering on the edge.

To put this matter into perspective, I am reminded of a vignette told by R. D. Laing about a woman who consulted him regarding her adolescent son. For the sake of convenience we will call him Julian. His behavior at home was becoming insufferable, and he had recently been diagnosed schizophrenic. While Julian wavered in and out of various delusional states, his mother noted, he always held fast to the conviction that the man she had married was not his real father, and that their familial relations were built on sham and pretense. But though he was an intolerable nuisance, she continued, she did not want her son drugged or shocked into submission, so she begged Laing to intervene before the situation spiraled out of control.

After a consultation with Julian, Laing invited his mother back and instructed her to be frank with him. After some prodding, she tearfully admitted that Julian had somehow intuited the truth; that he had really been conceived in the wake of a brief premarital affair. Laing then presented Julian's mother with two alternatives—tell her husband the truth and risk the future of her marriage, or maintain the status quo and risk ruining Julian's sanity and well-being. She chose the former, and though her marriage suffered, within three months Julian was off medication and virtually symptom free.

What bearing does this story have on Erikson's adolescence? Quite a lot, on reflection. Unlike Julian's hapless father, Theodor Homberger clearly knew the score when he married Karla, and Karla eventually admitted to Erik that Theodor was not his real father. So on the face of it, perhaps, the secrecy and duplicity in Erikson's home was not quite as thick as it was in Julian's, where husband and son were *both* kept in the dark. But unlike Julian's mother, who came clean in a crisis, Karla covered up her initial deception, and lied *a second time* when she claimed that his father was Valdemar Salmonsen. Moreover, Erik read his mother well enough to sense that this was so. And years later, when she was finally caught in this second deception, she *still* refused to divulge his father's identity. If she knew who Erik's father was, she took this secret to her grave.

As a result, though Erik's mother loved him and affirmed his uniqueness and promise with unwavering conviction, she also contributed to the sense of shame—a gaping hole in the middle of his being—that never entirely disappeared. For his entire life, Erikson evinced a deep reticence—a sense of not really belonging anywhere, which no doubt contributed to his restlessness and his willingness to move himself and his family about frequently. As Friedman notes, Erikson's shyness and diffidence sometimes evoked a fierce, maternal protectiveness, a desire to help and defend in friends of both sexes, which he made use of to advance his career. Friedman also suggests that Erikson's energetic pursuit of fame was animated by the desire to bring himself to his father's attention and to prove that he really amounted to something after all. This was doubtless part of his motivation. Next to his mother's love, his father's absence—and the various conflicts engendered by it—comprised the central theme of Erikson's existence, the source of his greatest vulnerability and of his greatest insights as well.

In view of its lifelong reverberations for Erik, Karla's steadfast refusal to disclose his father's identity invites closer scrutiny. While it is pointless to speculate who Erik's father was, Karla's motives for concealing his identity, though unknown to all but herself, are not irrelevant here. If we consider the situation logically, there are really only four possibilities, each of which presents us with a different emotional backdrop to the deeply convoluted relationship between mother and son.

One possibility is that when Salmonsen abandoned her, Karla embarked on a brief period of willful promiscuity, simply did not know the father's real identity, and concealed this fact to save face. This seems unlikely, in view of her character and circumstances. A second, more likely scenario, at least in her cultural setting, is that she was raped or seduced, perhaps while intoxicated, and wanted to spare Erik the shame of knowing or confronting her abuser—especially if, as rumor has it, he was a member of powerful and well-established Danish family, who might retaliate through the courts.

A third possibility is that, though a victim of some kind, she was not afraid of legal retaliation or economic misfortune but merely hoped to spare Erik the agony of imagining his mother in an ethically compromising situation. A fourth possibility, which is seldom discussed, is that Karla dearly loved Erik's father, and that their brief and heated affair was terminated due to the pervasive stigma on mixed marriages. Perhaps Erik's father was the great love of her life, who, for reasons of propriety and/or family pressure, felt constrained to break things off before he knew she was pregnant, while she, in turn, was too honorable to tell him about her condition when this fact finally came to light. However, to admit that—even to hint at it, at least publicly—might have caused poor Theodor heartbreak, and threatened the stability of her family. Apart from any adverse consequences for herself and her children, she may have hidden the truth as much out of loyalty to Theodor as to her erstwhile lover, because her devoted, hardworking Jewish husband simply did

not deserve such humiliation. So when pressed, she refused to reply to any inquiry that might have resulted in full disclosure or necessitated further lies
and evasions, thereby compounding the damage already done.

This is the explanation I favor. Though it can be neither proven nor refuted
in the current state of the evidence, it is completely in keeping with Karla's
romantic, contradictory character. Promiscuity wasn't her style, and to the
best of my knowledge there is no evidence that Karla ever experienced or described herself as a *victim* of Erik's father. If she did, I would wager this fact
would have registered strongly in the mind of the exquisitely receptive and
intuitive boy and featured prominently in both his youthful fantasies and adult
ruminations.

But regardless of what actually happened, or what Karla's motives for concealment were, the fact remains that Erik, her first born, was conceived in
tragic circumstances. And despite his mother's devoted efforts to make it up
to him—while denying that she was doing this, of course—he would never,
ever forget it.

Now that we've pondered her motives for deception—and later, for
silence—the next question is: How did her shifting attitudes strike Erik? Having learned that Theodor Homberger was not his real father and correctly intuited that Valdemar Salmonsen was not either, Erikson probably explored *all*
these imaginative possibilities in attempting to ferret out the real circumstances of his birth. Indeed, I would wager that during his adolescent wan-
derings, doing odd jobs or walking through woods and meadows, pondering
the words of Nietzsche, Angelus Silesius, and Lao Tzu, he probably spent
many hours weighing each one in turn, balancing the subtle undercurrents of
implication against the stubborn scent of evasion he had picked up in his increasingly frustrating exchanges with his mother.

And this prompts the question: Did these issues come up in Erikson's
analysis? Undoubtedly they did, at some point. But as Joan Erikson insisted
in her talks with Friedman, they were never properly addressed, much less resolved, by his analyst, Anna Freud. Why? In retrospect, with the benefit of
hindsight, we might say that this oversight reflected her shortcomings as a
therapist, and perhaps it did. But this way of framing the issue is also somewhat unfair because it neglects to point out that, in point of fact, the whole
psychoanalytic establishment was averse to addressing the pathogenic effects
of sustained parental secrecy and deception. Anna Freud was hardly unique.
Erikson himself tackled the problem briefly in "Psychological Reality and
Historical Actuality" (1964d). But Erikson's account of Dora's dilemma—
and of Sigmund Freud's inability to grasp its full developmental significance—was so tactful and understated that even he never addressed this issue
with all the seriousness it deserves.

That being so, it may be instructive to point out that though he seldom addressed the issue after his trip to America, Sigmund Freud addressed the child's response to parental duplicity in several papers between 1905 and 1910, in connection with what he termed *infantile sexual researches*. Prior to 1910 Freud usually attributed the pathogenic potential of childish sexual curiosity to the child's penchant for "naughty" ideas and the adults' desire to suppress them. According to Freud, the ensuing conflict in the child's mind, that is, the creation of internal censorship, results in a dissociation of the unwanted ideas and affects, engendered by the child's fear of losing the adults' love. This kind of inner "splitting," if taken too far, is serious enough. But more importantly, for our purposes, Freud said that when the child experiences the adult actually withholding information out of prudishness or some other ulterior motive, it erodes the child's trust and confidence in his or her adult caretakers, and can engender a deep estrangement that can last well into adolescence and early adulthood (Freud 1905, 1907, 1908).

At this stage of his theorizing, then, Freud implied that a child's rebellion against parental authority often has a rational basis and is not simply or primarily a reactive response to the adult's attempt to curb the child's precocious lust. On the contrary, the child rebels because the adult is deceptive and bent on withholding knowledge. So, for example, in a discussion of the Wednesday Night Meeting of November 25, 1908, Freud even declared that "the conflict with the father has its origin not in sexual rivalry for the mother, but in the father's concealment of the facts about the sexual processes concerned with birth" (Nunberg and Federn 1962, 72).

Obviously, in the father's absence these remarks would have a more general applicability, describing a potential arena of conflict with a mother (or stepfather) as well. Be that as it may, the most striking feature of Freud's formulations on infantile sexual researches prior to 1911 was their repeated emphasis on the child's thirst for truth, which gives birth to suspicion—or, in Eriksonian terms, mistrust—and an unwillingness to accept parental definitions of reality at face value. This idea informs Freud's study of Leonardo da Vinci, who became an exemplary scientist, said Freud, because he "escaped being intimidated by his father in earliest childhood" (Freud 1910a.) Unfortunately, after 1910 Freud lost interest in infantile sexual researches, parental duplicity, and the mistrust that it presumably engenders in young children.

The fact that all this seldom registers in the analytic literature prompts the reflection that Anna Freud's reluctance or refusal to explore the motives and consequences of Erikson's mother's duplicity may have been more than merely a personal shortcoming. After all, this was fairly typical of analysts then. When Erikson began analytic training in 1925, these were no longer perceived as important issues. Not only that, but there was an unspoken taboo on raising these issues—as Sándor Ferenczi did in 1933, at considerable cost to his reputation (Fromm 1970; Dupont 1988). For once the Oedipus complex was established as the "core complex" among Freud and his followers, rebellion and mistrust of adult authority were ascribed increasingly to an infantile antipathy to civilized constraints, which adults presumably enforce with more or less benign intent. As guilty Oedipus loomed large and little Leonardo receded from Freud's imagination, adult duplicity and the child's stubborn thirst for truth were no longer deemed relevant treatment issues (Burston 1994).

Though Freud averted his gaze from this issue almost two decades before young Erik entered his daughter's professional life, the fact remains it continued to bother Anna Freud's most famous analysand profoundly. Peter Blos, the friend who drew Erik into Anna Freud's circle, recalled him speculating often and at considerable length about the identity of his real father prior to his analysis, and weaving elaborate fantasies about what life would have been like if he had grown up in Copenhagen in his father's milieu (Friedman 1999). Young Erik was quite lucky to have Blos to confide in. Though it floundered somewhat later, in its initial stages his friendship with Blos was one of the most sustaining relationships of his early life. They met in the Karlsruhe Gymnasium and became fast friends shortly after they graduated. Peter's mother, like Erik's, was Jewish and artistic, while his father, though Christian, was a doctor like Erik's stepfather. As Friedman relates, Dr. Edwin Blos, Peter's father, was a kind eccentric steeped in Goethe. Despite his faith in the spiritual superiority of the German people, Edwin Blos also had a deep respect for Asian mysticism and helped lay the foundation for Erikson's book on Gandhi much later. Among Gandhi's distinguishing characteristics, according to Erikson, were his desire to fuse the wisdom of East and West and his stubborn determination to defy convention and turn reality itself on its head in pursuit of the truth—just as Leonardo and Freud did.

At any rate, before his graduation from gymnasium, Erik spent many happy hours in the Blos household and, as he later put it, "shared" Peter's father with him. And they did more than discuss philosophy. Erik was now approaching the age when he had to choose a career. He had shown great promise as an artist all along, and in addition to his skills in drawing, he had developed a particular talent for making wood-block prints. The Blos family all encouraged him to continue in that direction, though Theodor Homberger heartily disapproved. It was only after Erik despaired of becoming a truly *great* artist, and found himself wandering aimlessly around Europe without a clear direction in 1927, that Peter Blos issued an invitation to join him in Vienna, and replace him for the summer as a teacher at the Heitzing School recently founded by Anna Freud, Dorothy Burlingham, and Eva Rosenfeld.

ANNA FREUD, ANALYTIC TRAINING, AND
DISAPPOINTMENT IN DENMARK

Even by today's standards, the Heitzing School was an unusual setting. The pupils were the offspring of analysts, analysts-in-training, and foreign patients—mostly wealthy Britons or Americans—who came to see Freud or some other local luminary for treatment. While working there as a substitute teacher, Erik demonstrated a rare capacity to connect with children and was quickly invited to join the permanent staff, while getting his certification as a Montessori teacher, taking courses at the University of Vienna, and training to be a child analyst. As he later recalled, his initial perusal of Freud's work on Michelangelo's Moses disclosed to him that Freud possessed an inordinately strong "visual curiosity," and Erik would actually have preferred to work with "the Professor," who was now old and ill. But since a rare opportunity had emerged unexpectedly, he did not turn it down. Moreover, by way of compensation, his duties as Anna Freud's assistant included occasional encounters with the founder of psychoanalysis. As Freud's cancer of the mouth worsened, Erik sometimes drove him to and from the doctor's office. And since Anna shared her father's office suite, as her analysand Erik probably glimpsed Freud almost every working day before appointments (Roazen 1971.) Given the circumstances, as Paul Roazen points out, it is unlikely that they ever conversed at length about anything of importance. But Sigmund Freud and Erik Homberger were aware of one another's existence.

Though it started on a hopeful note, Erik's training analysis was marked by occasional turbulence. Shortly after his arrival in Vienna, Erik met and married Joan Serson, a Canadian student of dance who was in a brief and utterly disastrous analysis with Ludwig Jekels. As a result of her ordeal, Joan came to distrust Anna Freud—and psychoanalysis as a whole—intensely. Imagine being an analyst in training with a girlfriend, then a wife, who was injured or offended by another psychoanalyst!

Another emergent source of difficulty was the issue of dual relationships, which were ubiquitous in this milieu. During the course of his training, Erik was a teacher, and therefore in a position of some authority. And yet, like his own students, he was also in treatment with Miss Freud—a fact they were reminded of daily when Erik left the school for Miss Freud's consulting room. As Freidman rightly points out, in a certain sense, this put him on the same footing as his students. Though he favored a much more egalitarian stance with children than his analyst (and employer) did, Erik felt distinctly uncomfortable at having his authority eroded in front of the children this way (Friedman 1999).

As if all this were not bad enough, another serious source of tension lay in what Erikson later termed "a pervasive interdiction of thought" in Freud's circle. Owing to the previous "defections" of Alfred Adler, C. G. Jung, and Otto Rank, Anna Freud's insistence on ideological purity and personal loyalty to the Professor was simply ferocious. Already, the question of fidelity to Sigmund Freud was becoming a rhetorical device with which to intimidate potential innovators. Not surprisingly, Anna's efforts to polish and police the new recruits on her father's behalf occasionally blurred the boundaries between her father's work and her own. Indeed, at one point, while listening to a presentation of Erik's that demonstrated some originality on the subject of children's play, Anna Freud angrily reproached him with being a follower of Melanie Klein, who was her archrival in the sphere of child analysis (Grosskurth 1986; Roazen 2000c).

Apart from the mean-spirited, anxiety-provoking quality of this remark, the most striking thing about it is just how odd and off the mark it really was. Klein and Erikson both relied on play constructions and the cultivation of a nonverbal rapport with their young patients. But as John Bowlby remarked to me, Klein's interpretative schemata characteristically ignored the impact of real-life interpersonal and cultural determinants on children's fantasies, taking the analytical world's previous emphasis on "intrapsychic" and "instinctive" factors to absurd extremes. Moreover, her theories of infant development conjured with the "death instinct," which Erikson thought of as a philosophical, rather than a biological, concept—and a pretty dubious one at that (Evans 1967).

Why the charge of heresy, then? Though he probably only hinted at it obliquely in the course of his presentation, as Freidman points out, Erikson always cherished deep doubts about the epistemic validity and the clinical utility of making a rigid distinction between the patient's "inner" and "outer" worlds, as Anna Freud and Heinz Hartmann were both strongly inclined to do. Indeed, he felt that Freud and Hartmann minimized or devalued the importance of the cultural and interpersonal words in which children develop. Though somewhat reticent on this score initially, he became more candid on this point after he arrived in the United States. A vivid example is "A Memorandum on Identity and Negro Youth" (Erikson 1964e) in which he described a four-year-old African American girl who stared at herself in the mirror and scrubbed her face with soap incessantly in the vain hope of becoming white. This poor child had internalized the dominant culture's racist aesthetic, which devalued her appearance and culture of origin in conformity with the normative ideals of the culture at large. And this is hardly an isolated example. In fact, if you pause to think about it, Erikson's illuminating discussions of child-rearing practices among the Yurok and the Sioux in *Childhood and So-*

ciety (1950) were largely devoted to explicating the ways in which the person's "outer" world suffuses and informs his or her "inner" or "instinctual" one from early infancy onward.

In contrast with Erikson, Klein's views on fantasy and early childhood development depict the patient's inner world as being almost a closed system that is impervious to external influences, and therefore *radicalizes* and intensifies the very defect that Erikson was quietly calling attention to in mainstream ego psychology.

Though it is pure conjecture, of course, it is tempting to speculate that Anna Freud's obtuse attribution of Kleinian sympathies originated in feelings evoked by Erik's allegiance to Anna's *other* female rival, namely, Joan Erikson, who was quite critical of psychoanalysis and probably urging Erik to leave Anna's sphere of influence. Joan wished to leave Vienna because she was deeply alarmed by the political situation, which was becoming more ominous by the week. By contrast with Joan, and with many analysts, academics, and artists who fled Vienna in the early 1930s, Sigmund and Anna Freud were deep in denial, minimizing the scale and ferocity of the approaching crisis and urging all and sundry to stay and wait it out. In "Psychoanalysis: The American Experience" Robert Coles (2000) cites an interview in 1970 in which Erikson recalled the alarm and incredulity that he and his wife felt at the calm complacency of Freud and his circle. Erikson said:

> Our friends in the psychoanalytic community there kept telling themselves that when the German people got to see the truth, the truth of who—and what—the Nazis were they'd turn on them, vote them out. You see, you see there the faith of psychoanalysis—it's a part of the "liberal enlightenment": the truth will win out, will prevail over the "lower instincts," over "the base side of man." I often heard that back then—and what a price we all paid, eventually, to win that victory over the Nazis! (141)

Indeed. For the upshot of Sigmund and Anna's obstinate indifference to the "outer" world was that they lost some property, narrowly escaped with their lives, and inadvertently caused many others to lose theirs. Erikson was too tactful to broach this theme with Coles, of course. But in retrospect, one wonders what impact this experience had on Erikson's feelings toward his former analyst, who, whether she said so in so many words or not, construed his eagerness to flee as evidence of cowardice, opportunism, or betrayal of the cause. The fact that his judgment (and Joan's) proved superior in this instance was probably not lost on either party, and may have colored their galloping estrangement after the death of Anna's father, even though we may be sure that neither she nor Erikson ever alluded to these matters in conversation.

In any case, in 1933 Erikson graduated from the Vienna Psychoanalytic Institute as a member in full standing of the International Psychoanalytic Association, which entitled him to function as a training analyst anywhere in the world. This unexpectedly generous decision on the part of his teachers entitled him to be a training analyst anywhere in the world—in theory, anyway. This joyous rite of passage—which was a prelude to the more difficult one that awaited him—was rendered even more poignant by the fact that the honor was bestowed on him by Paul Federn (1871–1950), who was the vice president of the Vienna Psychoanalytic Society from 1924 until its dissolution by the Nazis in 1938.

Grateful and relieved, Erikson promptly left for Denmark, where he tried to revive his lapsed Danish citizenship with help from the dwindling Abrahamsen clan. They rallied impressively to his aid, but the Danish authorities were very wary of psychoanalysis, having recently admitted Wilhelm Reich into the country. An analysand of Sandor Rado's who became a training analyst in Berlin, Reich was also a former Communist who had urged Freud and the IPA to confront the fascists courageously, and was expelled from the IPA to placate Hitler. Having arrived in Denmark some months before, Reich was trying set up a practice and fighting ferocious polemical battles with Otto Fenichel, who was vying with Reich for the leadership of Freud's left-wing opposition, despite the fact that Fenichel's Marxist sympathies were becoming increasingly muted in public debates.

As he later remarked to Richard Evans, Erikson admired Reich's early work on character defenses and bodily rigidity, and credited him with advancing the clinical dimensions of psychoanalysis substantially (Evans 1967). But when he met Reich by chance on a Danish beach in the fall of 1933, Reich's behavior was so bizarre that it lent credence to Federn's suspicion that Reich was becoming schizophrenic—a suspicion that circulated as a rumor in analytic circles, to Reich's anger and dismay (Reich 1975). Reich had reason to be angry and suspicious, because a psychiatric diagnosis like this is the perfect pretext for dismissing someone else's political views, and because other disciples who had left the fold—including Rank, Rado, and Ferenczi—were saddled with specious "diagnoses" as punishment for their intellectual independence. But though he never impugned Reich's sanity, Erikson must have known that Reich's Danish interlude, which preceded and overlapped with his own, rendered his status there much more precarious than it would have been otherwise. So it is not surprising that his relationship with Reich ended there.

In any case, Erikson's failure to secure Danish citizenship was a source of great anguish and disappointment to him. Joan, who thought that all of Europe was menaced by the Nazi war machine, was actually somewhat relieved. But Joan was returning to a familiar world; Erik was not. Erikson had gradually made his way in Vienna, but now questions of belonging and blending in would become a nagging preoccupation once more, and his current stateless status unnerved him. After all, in the eyes of the world, he was neither German, being "Jewish," nor Danish, being "German." To complicate matters further, as Friedman points out, the national and religious coordinates of Erikson's identity were now hopelessly blurred *in his own eyes as well*—a fact that contributed to his unexpected love affair with America. As Erikson frequently pointed out, America encourages new immigrants to relinquish their older cultural identities and reinvent themselves within the framework of an all-inclusive American identity that rewards them for their forgetfulness of or indifference to the ways of their ancestors.

Having overstayed their official welcome in Denmark, Erik, Joan, and their two sons, Kai and Jon, aged two years and eight months, respectively, finally boarded the *Scanmail* in Copenhagen for passage to New York. It was a stormy thirteen-day journey that made Joan and Kai quite ill. Despite the rigors of the voyage, however, Erik profited greatly, as he befriended George Kennan, who occupied the adjacent cabin. An American diplomat who was fluent in German, Kennan was eager to help Erikson translate a paper he was working on into English. The paper in question would eventually be published as "The Legend of Hitler's Childhood," chapter 9 of *Childhood and Society*. As Erikson later recalled, Kennan was literally the first American he had met, and he was deeply appreciative of his enthusiasm and encouragement (Friedman 1999).

Meanwhile, having settled in America, Erikson had ample opportunity to refine his views on Hitler and National Socialism as World War II commenced and ground slowly toward its bloody conclusion. Some of them appeared in published articles; others, in a series of unpublished memoranda composed for the Committee on National Morale, entitled "On the Nazi Mentality" (1940), "Comment's on Hitler's Speech of September 30, 1942" (1942), "The Interrogation of German Prisoners of War" (1943), "Comments on Anti-Nazi Propaganda" (1945) and "A Memorandum to the Joint Committee on War Planning" (1945). These brief, but lively and engrossing, analyses appeared in print in 1987, in *Erik H. Erikson: A Way of Looking at Things*, edited by Stephen Schlein (1987). But as the war raged on they were read and discussed with vivid appreciation by many renowned figures in the mental health field, including Gordon Allport, Gregory Bateson, Edwin Boring, Kurt Lewin, Margaret Mead, Gardner Murphy, and Henry Murray. And with good reason: these memoranda demonstrate Erikson's subtlety as an analyst of social and historical trends. What they leave out, as Friedman points out, is any substantive discussion of Nazi anti-Semitism and the historic role of Jews in the emergence of modern German culture.

Though absent from his wartime memoranda, perhaps, Erikson addressed the issues of anti-Semitism and the German/Jewish relationship in "The Myth of Hitler's Childhood," which appeared as a chapter of *Childhood and Society* in 1950. Why the apparent delay?

Friedman suggests that the fleeting references to anti-Semitic stereotypes in Erikson's wartime memoranda reflect his ambivalence about his own Jewishness. Perhaps this is so; in view of his life experience until then, one cannot rule out that possibility. But other pressures were probably at work here, too. These war memoranda were solicited to illumine specific problems or processes that military and political leaders deemed critical to understanding, defeating, and, in due course, rebuilding Germany. Fathoming the roots of German anti-Semitism did not rank high on their list of priorities.

In any case, the subsequent appearance of some brief but searching reflections on European Jewry and their distinctive contributions to European culture in *Childhood and Society* indicates that, though dormant, these topics were definitely on his mind during the course of World War II. One only wishes he had been a little more forthcoming on this score. Had he demonstrated more interest in these issues early on, he might have avoided a barrage of reproaches that fairly engulfed him a quarter century later.

2

The New World

THE IMPOSSIBLE PROFESSION

In a foreword to *Wayward Youth*, written by August Aichhorn in 1925, Freud characterized psychoanalysis as an "impossible profession" (Aichhorn 1960), a bon mot popularized by Janet Malcolm in a book of the same name (Malcolm 1983). Malcolm glamorized Freudian orthodoxy (and slammed many of its critics) in ways that do her no credit, but the phrase itself is apt in more ways than one. Psychoanalysis *is* an "impossible" profession from several points of view. To begin with, there is constant debate between the natural science–based and hermeneutic and/or humanistic versions of psychoanalysis. Though it was not apparent at the outset, perhaps, this tension is now integral to, if not in some sense *constitutive* of, the whole Freudian field (Brunner 2001) Barring the abrupt collapse of the humanities and social sciences into the natural sciences, questions of method will always bedevil analytic discourse, with the result that its epistemic foundations are shaky, if not downright suspect—and not only to outsiders.

Another feature of the analytic field that causes interminable debate concerns the therapeutic rather than the theoretical side of things. Leaving issues of "technique" to one side momentarily, what are the goals of analytic therapy? After all, technique is a means to an end, and unless we are clear on the ultimate objective that informs a specific procedure, we may waste our ingenuity splitting hairs, losing the proverbial forest in the trees.

Though seldom addressed by practitioners, there is a profound tension between what I term the *philosophic* and the *instrumental* (or *pragmatic*) versions of psychoanalytic therapy. The philosophic view stresses what Erich Fromm termed the *disillusioning* function of the analytic dialogue (Fromm

1962). According to this view, only when a person relinquishes his or her most cherished illusions is deeper self-knowledge possible. And self-knowledge, by this account, is valuable for its own sake, irrespective of the degree to which it mitigates suffering or affords gains in terms of self-mastery, improved interpersonal relations, and so on. By contrast with the philosophic view, the pragmatic orientation holds that symptom alleviation and/or improved adaptation to the surrounding culture is the primary goal of the analytic encounter, and that self-knowledge is a merely a precondition or perhaps a bonus achieved along the way.

Evidently, Freud himself was unaware of the potentially disparate goals and priorities embedded in his therapeutic project—or if he was aware of them, he did not hasten to publicize this fact, perhaps for fear of sowing dissension in the ranks and/or discrediting his new discipline in the eyes of critics. Nevertheless, it is instructive to note that as his therapeutic pessimism deepened over the years, Freud valued psychoanalysis increasingly as an instrument for "research," justifying prolonged treatments that produced no tangible benefits to patients on that basis, to the shock and dismay of Sándor Ferenczi, galvanizing the latter's determination to experiment (somewhat recklessly) with analytic technique in the hopes of reviving its earlier therapeutic pretensions (Dupont 1988)

Nowadays, the only sizable school in the analytic world that openly attempts to justify its approach to treatment primarily on the basis of increments in self-knowledge are the followers of Jacques Lacan (Schneiderman 1984), though Kleinians still conduct lengthy analyses and bridle at the therapeutic pragmatism of the mainstream, or what is often called the Americanization of psychoanalysis. Lacan's courage—or intransigence—on this point is legendary, though in the eyes of his critics it was also the perfect rationalization for the grotesque mismanagement of many cases, rather than an issue of genuine principle.

In any case, Lacan deplored American ego psychology as a betrayal of Freud's radical vision, though Freud himself encouraged it in its early stages. In fairness to Lacan and his following, his virulent anti-Americanism, while distinctively French, is not new in analytic circles and can actually be traced back to Freud himself. Freud loathed America and made no secret of that fact. He thought it a misguided social experiment inimical to the development of psychoanalysis (Roazen 2000c) With rare exceptions like Erikson, who soon warmed to his adoptive homeland, Freud's anti-American bias colored the attitude of *most* European analysts who arrived in the United States prior to World War II, shaping their attitude toward their native American counterparts.

In fairness to the Europeans fleeing Hitler, American psychoanalysts did not welcome them with open arms, often refusing to recognize their credentials as lay analysts or constraining and encouraging qualified medical analysts to settle away from New York, Boston, and other urban centers where psychoanalysis was beginning to catch on. Undeterred by the envy and antipathy of their American counterparts, the Europeans who arrived in the 1930s slowly consolidated control over all the major institutes in New York, Boston, Chicago, and Los Angeles. Their superior training and prestige enabled them to ascend to positions of power and, eventually, to make the all-important determination regarding who was entitled to be (or become) a training analyst. No doubt they sought to make training more rigorous, but they also idolized Freud to such an extent that they turned psychoanalysis into a rigid and doctrinaire secular religion. As Douglas Kirsner put it in *Unfree Associations: Inside Analytic Institutes* (2000), the newly arrived analytic priesthood saw themselves as "the keepers of the flame," as "the anointed," or, in other words, as an epistemic elite uniquely in the know about the vagaries of the unconscious and the whole human condition, and therefore entitled to wield power ruthlessly to preserve "the truth" from foreign—that is, American—encroachments.

While they claimed to be uniquely qualified, having trained with Freud or members of his circle, the new analytic mandarins also lacked clearly articulated, publicly shared criteria of merit, or indeed, any fair and impartial way to assess competence in analytic theory or practice. The result, notes Kirsner, was the emergence of a "courtier culture," in which what you knew was utterly inconsequential by comparison with whom you knew, and whether or not you made the correct impression on the "right" people. The power elite did not have to explain or justify their attitudes or decisions to anyone but themselves. The predictable result was that many intelligent and outspoken trainees who were frank about their questions or misgivings were silenced or excluded before they qualified, ostensibly because of their psychopathology or lack of insight. Or, if they did qualify, they were not given referrals, to discourage them from practicing or affiliating with their accrediting body. Meanwhile, many flaming mediocrities advanced steadily through the ranks.

In short, by the 1950s, the halcyon days of psychoanalysis in America, a climate of anxious compliance and consciously cultivated docility replaced the exuberant enthusiasm that characterized European training institutes in the early days. In this stultifying atmosphere, a training analysis was often little more than an intensive, expensive, and lengthy course of indoctrination, and as a result, many qualified analysts lost the longed-for opportunity to explore their inner conflicts fully. The requirement of fitting their fantasies and feelings onto the Procrustean bed of orthodoxy—or their analyst's pet prejudices—robbed the whole process of authenticity and ensured that many of them remained profoundly neurotic or fixated in some fashion. Mindful of this shortcoming, many sought a second analysis freed from the strictures of their particular institute, whence the saying that the analyst's first analysis is "for the institute"; the second one, "for the analyst" (Malcolm 1983). And in the event of power clashes or ideological differences among the mandarins, various schisms erupted that sapped the energy and creativity of the psychoanalytic movement.

Fortunately for posterity, these developments did not stifle the intellectual creativity of the movement completely. The American refusal to recognize lay analysts as fully qualified practitioners, spearheaded by A. A. Brill, fostered a certain tunnel vision among American analysts. But most European analysts cherished a notion of psychoanalysis that is closer to the humanities and fosters more creative and interdisciplinary research. But as Kirsner points out, creative theorists who won a public following did not necessarily wield power in the inner sanctum. Analysts like Erikson, whose fame grew steadily because of the power and accessibility of their writing, were looked down upon by more powerful but less original and prolific apparatchiks as dabblers or popularizers who had lost or betrayed the essence of the analytic vision. And for various reasons, including loyalty to the movement, their need of referrals or teaching positions, creative theorists like these were often beholden to the bureaucrats and deferential to them in private and in public. So, strange as it sounds to the uninitiated, the fact remains that at the height of its popularity in the United States, there was no necessary correlation between an analyst's creativity and/or popularity, on the one hand, and his influence in inner circles, on the other. Indeed, in some instances, these traits were negatively correlated.

How did Erikson fare in the midst of these developments? He did very well, considering. When Erik Homberger arrived in New York in 1933, the one firm feature of his still-shaky identity was his vocation as psychoanalytic clinician. For this he had Anna Freud and the Professor to thank. Meanwhile, despite the approaching maelstrom, leaving Europe behind was not easy, and Erik's initial attitude toward America combined a subdued melancholy with the grim determination of a survivor. He later remarked to Huey Newton: "I will never forget the moment when our ship first sighted the coldly competitive skyline of New York. The sight more or less puts you in a state of psychic survivorship, both in the sense of having to accept, without looking back too much, and in the sense of having to survive as a family here too" (Friedman 1999, 110.)

Clearly, in addition to career considerations, family issues were very much on his mind. In fact, the two were inextricably intertwined. Erik's wife, Joan, was the daughter of an Episcopal minister, and, though artistic and outspoken—a protofeminist, in fact—she was also devout in her own fashion. This might have led to clashes had Erik embraced traditional Jewish customs, but soon after their marriage Erik dropped any pretense of keeping kosher or observing Jewish holidays—though, contrary to expectation, this did not damage his relationship to Karla and Theodor. After some initial misgivings, they sensibly decided to get over them, and welcomed Erik's spirited bride into their midst. Indeed, by 1929, three years before Erik's journey overseas, Theodor Homberger radiated with a newfound warmth and pride in his errant stepson, an attitude that was gratefully reciprocated on Erik's part. After all those years of dull estrangement, the positive change in his relationship with his stepfather must have been very gratifying.

Erik's sisters, Ruth and Ellen, both married Jews, but they welcomed Joan into the family as well, and credited this warm, focused, and outspoken beauty with transforming their confused and diffident brother, who could easily have become a loser, into a man of substance. Prior to Joan's appearance, they had liked their brother Erik in a distant, bemused way. But now that he was making his way in the world, with her help, they felt more comfortable in his presence.

In more favorable circumstances, this newfound family solidarity would probably have blossomed into a stable extended family, with Ruth and Ellen becoming devoted aunts, and Karla and Theodor exulting in their grandparental functions. After all, the first two children arrived promptly: Kai, the eldest, in 1930, and Jon, their second son, in 1933. But that was not to be. As Europe hurtled toward the abyss, Erik and Joan fled to America, where, with Erik's help, Ruth eventually settled with her husband, Paul Oppenheimer, in 1937. Ellen, an ardent Zionist, went to Haifa in 1933, where she met and married Yair Katz. When she returned to Karlsruhe to visit Karla and Theodor two years later, her parents' situation was quite desperate, and she persuaded them to leave their possessions behind and join her in Palestine. Since the Nazis had confiscated all their property, Karla and Theodor had lacked the resources to resettle there, so Erik sent substantial sums of money to the Haifa clan on a monthly basis. And, as Friedman reports, Theodor was deeply moved by his stepson's steadfastness. When Theodor died in 1949, says Friedman, Erik and he were close at heart, despite the vast geographical distance between them. And though he was drifting away from Judaism and often ducking the problem of anti-Semitism on the American campuses were he taught, Erik visited Haifa and Jerusalem often, and became an ardent admirer of Israel's resourceful and egalitarian kibbutzim and the bold strategic brilliance of its citizen army.

Meanwhile, after some initial setbacks in the New York area, Erik and family relocated to Boston, where Joan's mother, Mary Serson, helped them settle. There, in 1934, Erik got a leg up from Hanns Sachs and Irmarita Putnam, daughter of early American analyst James Jackson Putnam. Sachs and Putnam introduced him to William Healy, head of the Judge Baker Guidance

Center. Healy and associates were deeply impressed by Erik's ability to reach children deemed "hopeless cases"—an ability all the more impressive because Erik was still struggling to master English. So once again, his gift with children opened up unexpected doors. Child analysts were in demand, and despite his language difficulties, Erik Homberger thrived. In a letter to Helene Deutsch, one of Erik's former teachers at the Training Institute of the Vienna Psychoanalytic Society, dated February 9, 1935, Felix Deutsch—who was emigrating himself—recalled:

> I am trying to take up connections with a great variety of people, so as to get to know the lay of the land. For this reason I was at Homberger's today, to see how a man who certainly did not have the best pre-analytic qualifications, is able to make his way here. And he has done it! The means may not have been totally clean, but it can be excused by saying: the purpose sanctifies the means. He is now *the* child analyst. But he is working with utmost energy, and on the side he is completing the examinations for his doctorate in philosophy. I can forgive him for everything, who can only be compared with Hartmann's boys. (Roazen 1985, 280)

Among other things, Felix Deutsch's letter refers to the fact that Erik had gained admission to the doctoral program in psychology at Harvard—no small feat for someone who never completed an undergraduate degree! But that effort floundered. Harvard's psychology program was under the direction of Edwin Boring and Karl Lashley, and try as he might, Erik could not bring himself to reject or reformulate his analytic ideas and habits in behaviorist terms. He soon dropped out. Fortunately, however, he continued to cultivate ties with Harvard Psychological Clinic, founded by Morton Prince in 1927. The clinic was directed by Henry Murray, who had studied briefly with Freud and at greater length with Jung. There Erik was granted office space, periodic subsidies, and unlimited access to a fine library and many stimulating seminars. It was here, in 1937, that he met Scudder Mckeel, the first of many anthropologists he befriended, who later invited him to study the Oglala Sioux in South Dakota. Meanwhile, in 1938 Murray encouraged Erik to adapt some of his play therapy techniques to the testing of college freshmen. Erik's forays into psychological testing were largely unsuccessful, but they did provide his first exposure to college-aged Americans, who struck him as being very different from their European counterparts, prompting some searching reflections on the differences between American and European culture. Murray's emphasis on doing in-depth biographical studies of historical subjects was also very stimulating to Erik.

Between his various part-time jobs and his research at the Harvard Psychological Clinic, Erik also started a practice for adult patients. There he quickly abandoned the couch in favor of comfortable chairs. Early on, he even analyzed patients in his living room, where sessions were sometimes interrupted by his children's laughter or shouting, his requests for clarification of American English, and occasional forays to the fridge for snacks. For many patients, at least initially, these stark "deviations" from orthodox technique were profoundly reassuring, even endearing features (Friedman 1999). So Erik's reputation as a clinician grew steadily.

The problem with Boston was that while Erik was earning a decent livelihood, his attention was too fragmented by the demands of different employers to fully embrace his vocation as a researcher and a writer, which was chiefly what he wanted to do. So despite Joan's misgivings, the family moved to New Haven, Connecticut, in 1936. There, with the help of Lawrence Frank, Mark May, and Marian Putnam, Erik secured a three-year grant to work at Arnold Gesell's Child Development Clinic at Yale University. The arrangement was scuttled after eighteen months when Gesell denied Erik access to the clinic's research facilities. Gesell was alarmed and offended by Erik's frank interest in children's sexual behavior, and openly admitted to disliking "immigrants"—a code word for Jews. This crisis precipitated a move to Yale's Institute of Human Relations, under the command of John Dollard, where Erik met and studied with anthropologists Edward Sapir, Margaret Mead, and Ruth Benedict; pediatrician Benjamin Spock; psychologist Lois Murphy; and many others who would inspire, encourage, and applaud his work in years to come. (Dollard had been analyzed in Berlin, and written several books that Erik admired. Erik, in turn, analyzed Dollard's daughter, with very gratifying results.)

AN AMERICAN IDENTITY

While Dollard liked Erik, and did his best to keep him happy, the resources that were needed to free him up for research and writing were not forthcoming. Erik felt worried and unfulfilled, and in 1939 he accepted a job as a research associate and lecturer at the University of California's Institute of Child Welfare, directed by Jean Walker McFarlane, a friend of anthropologist Alfred Kroeber, who in due course introduced Erik to the Yurok tribe. Prior to his departure from New Haven, Erik had always gone by the name of Erik Homberger. But when he applied for naturalization, it was under the name "Erik Homberger Erikson," which became his legal name. McFarlane urged him to abbreviate Homberger to the initial "H.," and when Erikson published his first book, *Childhood and Society* (1950), that is how his name was spelled—Erik H. Erikson.

When pressed about this issue later, Erikson downplayed his former employer's role in precipitating the name change, and said that the original impetus for this idea came from Kai, who was tired of being teased for being a "hamburger" by his school mates. Joan thought a name change was a splendid idea too. After all, war was brewing, and Germany was the enemy once again. Even if America stayed out of the war, which didn't seem likely, Erik and Joan did not want their children tormented needlessly. And as he was about to transport his family across country to live on the Pacific shore, Erik reasoned that a Scandinavian name, honoring the existence of his (unknown) father would provoke less bigotry and ease their assimilation into the mainstream. And at that point in his life, acceptance was something he wanted.

Given his initial apprehensions and all the doors that had opened for him unexpectedly, Erikson was now quite fond of America, and its playful president, FDR. Why?

Unlike his adoptive homeland, Europe saddled each individual with a ready-made identity based on class, ethnicity, language, faith, and other historical accidents that were not of one's own making. From a European perspective, people may develop themselves in this or that direction more or less successfully, but they will never really transcend their cultural origins, which anchor their identity, for good or ill, even if they seek to deny it. And from a traditional European standpoint, Erik was a hopelessly hybrid entity.

By contrast with the Old World, America offered considerable scope and opportunity to the "self-made man" who renounced the beliefs of his ancestral home to embrace a new, more inclusive identity that transcended the conflicts and limitations of the old social order—a secular version of the Christian mythos that attracted Erik as a child. His analysis had not resolved the feelings of shame and the fear of ostracism that stemmed from the circumstances of his birth, so perhaps Erikson *needed* to take this step as an effort to transcend the memory of his own mixed and illegitimate parentage. As to the oblique implication that he was his now own father—Erik, Erik's son—he did not see the harm in that. As Freidman points out, consciously, at any rate, he wished to be done with the fantasy of finding and reuniting with his father—though in truth he had not resolved his issues on this score and remained somewhat preoccupied with it in years to come.

Though I suspect it never occurred to him at the time, Erikson would later be charged with insincerity, opportunism, and a desire to deny his Jewish heritage as a result of this name change. And in fairness to his critics, Friedman chronicles several instances when Erikson downplayed or avoided making reference to his Jewish upbringing. His name change was a part of an overall strategy for assimilation, and no doubt opportunistic motives played into his decision. But if we must be frank, let us also be fair. Many Jewish intellectuals and artists who "made it big" in America changed their names for similar reasons, and many of them were also analysts. Erikson was hardly unique. Moreover, unlike many of the Jews who pursued assimilation as a strategy for career advancement, Erikson's early religious upbringing was fraught with anguish, and his slow drift toward Christianity was more or less predictable given his temperament, childhood experience, and choice of spouse.

Finally, it is important to point out that none of these things hindered the eventual reconciliation of Erik with his stepfather, who, Erikson insisted, knew and approved of this development. And whether Homberger knew—or even cared—about this turn of events, it certainly did not harm their relationship toward the end of his life. And this is significant. After all, Theodor Homberger and his stepson got off to a very bad start, and given what each had to endure from proximity to the other for twenty years or so, their relationship ended as happily as one could imagine.

Another factor that may have prompted Erikson to change his name was a vague sense of guilt and a desire to compensate for hidden injuries of another kind. If he wanted to make life more comfortable for his family now, it may have been because his efforts to pursue his research career made it inordinately strenuous at times. In the summer of 1937, while Erik was away with Mekeel studying the Sioux in South Dakota, Kai got scarlet fever and was quarantined for a month and a half, with the result that Jon was on his own for long periods. Then, in the spring of 1938, Jon developed a mastoid infection, which required surgery followed by massive quantities of sulfa drugs to guard against a postoperative infection. These drugs triggered an allergic reaction that nearly killed him, and while Jon was recovering from this horrendous experience, a massive hurricane occurred to compound the horror of his recent trauma.

To make matters even worse, Joan, who was recovering from the mumps at the time, was devoting most of her available energy to their daughter, Sue, whom she had recently delivered, rather than to Jon, whose recovery took a long time. Arguably, the spread of serious illnesses among his family, a natural disaster, the arrival of Sue, and the hectic preparations for a move across the country should have prompted Erikson to stop his ethnographic efforts and return home to minister to his loved ones. But this he did not do, driven as he was by a desire to succeed and a deep aversion to domestic work of any kind. At the time he decided to change the family name, he may have vaguely sensed that his decision to pursue his career at the expense of his family had had some serious—if unforeseen—consequences. And if he did not, subsequent events would make that clear. Shortly after they all landed in Berkeley, Jon began to stutter, a problem that persisted for many years, and that Erikson, despite his clinical skills, could do nothing to ameliorate (Friedman

1999). Whatever developmental significance he may have attributed to it, Jon's stutter (and subsequent career difficulties) were probably experienced by Erikson as a standing reproach for his prolonged absences at a very critical juncture in his young children's lives.

At any rate, despite all the illness and the sense of dislocation that plagued members of his family in 1939, Erikson's career continued to flourish. In addition to working on a longitudinal study of healthy children with McFarlane, he taught the occasional seminar on child analysis at the University of California's Department of Psychology. When his relationship with McFarlane soured in 1940, he did very well in private practice and was appointed as a training analyst at the San Francisco Psychoanalytic Institute in 1942. Because of the glut of qualified Europeans and angry, disenfranchised American analysts about, he would never have achieved this status on the East Coast, and this fact was probably not lost on him when he decided to migrate westward. In 1943 he began working with war veterans at the Mount Zion Hospital, where he met and befriended two prominent Jungians, Joseph Henderson and Joseph Wheelwright. Despite the deep sectarian strife between Freudians and Jungians during World War II, Wheelwright in particular became a close and treasured friend (Erikson 1982a).

THE END OF THE BEGINNING: MIDDLE AGE AND ITS VICISSITUDES

Though he qualified to be a training analyst anywhere in the world in 1933, the fact remains that Erikson had to wait ten years and journey halfway around the world before he could achieve that status. But though he flourished in this training and supervisory role, Erikson was also appalled at the avid, grasping, and materialistic quality of many of his American trainees, who seemed much more interested in making money than in really helping their patients. Despite deepening dissatisfaction with the rigid ideology and teaching methods of the analytic establishment, Erikson was still gripped with the quasi-religious fervor of the European pioneers (Fromm 1959) and intent on imparting a more flexible, inclusive, and judicious tone to analytic training.

Then in 1944, when Joan was forty-one, their fourth and final child arrived. Unfortunately, the new arrival, Neil, had Down syndrome, and while Joan recovered from an unusually difficult birth in hospital, Erik consulted with Margaret Mead, now a close friend, who urged that the child be institutionalized. Joan and Erik were mortified at the prospect of taking this step, but on reflection deemed it necessary for the well-being of themselves and their other children—an attitude that is deplored nowadays, but was quite common at the time. While Erik eventually told Kai what happened at the hospital and afterward, he lied to Jon and Sue, telling them that the baby had died. This proved to be a big mistake. An analyst whose entire life was deranged by furtive family secrets lacked the courage and the candor to dispense with them in raising his own children—until seven years later, when the family was preparing to return to the East Coast and settle in Stockbridge, Massachusetts. Unfortunately, as Friedman points out, by then, the damage was done. The discovery that they had a younger brother who was deformed and institutionalized had a profoundly unsettling effect on Jon and Sue. Just what it signified to them at that time about their parents, their family, or life in general is unknown, perhaps, but it clear that this discovery, and the knowledge that they had been deceived, eroded their trust and confidence in both parents—but especially in their father, who was now engrossed in his writing and clinical work, and generally unavailable for extended periods.

Neil's birth and the decision to institutionalize him also put a strain on the relationship between Erik and Joan, who briefly contemplated divorce. Why? Looking back, Sue Erikson Bloland remembers just how easily her father was overwhelmed by any display of emotional neediness or distress on the part of any of his three young children (Erikson Bloland 1999). In such circumstances, she recalls, he would invariably call for Joan to intervene, feeling helpless and ineffectual to cope with such commonplace occurrences. Moreover, Joan revealed to Friedman that though he needed no encouragement to write, Erik was completely dependent on her to oversee the details of his diet, exercise, and wardrobe to stay on an even keel—so much so, in fact, that his insistent neediness rendered him like a fourth child.

Moreover, and perhaps more importantly, Joan had career aspirations of her own that had lain dormant, but not forgotten, for some time. She had diligently assisted her husband with his writing and research, but wanted to write books and papers of her own. Her devotion to her family left no time for that purpose. So in addition to echoing the prevailing medical consensus, the decision to institutionalize Neil probably reflected the Eriksons' awareness that they had reached middle age, that their energies were waning, and that the time allotted to them to accomplish their hearts' desire was finite. If they hoped to leave something valuable to posterity, they would have to do it soon. In short, they were experiencing what Erikson would later call *a crisis of generativity*.

So, though he scarcely knew them, the fact remains that from the moment of his birth until his death in 1965, poor Neil Erikson had a profoundly disturbing effect on the lives of his parents and siblings. But as Freidman rightly points out, the effort to understand and cope with this new situation brought some of Erikson's slumbering creative energies back to life. Erik and Joan now read a great deal about how the development of Down syndrome children deviates from the normal maturational trajectory, both in utero and afterward. The notion that mental health—or what Erikson called *ego strength*—is sustained by development that unfolds at a "normal rate" and in the proper sequence may have been influenced by their extensive reading.

In any case, in a concerted—and ultimately very successful—effort to save their marriage, Erik and Joan now joined forces to "map" the human life cycle after birth and explore its normative and/or psychopathological dimensions. Indeed, this joint project soon absorbed them both, and Erik never failed to credit Joan with coauthoring the basic developmental schemata in his eight-stage life cycle model. Though they drew inspiration from Freud and Shakespeare, among others, when he published their joint reflections in *Childhood and Society* (1950), Erikson invoked the epigenetic principle to explain human development.

The epigenetic principle, which derives from embryology, states that the development of neurological and anatomical features in the growing fetus must unfold in an orderly, preordained sequence; otherwise, morbidity ensues. The timing of these developmental stages is quite precise, and the precocious or belated appearance of specific morphological features in utero has adverse consequences, whether the pregnancy miscarries or is brought to term.

When applied to psychological growth, the epigenetic principle stipulates that there is an orderly sequence of stages that the developing person must traverse on the road to maturity, and that arrested development or extreme precocity are often indicative of psychopathological trends. However, in psychological growth, there are also some mitigating circumstances noted by Freud and his followers that Erikson took into account and wove into the fabric of his evolving theory. For example, in Freud's psychosexual theories, developmental arrest or precocity need not do irreversible damage if these untoward deviations from the norm can be remedied through appropriate therapeutic interventions. Moreover, while processes of physical maturation are irreversible in character, a temporary lapse into a an earlier stage of development may facilitate creativity or even herald a great leap forward in growth—what analyst Ernst Kris called "regression in the service of the ego." Finally, Freud also allowed that in the absence of psychotherapeutic intervention, some forms of arrest and/or precocity can be turned to account in the person's artistic or intellectual development as a result of sublimation, as in Freud's study of Leonardo da Vinci (Freud 1910a)

Even with these caveats in mind, however, one problem with Freud's epigenetic theory was that it only addressed human development from birth until the childbearing and/or child-rearing years, neglecting middle and old age—something Henry Murray, who had mentored Erikson at Harvard, did not do, thanks to his analysis with Jung. Indeed, if Freud overemphasized the determinism of early childhood experiences, Jung erred in the opposite direction, with an emphasis on the vicissitudes of aging and the challenges of facing approaching death.

Unlike Freud and Jung, however, Erikson tried to create developmental schema that did ample justice to the complexities of development on *both* sides of the life cycle and emphasized the cultural relativity of the timing of specific stages. So while the character or content of a specific stage has some generic properties that apply across all cultures, the precise timing of each stage may vary somewhat from one culture to the next, with some cultures prolonging or intensifying "oral" traits (e.g., the Sioux) and fantasies among their adult population, others more "anal" characteristics (e.g., the Yurok), while others prolong adolescence, and so on. In other words, by Erikson's reckoning, all human beings must traverse the same set of developmental hurdles and face the same basic psychological challenges. But the timetable for doing so is not as rigid or inflexible as a straightforward transposition of an embryological perspective might suggest.

Another novel feature of Erikson's developmental model is his insistence that the transition from one stage of development to another is mediated by a crisis. However, the term *crisis* does not refer here to a brief temporal interlude characterized by an urgent need to address some external threat. On the contrary, the crisis is an internal one, and, though it passes, presumably, with the emergence of a new developmental phase, in a vital sense the crisis in question is already prefigured at the very outset of every new phase of life. There is no getting around it.

Erikson's notion of developmental crisis was not unprecedented, of course. Though they did not employ the concept of identity to address it, as Erikson would later, Anna Freud and her circle had long recognized that adolescence inevitably entails a crisis of sorts, and Jung had already waxed eloquent about crises in midlife and old age. But due to the reciprocal antipathies between Freudians and Jungians that prevailed at the time, there was little or no attempt to bridge the gap between these discourses. A little closer to home, Søren Kierkegaard, whom Erikson studied closely, argued that there are three basic stages to adult development and that the transition from one to another is always mediated by a distinctive kind of crisis—and one can get "stuck" in the first or second stages and suffer a corresponding impoverishment or deformation of subjectivity (Friedman 1994).

Having said that, however, it is important to emphasize that the resolution of a specific stage's crisis does not entail the definitive transcendence of the conflict that gave rise to it. For another distinctive feature of Erikson's theory is that the resolution of all such developmental crises, from infancy onward, involves a kind of Hegelian dialectic in which antithetical attitudes or impulses struggle within us, only to yield an eventual synthesis in which the negative term is subdued or contained rather than abolished outright. In Hegelian terminology, the antithesis is said to be *aufheben*, or incorporated somehow into the emergent synthesis, rather than annulled completely. As it happens, this is the aspect of Erikson's work that he felt was the most widely ignored and misunderstood by mental health professionals (Evans 1967) That being so, we should at least pause to consider the first crisis in the epigenetic series that Erikson depicted to illustrate this process in more detail.

According to Erikson, the newborn infant is disposed to trust his or her caretakers when and if it can rely on responsive care on a more or less continuous basis. When such care is provided, the infant acquires an attitude of "basic trust" that facilitates the emergence of initiative, or active and exploratory behavior. When such care is lacking, however, or is provided erratically and episodically, the infant acquires an attitude of "basic mistrust," which, in pronounced form, obstructs or derails development, leading to hostile and/or psychotic trends.

Unfortunately, the exigencies of life are such that interruptions in the quality or continuity of care for infants are more or less inevitable. So despite the best of intentions and the most diligent efforts on a parent's behalf, transient experiences of mistrust are unavoidable in infancy. Moreover, while basic mistrust has pathological sequelae if taken too far, some degree of mistrust is actually adaptive as a spur to reality testing and as an antidote to excessive credulity and suggestibility. Another way of putting this is that people who trust others too much lack trust in their own judgment, and if they fail to learn from experience, their prospects for survival may be impaired accordingly. On the road to maturity, some measure of mistrust must enter into our dealings with significant others lest we remain naive in our attachments to them. What is vital for health, said Erikson, is not the mere presence of mistrust, but the ratio of trust to mistrust. If trust prevails, by and large, we thrive. However, if trust is eroded and our tendencies to mistrust exceed a certain threshold, our relationships with others become more fraught with conflict and suspicion, and, in due course, impossible to sustain. And when that is so, we can lay waste either to our (real or imaginary) adversaries, or to our own sanity — or to both.

Later on, in *The Golden Rule and the Cycle of Life* (1962) and "The Ontogeny of Ritualization" (1966a), Erikson would emphasize that the gradual ascendance of basic trust over mistrust in the infant results in a mood of hopefulness about the present and the immediate future, adding that the "virtue" of hope precedes and, in a certain sense, supercedes all others. No matter what stage of life we are in, no attitude is more vital to the maintenance of our mental health than a hopeful disposition, even in the face of circumstances that are calculated to defeat it. Moreover, our sense of the numinous, of the holy, is rooted in our first encounter with the mother (or mother surrogate), whose tender ministrations create the first experiential template for the sense of a "hallowed presence." Though different cultures divert or develop this sense of the holy in diverse ways, they all draw on this primordial experience of infancy to articulate their sense of the divine being, or of providence, or grace.

Erikson went on to add that it is foolish to characterize the acquisition of basic trust as a purely intrapsychic process. As Urie Bronfenbrenner later emphasized, albeit in much greater detail (Bronfenbrenner 1988), the parents' ability to provide loving, continuous care to a child must also be supported by faith in the future—a faith often sustained in the face of adversity by organized religion. And even when it lacks a religious coloration, parents' faith in their ability to nourish and educate their young and bring them to wholesome maturity, despite the challenges posed by encircling threats of one kind or another, is necessary to evoke and sustain the hope of their children. The faith parents have that they can meet such challenges depends in part on their own earliest experiences of loving kindness, that is, on their own parents, living and dead. So though it manifests locally in the radiant expression of the healthy, growing child, from the very outset the production and sustenance of hope is actually a societal affair, one that Erikson—borrowing from David Rapaport (1951) in another context—called *cogwheeling*, or the intricate and ongoing intermeshing of the hopes, expectations, and activities of differing generations simultaneously.

While many of these ideas were foreshadowed in *Childhood and Society*, many had to wait a decade or more to be fleshed out in detail. Meanwhile, however, though *Childhood and Society* showed great promise and originality, some aspects of the book were somewhat derivative, and because Erikson's intellectual influences were quite heterodox, as it turns out, he sedulously avoided citing them. For example, Erikson said nothing here about the work or ideas of Joseph Wheelwright, the Jungian who collaborated with him in the treatment of veterans at Mount Zion Hospital and who influenced him in various ways. Another person whose works are conspicuous by their absence in his index, bibliography, and footnotes is Fromm, who was drummed out of the IPA in 1954 (Roazen 2001), and whose first book, *Escape from Freedom* (Fromm 1941), had a considerable impact on Erikson's thinking.

In short, though Erikson disguised this fact as cleverly as he could, there are both Jungian and Frommian tropes in *Childhood and Society*. Despite protestations of undying loyalty to the Professor, Erikson was beginning a lifelong program of adopting and obliquely legitimating revisionist perspectives under the guise of orthodoxy. For *Childhood and Society* sought to embed Freud's theory of infantile sexuality in a larger, more encompassing theory of human development that involved eight distinct life stages and did not disparage spiritual experiences or ideals.

While many people greeted *Childhood and Society* with considerable enthusiasm, Anna Freud claimed not to understand a word of it. In *Freud and His Followers* (Roazen 1971), Paul Roazen points out that her father, Sigmund Freud, professed not to understand ideas somewhat at variance with his own, and that Paul Federn, whom Erikson admired, deemed his apparent inability to understand another point of view a symptom of "resistance"—or, more bluntly, disapproval. No doubt Erikson greeted Anna Freud's avowed perplexity in the same frame of mind. Anna Freud's diffidence and apparent perplexity over the direction of *Childhood and Society* changed to deep indignation when Erikson published "On the Dream Specimen of Psychoanalysis" in the *Journal of the American Psychoanalytic Association* in 1954. The fact that Heinz Hartmann endorsed the paper, which purported to elucidate a "crisis of generativity" in the founder of psychoanalysis, did nothing to diminish her wrath. After all, her pupil—or, figuratively speaking, her son—had dared to analyze her father (and analyst), his own analytic "grandfather," in public. And not only did Erikson use Freud's first "specimen" dream and his free associations to buttress his own epigenetic theory, which was markedly different from her father's (and hers), he even had the effrontery to draw attention to the sexual (and homosexual) symbolism of "The Dream of Irma's Injection"—dream elements that were patent enough to discerning readers, but had gone conspicuously unremarked upon in Freud's analysis, and were tactfully overlooked by other, more orthodox commentators ever since then. (For more on this dream of Freud's, see chapter 7.)

Anna Freud did not voice all these objections in quite so many words, but that is probably a fair summary of her position. In the years that followed, Anna Freud's anger at Erikson was also reflected in the verdicts of two close colleagues, Kurt Eissler and Robert Waelder. Reversing the decision of Freud's own circle in 1933, Eissler, for example, declared that Erikson, who was credentialed in 1933, and became a full training analyst in San Francisco in 1942, was really a mere "psychotherapist"—a very grave insult to analytic insiders (Roazen 1976). And in *The Basic Theory of Psychoanalysis*, Waelder volunteered that the identity crisis Erikson said is characteristic of adolescent development, and therefore normal up to a point, is really a peculiarity of a particular subgroup of those who suffer from the "As If" personality described by Helene Deutsch (Waelder 1960, 210). The drift of these remarks is crystal clear, even if deliberately understated; in Waelder's view, Erikson took a relatively rare type of psychopathology and gave it a universal significance that is completely unwarranted by the facts.

Other establishment figures—Hartmann and Rapaport, the most prominent—leaped to Erikson's defense, however. But whatever the source or meaning of the insults radiating from Anna Freud's circle, Erikson had no choice but to affirm the validity of what he himself experienced firsthand. Leaving his own adolescence aside for the moment, Erikson observed identity confusion as a palpable source of disturbance among American war veterans, new immigrants, and, to a lesser but significant extent, Americans generally. For one of the risks we run for abandoning the Old World outlook and embracing the more inclusive and encompassing American approach to identity is the threat of uprootedness, epitomized in the dreams of many of his patients—immigrants and natives alike. Or, put another way, in embracing the New World, Americans are exchanging an identity that is too narrow and constraining for one that, perhaps by virtue of its very inclusiveness, is too vague and diffuse, too ill defined, and too subject to change, thanks to American culture's restless penchant for movement and self-invention, which are accelerated by ceaseless technological innovation.

So strangely enough, displaced Viennese like Eissler and Waelder, who were loyal to Anna Freud, trashed Erikson's identity concept even though it was widely applicable in their new cultural surroundings. Among other things, no doubt, this was a measure of their obliviousness to (and distaste for) their adoptive homeland, as well as an oblique affirmation of fidelity to Freud. Physically, they were in America; but mentally, they were still in Vienna, according to classical Freudianism a timeless, universal validity that was obviously quite discrepant with the turbulent realities of the New World.

Though he was never tactless enough to say so publicly, Erikson probably interpreted the provocations of Eissler and Waelder as the indirect expression of a strong defensive posture resulting from attempts to cling to their old cultural identities by selectively screening out ideas and experiences that conflicted with their sense of cosmological coherence. He had to, to be consistent with his own emerging insights. In any case, despite subsequent efforts on both sides to smooth things over, this was an intractable situation and was bound to end badly. Anna Freud and her circle suspected Erikson of calculated insincerity and barely disguised revisionist intentions, while he saw her friends and representatives in America as operating in a state of near denial and being furtive and dishonest about their personal animus toward him.

And here is another curious irony. In fairness to Anna Freud, Erikson was not entirely candid—with himself or with others—about his revisionist agenda. But, in fairness to Erikson, his evolving identity theory and its application to American life shows that he was much more open to—and honest about—the challenges of his new environment than they. As a result, perhaps, Americans warmed to his ideas and were often quite oblivious to the implicit critique of their way of being that was subtly inscribed in Erikson's writings. If Americans tended to ignore the critical component of Erikson's ideas, they were encouraged in that direction by Erikson himself, at least initially. For Erikson's eagerness to succeed, his characteristic emphasis on health rather than illness, and his deep and genuine reluctance to offend prompted him to accentuate the positive dimensions of American culture until the mid-1960s, when latent misgivings about imperialism, racism, nuclear arms, and horror at the Vietnam War prompted a dramatic reappraisal and shift in tone.

FROM BERKELEY TO STOCKBRIDGE

While Erikson was working on *Childhood and Society*, his growing prominence in San Francisco's psychoanalytic community brought him to the attention of the Menninger Clinic in Topeka, whose chief of staff, Robert Knight, repeatedly attempted to lure him to Kansas. But the prospect of life on the prairies did not appeal to Joan, so in 1949 Erikson accepted a full professorship in psychiatry at the University of California, Berkeley, and shortly thereafter was drawn into the controversy about the university's loyalty oath and the McCarthyite hysteria that was gripping the nation. Erikson refused to sign the oath, but found the experience of taking a stand and speaking out publicly against it deeply distressing. And despite his vocal objections to a public oath, as Freidman points out, Erikson made the curious (and deceitful) concession of signing a somewhat watered-down version of the loyalty oath secretly to placate his employers—an odd and unnecessary gesture that probably bothered him later.

Fortunately, he did not have to stay there long, because in 1950 Knight left the Menninger Clinic to assume the directorship of the Austen Riggs Center in Stockbridge and immediately invited Erikson to join him there. In addition to a generous salary, Knight offered Erikson the opportunity to work a few days every other week with Benjamin Spock at the Arsenal Nursery School of the Western Psychiatric Institute at the University of Pittsburgh. Erikson accepted gladly and moved his family to Stockbridge in 1951.

When Erikson arrived at Austen Riggs, he began to thematize the issue of identity formation for and with his adolescent and young adult patients. At this point in his career, Erikson was apt to emphasize that the adolescent is torn between simultaneous needs for repudiation and devotion—needs he found vividly and acutely expressed in young Martin Luther. The adolescent also renews the infantile search for recognition and validation from the other, but in the effort to separate from its parents displaces its longing onto the larger community in a number of potentially conflict-laden or conflict-inducing ways. For example, said Erikson, a mistrustful adolescent typically tests her elders more ingeniously and insistently than a child does because she understands their vulnerabilities better, and needs to strenuously *reject* those features of the parental world (and worldview) that she embraced as a child but finds to be an obstacle to her autonomy now. On the other hand, said Erikson, while emphatically rejecting certain things, she must also embrace a political or religious ideology and/or answer to some sense of vocation before pledging herself irrevocably to a committed relationship with another human being and achieving genuine intimacy.

To achieve these goals, said Erikson, the adolescent requires a period of experimentation or a "psychosocial moratorium" in which to immerse himself experimentally in different ideological frameworks and vocational settings and communities. It is a period characterized by freedom from commitment while the adolescent "tries on" different identities to see which one suits him best. As the adolescent finds his way, spiritually, politically, and professionally, often at some distance from the parents, recognition from the community at large helps to consolidate his sense of worth and future promise, and to avert the danger of what Erikson variously termed *identity diffusion* or *role confusion*. Another, more Hegelian way of expressing this is that one cannot define oneself exclusively by way of negation, by reference to what one is not, by what one rejects. That is necessary, perhaps, but not sufficient to finish the job. A stable adult identity is also defined positively by one's commitments and the ability to commit oneself irreversibly to a person, position, mission, or ideal (Erikson 1956a)

That being so, said Erikson, the adolescent needs to be faithful to herself and to her principles, and must be valued and recognized by others and put to good use in order not to succumb to the kind of sterile negativism that comes with a refusal or inability to commit oneself to a particular course in life (Erikson 1958b). And when this process miscarries, said Erikson, it is often the result of what he termed a *missed mutuality* or a disruption in *intergenerational identification* in early development that is evidenced repeatedly in the patient's dreams and symptoms.

We'll say more about all this later. For now, suffice it to say that Erikson was able to describe the inner struggles of adolescents (and fixated adults) with such insight and sensitivity because he identified strongly with his patients' struggles and saw the potentially constructive side of their conflicts in ways that other analysts, whose sense of intergenerational continuity was relatively intact and therefore taken for granted, could not. Moreover, while becoming a healer of troubled youth, Erikson was also attempting to fathom and resolve many of his own lingering conflicts, and he used the experiences gleaned in this way as raw material for many books and papers.

Erikson's Stockbridge period was probably the most rewarding and productive period of his life. Despite subsequent moves, he always considered Stockbridge his home. Its splendid wooded surroundings afforded Erikson plenty of opportunity to indulge his adolescent passion for walking, while Riggs itself offered Erikson sustaining friendships with colleagues such as Robert Knight, Margaret Brenman-Gibson, Merton Gill, Roy Schafer, Stuart Miller, Allan Wheelis and, above all, David Rapaport, whom Erikson described as his "analytic conscience." In retrospect, however, it is clear that despite (or because of!) the warm relationship between them, Rapaport suffered from the delusion that Erikson's work-in-progress was completely compatible with Freudian metapsychology, as well as with the work of Hartmann (Friedman 1999, 288; Meyer and Bauer 2002). In truth, however, Erikson's vision represented a dramatic departure from both Freud and Hartmann, as we shall see. Nevertheless, Rapaport's perverse insistence to the contrary was so eloquent and authoritative at the time that it provided Erikson with some much-needed cover from orthodox critics. While warmth of feeling my have led his judgment astray, Rapaport's intentions were good, his interest strong, and his support for Erikson unflagging, despite Anna Freud's strictures.

Another factor that made the Stockbridge years productive was that Joan flourished in these surroundings, too. Joan had always been a diligent wife and mother, and had helped Erik master English and, in due course, to map the human life cycle. On her arrival in Stockbridge, however, Joan was placed in charge of Riggs's burgeoning activities program, and saw to it that theater, dance, painting, sculpture, woodwork, gardening, and music, all mentored with patience and zest by a stable community of local artists, became an integral part of patients' daily lives. She even started a Montessori kindergarten for local families and the staff at Riggs, in which patients could apprentice and study child development firsthand. These new challenges brought all her creative energies to the fore. Thanks to her imagination and initiative, the Activities Program at Riggs became a unique, engrossing, and deeply healing experience for many patients, which stood in stark contrast to the enforced passivity, boredom, and/or utter self-absorption that prevails in many treatment settings. Moreover, it is instructive to note that at her insistence, the artistic, literary, dramatic, and horticultural activities of the patients at Riggs were deemed "an interpretation-free zone"—one where disciplined effort and reciprocity, not introspection, were the norm (Shapiro and Fromm 1999). Whether this policy reflected her earlier antipathy to psychoanalysis or a judicious appraisal of the human need for meaningful work and communal involvement—

or both, in some measure—is a matter for conjecture. But what cannot be doubted is that the patients' efforts and accomplishments in these diverse projects were remarkably sophisticated and successful, building skills, knowledge, and confidence while they were in treatment. Erik, for his part, was deeply impressed with Joan's results. Pondering the effectiveness of her programs, he wrote appreciatively about the importance of work and recognition from the community in the healing of troubled adolescents (Shapiro and Fromm 1999). And in response to the newly published work of Kai, who was now a sociologist at the University of Pittsburgh, Erikson also wrote about the potential pitfalls of succumbing to the narrow, negative identity imposed by lengthy immersion in "the patient role"—something Joan's activities program clearly helped many patients to avoid.

In addition to the splendors of nature and gratifying work for Erik and Joan alike, Stockbridge offered the Eriksons a wonderful social circle, including friends like Norman Rockwell and Reinhold Niebuhr, who was just around the corner and always willing to converse with Erikson about his book on Martin Luther, which was beginning to take shape. Though not a neighbor, as it happens, in 1956 a young man named Robert Jay Lifton also became a frequent visitor at the Erikson home. Lifton and Erikson soon became close friends, and in years to come would launch the psychohistory movement that defined Erikson's public profile in the 1960s (Lifton and Olson, 1974).

IN HIS OWN VOICE

Meanwhile, his reputation abroad was growing. In 1956 Erikson was honored with an invitation from the Frankfurt Institute for Social Research and the University of Heidelberg to join Hartmann, Franz Alexander, and René Spitz on the speaker's podium on May 6 at a celebration of Freud's centenary in Frankfurt. After introducing himself in a modest, muddle-headed, and somewhat misleading fashion as a "student" of David Rapaport's, Erikson presented an illuminating paper entitled "The First Psychoanalyst," which was subsequently printed in the *Yale Review* (Erikson 1956b), in which he shared his youthful impressions of the elderly Freud as a man of "rare dimensions, rare contradictions." He then presented the first in what would become a long series of meditations on the similarities between Darwin's and Freud's episodes of "creative illness," followed by brief reflections on Freud's "Project for a Scientific Psychology," his abandonment of the seduction theory of hysteria, his peculiar relationship with Wilhelm Fliess, his self-analysis, and the gradual emergence of the dynamic, economic, topographical, structural, and genetic "standpoints" in psychoanalysis. While thought provoking and pleasingly phrased, there was nothing deeply controversial or provocative about his paper until the very end, where he noted:

> Today, the student of psychoanalysis receives a training analysis which prepares him for the emotional hazards of his work. But he must live with the rest of mankind in this era of what we may call anxiety-in-plenty, and neither his personal life nor in the progress of his work will spare him renewed conflicts, be his profession ever so recognized, ever so organized. Wide recognition and vast organization, in fact, will not assure—they may even endanger—the basic triad, for which the psychoanalyst makes himself responsible, to wit: that as a clinician he accept his contract with the patient as the essence of his field of study and relinquish the security of seemingly more "objective" methods; that as a theorist he maintain a sense of obligation toward continuous conceptual redefinition and resist the lure of seemingly more profound or more pleasing philosophic short cuts; and finally, that as a humanist he put self-observant vigilance above the satisfaction of seeming professional omnipotence. For, in a sense, the psychoanalytic method must remain forever a "controversial" tool, a tool for the detection of that aspect of the total image of man which in a given historical period is being neglected or exploited, repressed or suppressed by the prevailing technology and ideology—including hasty "psychoanalytic" ideologies (Erikson 1956b, 42–43)

Due to the emergence of psychoanalytic training organizations that rival the International Psychoanalytic Association, Erikson's remarks will not strike many contemporary analysts as being particularly bold or outspoken. But Erikson was still operating in an environment that required more doctrinal purity and more public gestures of conformity than is generally the case today. So in effect, if not in so many words, Erikson was using the occasion of Freud's centenary to caution colleagues and prospective psychoanalysts to be wary of success, or, more precisely, of the unanticipated side effects of their newfound respectability and their large international administrative apparatus, which tends to obscure the risks and the responsibilities inherent in becoming an analyst. The dedicated clinician has to take responsibility for himself, exercise "self-observant vigilance," and continuously redefine his concepts in the light of experience. He cannot trust the bureaucracy to be his scientific conscience, nor allow it to wrap him in a rigid dogma, dutifully handed down, and he must resist the temptation to embrace any fashionable and newly contrived "psychoanalytic" ideology that comes along. In short, Erikson was suggesting that the real psychoanalyst must engage in a rigorous, lifelong "*imitatio* Freud," but according to his own lights, rather than letting others prescribe for him how to do this according to an acceptable formula. (Shades of Jacques Lacan!)

Finally, Erikson appended another task to those traditionally assigned to the psychoanalytic clinician, namely, to detect "that aspect of the total image of man which in a given historical period is being neglected or exploited, re-pressed or suppressed by the prevailing technology and ideology." The faith-ful fulfillment of this task will presumably ensure that psychoanalysis will al-ways remain controversial, no matter how prosperous or deeply sunk in middle-class respectability individual practitioners may be. So according to Erikson, a real analyst is duty bound to harness his skills in the service of cul-tural critique and collective emancipation as well as the remediation of indi-vidual suffering.

And Erikson did not stop there. Two years later, in *Young Man Luther*, he gave his wariness toward the analytic mainstream even clearer expression. Here, however, his misgivings were expressed somewhat obliquely, by way of some provocative and illuminating comparisons he made between psycho-analysis and monastic orders. While discussing Luther's monastic training, for example, he said:

> I am led to think of my own profession: let me make the most of a strange par-allel. Young (and often not so young) psychoanalysts in training often undergo a training procedure which demands a total and central personal involvement, and which takes greater chances with the individual's relation to himself and to those who up to then shared his life, than any other professional training except monkhood. Because the reward for psychoanalytic training, at least in some countries, is a good income; because, for decades, the psychoanalyst seemed primarily preoccupied with the study of sexuality; and because psychoanalytic power under certain historical conditions can corrupt as much as any other power, an aura of licentiousness is often assumed to characterize this training.
>
> The future psychoanalyst, however, must undergo a personal psychoanalysis. This is a "treatment" which shares fully with the treatment of patients a certain systematic interpersonal austerity. Over the decades, psychoanalysts have ac-cepted the formal setting of the almost daily appointment as the natural arrange-ment for eliciting the analysand's free associations. However, this natural setting for a spontaneous production is both an exercise in a new kind of asceticism, and a long-range experiment determining in large measure the free verbal material that it provokes (Erikson 1958b, 151.)

This last sentence is striking. It bristles with gentle irony, poking fun at the laboriously contrived conditions necessary to engender the kind of lucid, self-referential reverie deemed "natural" or "spontaneous" by the analytic profession. Erikson then enumerated the "ascetic" dimensions of the analytic setting—the restriction of the visual field, the prohibition of movement, ab-sence of facial communication, the "deliberate exposure to emerging thought and imagery," all of which run contrary to the conventions governing normal conversation—and concluded that these basic conditions "produce, as they are intended to, a transference neurosis" (151). Another striking statement.

But unlike critics of psychoanalysis, who dismiss both the process and the results of free association as pure artifact, and therefore as worthless—or worse, scientifically speaking—Erikson insisted that "psychoanalysis helps those who are well enough to tolerate it, and intelligent enough to gain by it over and above the cure of symptoms. As an intellectual experience, however, it is like other ascetic practices in specifically arousing and giving access to certain recesses of the mind otherwise completely removed from conscious mastery."

This passage is noteworthy because it attests to the value of an analytic therapy as an "intellectual experience" that—for some, at any rate—may be valuable "over and above the cure of symptoms." But there are potential drawbacks to this method as well. Erikson cautioned that

> [i]t stands to reason . . . that when a devotional denial of the face, and a systematic mistrust of all surface are used as tools in a man's worklife, they can lead to an almost obsessional preoccupation with "the unconscious," a dogmatic emphasis on inner processes as the only true essence of things human, and an overestimation of verbal meanings in human life. The risks and the chances inherent in this method are analogous to those in Martin's scruples. Into the ears of a master whose face is averted, and who refuses in any personal sense to either condemn or to justify, temptations are revealed which one never dreamt of, or never knew one dreamt of until one began to understand dreams and to recognize the maneuvers of self-deception (152).

While discussing the many similarities between monastic discipline and psychoanalysis, Erikson credited Luther's confessor, Dr. Johannes von Staupitz, with rare therapeutic acumen that supposedly saved the sanity of this prodigiously gifted but deeply disturbed young man. A more recent biographer, Richard Marius, contradicts Erikson, arguing that Staupitz was a genial but shallow and self-centered fellow who did not care deeply about Luther, but simply muddled through his interminable confessions and monumentally petty self-reproaches in a steadfast, even-tempered way, offering solace and inspiration where he could (Marius 1999). In other words, hints Marius, using Staupitz as a prop, Luther cured himself—if "cure" is the appropriate way of framing the young monk's newfound determination to confront the powers that be.

Either way, the monastic injunctions to confront temptation and root out self-deception, as taught to Martin Luther and as depicted subsequently by Erikson, are really not the central issue here. Whether Erikson's account of Luther's monastic training was accurate, and the parallels he adduced between monastic discipline and a training analysis are valid, the more pertinent fact is that Erikson devoted five full pages to elucidating these ostensible parallels in the interests of clarifying the background and nature of Luther's existential crisis. To put the matter bluntly, the fact that he spent so much time and attention elucidating these parallels says something striking about Erikson himself: He clearly took the parallel between psychoanalysis and religion—which was anathema to Sigmund Freud and to the vast majority of his colleagues—very seriously indeed. Moreover, he used this parallel to level a frank and illuminating critique of his own profession's training procedures. At the end of these reflections, for example, he wrote:

> When such a responsible invention for the disciplined increase of inner freedom becomes widely used as a therapy and as a method of professional training, it is bound to become standardized so that many will be able to benefit from it who of their own accord would never have thought of such strenuous self-inspection, and who are not especially endowed for it. A standardized procedure calls for uniform application, an application which would have been much too uniform for those who initiated the method. Here training analysts are—on rare occasions, to be sure—aware of the other side of the coin: the predicament of the young Martin's superior's when they found that they had a young great man on their hands. If such a man, possessing the truly original self-inspection and the fierce pride that is attached to originality—if such a man should apply to us for training, would we recognize him? Could he fit his budding originality into our established methods? And could we do justice to him, within a training system increasingly standardized and supervised? (Erikson 1956b, 154)

Though stated as tactfully as possible, under the circumstances, this was actually a powerful indictment. In his quiet, understated way, Erikson was declaring that he had had enough and was now throwing down the gauntlet, respectfully thumbing his nose (in print) at many people whom he had to treat cordially (in person). Now that he was approaching his sixtieth year, he would speak his mind about these systemic evils in his profession, even if he would not point a finger of blame at specific individuals. And what were these systemic evils?

Judging from his remarks, Erikson saw analysis primarily as "a responsible invention for the disciplined increase in inner freedom"—one that had been adapted to therapeutic and professional uses. By Erikson's reckoning the (inevitable) routinization and standardization of psychoanalysis favored the reception and training of many who, in other circumstances, would have avoided strenuous introspection and "are not especially endowed for it." And while the inevitable routinization and standardization that the method undergoes benefits people like these, said Erikson, those rare souls capable of "truly original self-inspection, and the fierce pride that is attached to originality"—like Freud, perhaps?—seldom thrive in such an environment.

Many training analysts circa 1958 probably shared Erikson's misgivings, but few, if any, had the courage to voice them publicly. And therein lay the problem. Doing the whole clan's dirty laundry in full view of the general public is greatly frowned on in most professions. While it took courage to express, we should ask ourselves whether Erikson's bold questioning, and the critique it entailed, was sound on the whole. Erich Fromm certainly thought so, and was drummed out of the IPA in 1954 for uttering similar sentiments (Roazen 2001). And in 1959, one year after *Young Man Luther* was published, R. D. Laing was almost disqualified by the London Institute of Psychoanalysis for possessing the kind of fierce pride and originality Erikson applauded in Martin Luther (Burston 1996, chap. 3). If their stories are any indication, Erikson hit the nail squarely on the head. Meanwhile, Robert Jay Lifton took a somewhat different route than Fromm and Laing. The latter were qualified analysts who were marginalized within their own profession, despite—and because of—their large public followings. But Lifton, who was nearing the end of his analytic training, was a relative unknown who decided to drop out altogether because of the similarities between psychoanalysis and the practice of "thought-reform" or "brainwashing," which he was studying intensively at the time (Lifton 1961). It is a testament to Erikson's openness and respect for other people's points of view that he never tried to dissuade Lifton from abandoning the analytic vocation and remained his good friend in the ensuing years.

Meanwhile, leaving cases like theirs aside, sociologically minded readers will note the parallel between Erikson's critique of psychoanalysis circa 1960 and Max Weber's ideas about the "routinization" of charisma (Gerth 1946). Similarly, Christians may discern a parallel between Erikson's plaint and Kierkegaard's *Attack on "Christendom"* (1845–1855), which lashed out at the growth of the church, its embrace of respectability, and the corresponding death of the spirit that had animated its inception (Kierkegaard 1968). It was as if Erikson was gently scolding his contemporaries for abandoning, disfiguring, or obscuring the spirit that gave rise to their movement while clinging desperately to the letter of their "law." Similarly, he seemed to imply that he adhered to a higher standard of intellectual integrity, one that was more consonant with the founder's real intentions.

But despite his manifold misgivings about the impossible profession, Erikson was not about to abandon ship like his friend Lifton. This fact is reflected in another remark in *Young Man Luther*, where Erikson observed that "the first discipline encountered by a young man is the one he somehow must identify with unless he chooses to remain unidentified in his years of need. The discipline he happens to encounter, however, may turn out to be poor ideological fare; poor, in view of what, as an individual, he has not derived from

his childhood problems, and poor in view of the irreversible decisions that begin to crowd in on him" (1958b, 90).

As Paul Roazen discerned many years ago, Erikson was not talking merely
about Luther here, but also, and quite consciously, about himself. If one were
to adopt a skeptical view of his motives for remaining a psychoanalyst, one
might well ask: What else could he do? He had failed as an artist and had no
professional credentials beyond those conferred on him by Freud and his circle. But even if we take this uncharitable view of matters, it is clear enough
from context that Erikson was somewhat ambivalent about "the impossible
profession" and acutely mindful of various disappointments and deprivations
imposed by his disciplinary affiliation. Moreover, as the emerging psychohistory movement would eventually demonstrate, he was determined to
make up for these built-in constraints with creative interdisciplinary research,
which would obligate him to wrestle with his vocation anew and make it
uniquely his own. In a certain sense, this makes his candid comparisons between psychoanalysis and religious introspection all the more impressive.

3

A Crisis of Integrity

ERIKSON AT HARVARD

The Austen Riggs Center was very kind to Erikson. Thanks to Robert Knight's wise stewardship, it provided him with supportive and congenial colleagues, a constant flow of intriguing patients, and all the artistic stimulation and natural splendor he required to clear his mind and rejuvenate his spirit when circumstances required. Despite its benefits and attractions, however, Erik was getting restless again, and so the Eriksons left Stockbridge for Cambridge and Harvard University in 1960—the same year Karla Homberger and David Rapaport died.

Unlike most academics, who apply and compete for jobs like everyone else and are attached to a specific department, Erikson was designated as a University Professor, and therefore tied to no single department. This fact speaks to his growing fame, to the temper of the times, and to the background and interests of Michael Maccoby, a doctoral student in psychology at Harvard who was using *Childhood and Society* in his undergraduate tutorials and had recently read *Young Man Luther*. Maccoby went to visit Erikson in Stockbridge and brought him to the attention of McGeorge Bundy, Dean of Harvard College, and then sought endorsements for his appointment to a University Chair from David Riesman, Talcott Parsons, and Robert White, who valued Erikson's interdisciplinary orientation and enthusiastically endorsed the idea of bringing him on board (Friedman 1999).

Despite some previous experience teaching small graduate seminars in Berkeley in the forties, Erikson felt utterly unprepared for the large undergraduate audiences that awaited him, and to assist him with this transition, Maccoby dispatched Kenneth Keniston to Stockbridge that summer to help

49

him prepare and to ensure he'd be ready in the fall. In the years that followed, a series of diligent and helpful graduate assistants—many of whom went on to establish successful careers of their own—were employed to help Erikson manage his undergraduate courses. One of them, Virginia Demos, remembers his classroom delivery as somewhat scattered and elliptical at first. Typically, his lectures started to cohere only toward the middle or the end of his talk— by which time he had the audience in the proverbial palm of his hand. Though he lectured at length, Demos recalls, Erikson did not just drone on monotonously, as many of his colleagues did; instead he enlivened students with curious anecdotes and self-disclosure, making jokes and frequent eye contact. But despite his playfulness, he did not pander to students, and he spoke with a quiet sense of conviction that many students found compelling. And after every lecture he would ask his assistant, with genuine concern and without a trace of false modesty: "Was I OK?" (Demos, personal communication, 2000).

Erikson was not merely "OK." In fact, he was a big hit with students, becoming one of the most sought-after lecturers on campus. From the beginning, Erikson's popularity with students was remarkable—and a relief both to himself and to the Harvard brass, some of whom regarded his presence there as quite a gamble. After all, as Lawrence Friedman points out, though he gleaned the support of some powerful people there, no department or discipline at Harvard really wanted him—which is not surprising, considering the depth and extent of his interdisciplinary efforts. Though he had an exquisite sensitivity to the boundary issues of his patients, Erikson was an inveterate boundary transgressor in the realms of expert knowledge, and his efforts to blend clinical work with the findings of ethology, anthropology, sociology, history, theology, and comparative religion were bound to offend specialists in all of these fields.

Though somewhat unexpected, perhaps, in retrospect Erikson's popularity is no mystery. After all, this was the era of the "generation gap," when young people complained that their elders had abdicated their ethical responsibilities, embracing a deadening complacency and a mind-numbing conformity that robbed them of the capacity to inspire trust and respect in their offspring. Though they could seldom say so explicitly, perhaps, many of them felt cheated and yearned for connection with elders whom they could trust and emulate, or, failing that, love and respect without too much ambivalence. This diffuse yearning for connection in the face of disillusionment was expressed in many underground anthems of the day, some of which made their way into the musical mainstream. For example, take the title of the Moody Blues' memorable 1970 album, *To Our Children's Children's Children*. The title alone expressed a yearning for intergenerational connection and the implicit hope that the experiences and sensibilities of young adults in those turbulent times would still have resonance for their distant progeny three generations hence.

More often than not, however, it was not entire albums but individual songs that evoked or expressed the yearning for intergenerational connection, or angry reproaches attendant on its continued frustration. Among the most memorable anthems of that era was Crosby, Stills, and Nash's song "Teach Your Children," which was recorded on the album *Déjà Vu*. Others included Cat Stevens's beloved song "Father and Son" from the album *Tea for the Tillerman*, and, less obviously though no less profoundly, Procol Harum's epic fantasy "Salty Dog" from the album by the same name. Many songs of this type addressed the seemingly insurmountable estrangement between youth and middle (or old) age, and the deep incongruities between their perspectives on life. Joni Mitchell's folk classic "The Circle Game" was an atypical example of this genre, dwelling in a lilting, elegiac way on the frustrations inherent in each stage of life and the inexorability of aging, hinting that despite our disparate perspectives and frustrations, in the end we all share the same biological destiny, and are therefore one. But this lovely melody stood in palpable contrast to her most popular dirge, "Woodstock," which Crosby, Stills, and Nash covered on *Déjà Vu*, which stressed the disenchanted and apocalyptic sentiments of the "back to the land" and environmental movements at that time. Similarly, Crosby, Stills, and Nash's song "Wooden Ships" contained the plaintive but undisguised reproach to the elders, "We are leaving; you don't need us!" while "My Generation" sung by Roger Daltrey of the Who and released much earlier, in 1964, is almost inarticulate with rage, spluttering angrily, "Why don't you all f-f-f-fade away!"—a thinly disguised obscenity and a veiled death wish.

Songs like these were quite common between 1964 and 1970, when Erikson's popularity peaked at Harvard. The fact that songs of this type elicited such a powerful response—and have since disappeared from popular and "alternative" music—tells us a lot about the temper of the times. Though they often despaired of finding it, most young people of that era yearned to connect with older adults whose values were unimpaired by the process of growing older and embracing professional roles and responsibilities. Erikson came to the classroom with a strong and conscious desire to assure students that one can grow older without losing one's moral or spiritual compass, and to caution them that the process of succumbing to bitter estrangement or despair in youth breeds cynicism in old age, which damages the next generation (Erikson 1962, 1972).

Another source of Erikson's popularity was his willingness to criticize the mental health professions for their unconscious complicity in perpetuating racist or ethnocentric stereotypes. For example, in the concluding chapter of *Identity, Youth and Crisis* (Erikson 1968) Erikson challenged Thomas Pettigrew's analysis of the prevalence of sexual identity problems among African American males. Using the supposedly "objective" measure of sexual identity afforded by the "masculinity-femininity scale" of the Minnesota Multiphasic Personality Inventory (MMPI) on a large group of African American subjects, Pettigrew concluded that a disproportionate number of African American males suffered from a deficient sense of masculinity because they endorsed such "feminine" items on that test as "I would like to be a singer" and "I think that I feel more intensely than most people do."

By way of a response to Pettigrew's analysis, Erikson pointed out that the large differences in test scores between whites and blacks may indeed reflect modal differences between the two groups, but that there is no warrant for assuming a priori that these differences reflect some pathological deficit. In his own words:

> That a test singles out as "feminine" the wish to be a singer and "feeling more intensely than most people do" suggests that the choice of test items and generalizations drawn from them say at least as much about test and the testers as about the subjects tested. . . . To be a singer and to feel intensely may be facets of a masculine ideal gladly admitted if you grew up in a Southern Negro community (or, for that matter, in Naples), whereas it would be a blemish in a majority having adjusted to other masculine ideals. In fact, in Harlem and in Naples an emphasis on artistic self-expression and intense feeling—and this is the point to be made—may be close to the core of one's positive identity, so close that the loss or devaluation of such emphasis by way of "integration" may make one a drifter on a murky sea of adjustable "roles." In the case of the compact White majority, the denial of intense feelings may, in turn, be part of a negative identity problem which contributes significantly to the prejudiced rejection of the Negro's intensity. Tests harboring similar distinctions may be offering "objective" evidence of racial differences and yet may also be symptomatic of them. (306)

While Erikson did not shirk controversial issues like racism and colonialism, he was also mindful of the fact that students who were distressed by the disparities and injustices in American society were increasingly torn between violence and nonviolence as methods for social change; hence the interminable debates between the perspectives and agendas of Frantz Fanon and Mohandas K. Gandhi, Malcolm X and Martin Luther King Jr., and so on. While Erikson favored nonviolence, he did not disparage or diminish the urgency of the issues raised by Fanon or Malcolm X, or indeed by Huey Newton, whom he even likened to Gandhi—an odd comparison we will look at a little later (Erikson 1975).

Having said all that, however, Erikson was not uncritical of American youth or their leaders. Though he supported the ethically responsible students who opposed nuclear proliferation, the Vietnam War, racism, poverty, and so on, he deplored the slick salesmanship of Timothy Leary and the regressive inwardness of the psychedelic movement. He was also alarmed by the self-centeredness of many students, who ignored his overarching life cycle perspective in classroom discussion, homing in repeatedly and relentlessly on the identity crisis of adolescence as if that were all that mattered. Though doubtless the result of unmet needs in many instances, this insistent focus on oneself and one's peers was contrary to what Erikson stood for and to what he was trying to impart, and he spent many hours with colleagues discussing how to get students away from their preoccupation with themselves and their peers. That he was never entirely successful was probably due less to his shortcomings as a teacher than to features of American culture that he himself had analyzed astutely some time before.

Ideally, said Erikson, adolescence is a "psychosocial moratorium" marked by a postponement of the binding and irreversible commitments that characterize adult life. During this transitional interlude, the young person plays with different social and vocational roles, and different religious and political perspectives, sizing up which role one "fits" best. Meanwhile, Erikson noted, the tendency to repudiate children and adults alike is most pronounced in adolescence, when young people are poised precariously between childhood and adulthood. In the absence of patient and discerning adult support and recognition, adolescents tend to emphasize the unique and incommensurable quality of their own needs and experiences and to define themselves negatively, by what they are not, rather than embracing a more encompassing sense of human solidarity. And for one reason or another, many adults get caught in this adolescent mode indefinitely (e.g., Erikson 1968, chap. 4).

Unfortunately, said Erikson, American culture tends to prolong the psychosocial moratorium and seems to incorporate some version of it into the cultural vision of adulthood, such that formerly irreversible commitments and identities are easily thrown over and new ones assumed without much inner turmoil. The "identity crisis" becomes prolonged indefinitely or revived instantaneously the moment the individual finds her life situation too constricting.

In any case, to counter the self-centeredness of his late and postadolescent following on campus, Erikson often dwelt deliberately on the vicissitudes of old age and its place in the life cycle. Indeed, one of his favorite (and, in due course, most popular) classroom talks was about the film *Wild Strawberries* by Swedish director Ingmar Bergman, which examines a crisis of integrity in an elderly protagonist, Dr. Isak Borg, a Swedish physician who embarks on a searching retrospective appraisal of his life as he drives across country

to receive an honorary degree (Erikson 1976). This film had a very deep resonance for Erikson, for whom it epitomized "the most perfect combination
of artistic form and psychological comprehension and existential religiosity"
(Friedman 1999, 440).

Like many of Erikson's classroom talks, this one went through many
drafts, the last of which appeared in *Daedalus* in 1976. "Reflections on Dr.
Borg's Life Cycle" used Bergman's film as a springboard for an illuminating
elucidation of his life cycle theory, but this time with special emphasis on the
vicissitudes of old age. Nevertheless, the paper continued to call attention to
Erikson's central contention that ego strength (or mental health) is contingent
on the reciprocal recognition and affirmation of individuals in different
phases of the life cycle at every stage of development. Children and adolescents need parents and grandparents, and we, in turn, need them. Unfortunately, this ontic interdependence is often misconstrued by all concerned as a
one-way street, in which they need us and not vice versa. Nothing could be
further from the truth. Absent the maintenance of vital contact with and disinterested concern for the welfare of the coming generation, we become self-
ish, grasping people or detached, schizoid types seeking an imaginary self-
sufficiency—like Ebenezer Scrooge in Charles Dickens's celebrated story *A
Christmas Carol*.

Like any cultured European at midcentury, Bergman was doubtless exposed to psychoanalytic ideas, and often seemed to weave them into his films
quite deliberately. The same cannot be said of Dickens, who published *A
Christmas Carol* in 1843, more than half a century before Freud published
The Interpretation of Dreams (Freud 1900). Still, the resemblances between
the two tales are striking. Like Bergman's protagonist, Scrooge is a lonely old
man haunted by thoughts of impending death, who is flooded by memories of
earlier periods of his life triggered by a series of fortuitous events. These
abruptly rekindled memories demand much soul-searching before the central
character finds inner peace. Indeed, if *Wild Strawberries* was a cinematic
meditation on Eriksonian themes, then Scrooge is the perfect literary illustra-
tion of Erikson's notion of old age, and the processes of internal life review
that ensue as death approaches. And since the character of Scrooge is more
familiar to most of us than Bergman's Dr. Borg, let us revisit Dickens's timeless tale of crisis and renewal to illustrate these issues clearly.

A CHRISTMAS CAROL

One Christmas Eve, a miser named Ebenezer Scrooge retreats to his home
alone. He steadfastly refuses to celebrate this holiday, having already scorned

the advances of alms seekers and the generous friendship of his nephew, and heaping abuse on poor Bob Cratchit, his sole employee, whose family teeters on the brink of starvation. On reaching home, he is briefly confronted by an apparition—the face of his dead business partner, Jacob Marley—on his front door: an unwelcome sight, which he dispels by hurtling headlong upstairs. As he sits anxiously over the feeble fire, hoping that indigestion is the source of his recent upset, his mind is suddenly crowded with the biblical images that decorate his fireplace, including Cain and Abel, Pharoah's daughter, the Queen of Sheba, angelic messengers, Abraham, Belshazzar, the apostles. But while distracting himself with these biblical motifs, the unwelcome and un-expected "face of Jacob Marley, seven years dead, came like the ancient Prophet's rod, and swallowed up the whole" (Dickens 1986, 12). The Day of Judgment—a crisis of old age—is at hand, and the question of whether Scrooge's judge is the Almighty or his own feeble conscience sputtering back to life is quite immaterial to the outcome.

Next, Scrooge hears the clanking of chains; Marley's ghost arrives in shackles, which the ghost describes as fitting punishment for his heartless conduct while he was alive. He then predicts that unless he changes his ways, Scrooge awaits a similar fate, and announces the imminent arrival of several shades, and a much longer ordeal that awaits Scrooge, which cannot possibly be averted. In the pages that follow, Dickens uses Scrooge's journeys with the Ghost of Christmas Past to illustrate how young Ebenezer's early develop-ment was blighted by the death of his mother in his infancy, and the distant, infrequent attentions of a cold, rejecting father while he was a child. Without saying so in so many words, of course, the ghost implies that his trust in life was severely eroded as a consequence.

Moreover, as the Ghost of Christmas Past reminds him, Scrooge floun-dered again in early adulthood, when Scrooge's fiancée rejected him. In the memory that the Ghost of Christmas Past rekindles for Scrooge's edifica-tion, his former fiancée explained her rejection of him on the grounds that Scrooge had a new "idol," namely, the single-minded pursuit of money, which he grasped avidly as a shield against adversity and a substitute for genuine hope and faith. This was not the man she had hoped to marry, and the implied infidelity, she said, rendered real intimacy impossible. Those versed in Erikson's epigenetic theory will recall that the search for fidelity and the need to establish intimacy are the distinctive tasks of adolescent and early adulthood, and that by his fiancée's reckoning, Scrooge is a failure de-spite his success as a man of business. The bitterness occasioned by her re-jection, and the subsequent loss of his beloved sister, fuelled the relentless pursuit of solitude, power, and cold, hard cash that Scrooge used as a de-fense against the world, which led inexorably to partnership with the equally hardhearted Jacob Marley, and in due course, to his own despair, which surfaced suddenly in his dark night of the soul.

As it turns out, whatever else she may have meant to him, Scrooge's fiancée was an astute observer who vividly diagnosed his central disorder, that is, a failure of intimacy, preceded by mistrust of the world. From an Eriksonian perspective, she represents the principle of charitable love, the spirit of human solidarity and forgiveness—more so than Eros, given the stage of life at which Scrooge reluctantly rekindles his memory of her. By contrast, young Scrooge's former employer, old Fezziwig, who is also rekindled in memory at this time, represents what Scrooge might have become had he not given up hope and embraced the Golden Calf. After all, though he is diligent and successful businessman as well, Fezziwig differs dramatically from Dickens's haunted bachelor because he successfully negotiated the search for intimacy and embodied that zest for life that accompanies a firmly rooted experience of midlife generativity, joining the generations in a festive Christmas dance—a dramatic contrast to Marley, and to Scrooge's own father, whose lonely example Scrooge was unconsciously emulating.

In any case, though couched in the traditional religious imagery of sin and repentance, *A Christmas Carol* is a remarkably modern and psychologically sophisticated tale. A summary this brief simply cannot do justice to all the nuances and insights it affords. Suffice it to say that by engendering a dramatic return of the repressed, Scrooge's ghostly interlocutors gradually enlighten him on the nature of his existential dilemma. Unless he changes course and connects himself to others in bonds of love and concern, there will not be a single mourner at his grave, and all those whom he could have helped with his generosity while he was still alive will go on living—or dying—without anyone else to address their needs and feelings. By the story's conclusion, Scrooge experiences a spiritual rebirth, reinserting himself in the cycle of generations by opening his heart to his unfortunate nephew and his family, the even less fortunate Bob Cratchit and his children, and above all, to Cratchit's youngest child, Tiny Tim, who plays a special role in the fantasies that bring about Scrooge's miraculous transformation.

Apart from emphasizing the interconnectedness between the generations as being integral to the health of elderly adults, married or single, there are other features of Dickens's tale that have a distinctly Eriksonian character. Consider the constant interplay of temporal perspectives in Scrooge's reverie, in which the present is poised, so to speak, between past and future, and always enfolds and encompasses them both. By exhuming his past, illuminating his present, and clarifying his options for the future, Scrooge's "ghosts" perform an exemplary existential analysis of Scrooge's dilemma, and with good therapeutic results. Scrooge resolves to die a Fezziwig, rather than follow in Marley's—and his own father's—footsteps. Dickens's approach to psychic causality stands in striking contrast to Freud's *psychic determinism*, in which our present ideas, experiences, and attitudes are always essentially "overdetermined" by our past experience, such that current conflicts are always disguised or distorted derivatives of older childhood templates. This way of framing the vicissitudes of conscience and the search for intimacy in adulthood leaves little or no room for genuinely new or unprecedented conflicts and experiences, and the kind of indeterminacy and openness to possibility and to the future that Erikson had already built into his notion of identity formation. In a similar vein, the notion that our memory is tendentious, furnishing us with childhood recollections that are pertinent to our present day conflicts, is one that Erikson stressed frequently in his earlier reflections on identity formation. Another Dickensian theme found in Erikson—and a few other psychoanalysts—is the traditional humanist emphasis on self-authorship—of choosing what kind of person you become, and what kind of person you want to have been at the moment of your death.

EXISTENTIALISM, JUDAISM, AND CHRISTIANITY

In light of the preceding discussion, it is instructive to point out that the perspectives on time, memory, and the role of choice in human development that Dickens deployed so skillfully as a storyteller are all broadly consistent with an existentialist perspective on psychology, as well as with an Eriksonian approach. But though generously acknowledged by some existentialist authors (Knowles 1985), Erikson often disparaged existentialism as "an ideology of parallel isolation," which stresses the stark isolation at the root of human subjectivity and denies the possibility of real and abiding love or intimacy between human beings. While this description rings true (to varying degrees, and for different reasons) for Friedrich Nietzsche, Martin Heidegger, and Jean-Paul Sartre—all of whom were atheists, incidentally—it is completely off the mark where religious existentialists like Max Scheler, Karl Jaspers, Martin Buber, Paul Tillich, Gabriel Marcel, or Emmanuel Mounier are concerned (Friedman 1994; Burston and Frie 2006).

Was Erikson conversant with their work? With the exception of that of Tillich, probably not. But when he finally arrived at Harvard, Erikson attended Tillich's graduate seminars at the Divinity School and became a close friend of his, delivering the eulogy at his funeral in 1965 (Erikson 1966b). As Friedman points out, Erikson and Tillich shared an abiding interest in Kierkegaard, and a deep commitment to wedding the spiritual and the sensuous dimensions of human life. Of course, Erikson's admiration for Tillich prompted many questions among his friends about his own religious identity. Indeed, Robert Jay Lifton once asked Erikson if he was Jewish or Christian, to which he replied: "Why both, of course." While this remark was made with tongue in cheek, perhaps, in a certain sense, it was also profoundly true.

While they are irreconcilably at odds on the divinity of Jesus, Judaism and Christianity share the conviction that each and every human being is made in the image and likeness of God, and converge impressively in their emphasis on the virtues of justice and mercy, and their urgent desire to foster a truth-loving disposition. Yet paradoxically, Judaism and Christianity also caution us that each and every human being has innate propensities to violence, greed, and deception that can be averted only through conscious choice and decision, and a resolute determination to hold adult human beings account-able for their choices. This emphasis on individual accountability for sin and righteousness underscores the teaching on the Day of Judgment, in which the Almighty, who knows the innermost recesses of our hearts and is indifferent to worldly status or accomplishments, weighs the person's good deeds against his evil ones and rewards him accordingly.

Admittedly, one does not have to believe in a final day of reckoning to take the ideals of justice, mercy, and a truth-loving disposition seriously. Indeed, Erikson would have insisted that literalism and dogma on issues pertaining to the "afterlife" or "world to come" are counterproductive or even beside the point here. For whether one believes in the afterlife or is firmly convinced of the finality of death, the fact remains that, as Immanuel Kant pointed out, an ethical person must conduct her life as if the Day of Judgment will come to pass. This is so even if the person's resolve to be just makes them unpopular, or complicates her life in ways that less principled pleasure seekers would wish to avoid. In other words, one must internalize and embrace some version of the aforementioned ethical ideals to be an authentic Jew or an authentic Christian, even if only at a symbolic level. That is why *A Christmas Carol* is such a moving and illuminating story, even to those with no faith or affilia-tion in the field of organized religion.

Why do Judaism and Christianity share these core convictions? Quite sim-ply, because they were rooted in the religious environment that Jesus grew up in. This fact is not controversial, at least among scholars, who universally ac-knowledge that the content and the style of Jesus' teaching were deeply rooted in Jewish tradition. But it was not always so. In an influential book en-titled *Das Wesen Des Christentums* (1900), published two years before Erik-son's birth, Protestant historian Adolph Harnack attempted to uproot and dis-tance Christianity from its Jewish antecedents and define the core of Christian faith in a completely ahistorical fashion. He even chastised Luther and the other Reformers for not eliminating *all* traces of lingering Jewish influence, catalyzing a vigorous (and highly successful) movement to expunge words like "Hallejujah" from the Lutheran liturgy because of their Hebrew provenance.

Harnack's pejorative assessment of the Jewish faith catalyzed some cogent and forceful rejoinders from Jewish luminaries like Solomon Schechter, Leo Baeck, and Martin Buber, who likened Harnack to Marcion, a second-century theologian who sought to sever any remaining links with Jewish doctrine and religious practices (Friedlander 1968), and was ultimately excommunicated for heresy. That being so, it is instructive to note that when Erikson published his personal reflections on Jesus' life and teachings in "The Galilean Sayings and the Sense of 'I'" (Erikson 1981), Christian scholars were finally beginning to reconsider and reinterpret the relationship between Judaism and Christianity. But judging from their tone and content, Erikson's views were not influenced by Harnack and his followers, or by the emerging scholarly consensus. Indeed, they were based on convictions he had cherished privately for many years—possibly since late adolescence. Erikson's reflections on the Lord's Prayer, the parable of the prodigal son, and the inescapable embeddedness of the "I" in a sense of "we" that unites the living and the dead in bonds of fellowship, were offered up as psychoanalytic interpretations of the Gospels. But on reflection, they bear a closer resemblance to the ideas of religious existentialists like Martin Buber, Ferdinand Ebner, and Gabriel Marcel, among others (Friedman 1994).

Moreover, in addressing these themes, Erikson drew on his (limited) knowledge of Jewish history, ritual, and prayer, but ignored learned Jewish commentaries on the Gospels, of which there were several (e.g., Maccoby 1980; Sandmel 1978): a significant omission, to say the least. But he did acknowledge a nodding acquaintance with an earlier generation of Christian New Testament scholars—Dibelius, Bultmann, and Jeremias—and demonstrated a competent grasp of Norman Perrin's *Rediscovering the Teaching of Jesus* (Perrin 1967). As a result, when it came to authenticating his own perspective on the kinship and continuity between the two faiths—on which he laid considerable emphasis—Erikson largely ignored biblical scholarship, Jewish and Christian, and cited a freethinking, pantheistic Jewish physicist, Albert Einstein, who stressed the Prophetic tradition as the fundamental link between them (Erikson 1981). Evidently he felt Einstein's authority would suffice. He also identified himself as "a psychoanalyst in the Judaeo-Christian orbit," rather than simply as a Christian psychoanalyst, which is how many sympathetic critics had since come to see him (Browning 1975; Homans 1978). For though he never repudiated his Jewishness as such, with the passage of time Christian sentiments and images clearly came to dominate Erikson's perspective. This gradual shift in perspective was evident in *Young*

Man Luther (Erikson 1958), and influenced by his early exclusion from the Jewish community, the unresolved longing to know his Christian father, and the fact that his wife was an ardent Christian (Erikson 1970).

As we will see presently, Erikson paid dearly for his cherished ambiguities on this score. And as Lawrence Friedman explains, many of the antipathies engendered by Erikson's dual allegiance were due to contemporaneous events and issues pertaining to anti-Semitism and the Shoah. But on closer inspection, the roots of Erikson's credibility problem actually lay much deeper, in the tensions between the processes of Jewish and Christian identity formation, which, strangely enough, Erikson never addressed in quite so many words.

One thing that differentiates Judaism from Christianity is the way it enfolds sacred history into its sense of collective identity. Like his Christian counterpart, the average Jew's sense of history is punctuated by pivotal events—the Creation, the Flood, the Exodus, Sinai, the Temple, the Exile and return, and so on. But for the average Christian, the pivotal events that occur in the Hebrew Bible merely *prepare the way* for Jesus' ministry, and the episodes that are most pertinent to the Christian's faith are the (real or alleged) predictions or premonitions of Jesus' arrival and the events surrounding Jesus' birth, his ministry, his trial, and his crucifixion and resurrection. Jesus' religious education and development, on which the Gospels are strangely silent, and events that unfolded in the aftermath of his crucifixion are of interest to scholars, perhaps, but are either irrelevant or relatively inconsequential to the average Christian. For the Christian believer, everything hinges on this particular story, which is as timeless, fresh, and relevant today as it was two millennia ago, when Jesus first preached his message.

In contrast with Christians, who are apt to forget or to minimize the importance of events that occurred before and since Jesus' crucifixion, Jews are commanded to remember them vividly. In Hebrew, this injunction is summed up in a single word—*zachor*. This injunction is inscribed in the name of the Jewish New Year—*Yom Ha'Zicaron*, or Day of Remembrance—and stated repeatedly during the Passover Seder to foster *intergenerational identification* and to underscore the need for continuity as an antidote to the threat of identity diffusion, assimilation, or conversion.

So what does the Jew remember? Among other things, the Jew remembers—and is sharply reminded when he or she forgets—that more than ten thousand Jews were crucified by their Roman overlords in the first century CE. Some were slaughtered against their will, no doubt, but many risked their lives willingly and died *al Kiddush Ha' Shem*—sanctifying the name of the Almighty. Jesus died this way too, no doubt, but Jews do not construe this tragic event as being the pivotal event in human history. For Christians, yes; but for everyone else, presumably, no.

So at a minimum, Jewish and Christian identities hinge on different hermeneutic strategies, different ways of interpreting scripture, and different idioms to elucidate and express the nature of their covenant with God. The average Christian's sense of cosmological coherence and of personal identity hinges on the life and example of a single man, coupled with a relative indifference with respect to other events before, during, and after Jesus' life, including many events that have a crucial bearing on how Jews are apt to interpret this same man and his teaching. By contrast with the average Christian, who emulates and identifies with Jesus, the average Jew is exhorted to identify with *all* his ancestors and emancipators, but not to divinize *any* of them—including Isaiah's suffering servant. And no one—not Adam, Noah, Abraham, Moses, Elijah, David, or Solomon—is as *central* to Jews as Jesus is to Christians.

Was it ever thus? Evidently not. In the first and second centuries, the boundaries between the two faiths were much more fluid than they are today (Ruether 1997). These divergent identity patterns, rooted in shared idioms and ways of reading and interpreting texts, took almost two centuries to crystallize (Reary 2006). Moreover, despite their general validity nowadays, these disparate identity patterns can still be invoked in a heavy-handed, overly dichotomous fashion. If you shun generalizations like these and look at the historical record, you find many Christians whose theology remained remarkably prophetic, and many prominent Jewish thinkers who absorbed Christian traits and tendencies unawares. How could it be otherwise after two thousand years of shared history?

In any case, in a manner of speaking, Erikson was stranded at the interstices of these two religious identities, and he steadfastly refused to choose between them, though he felt strongly pulled in the direction of Christianity. And the fact that this was a lifelong conflict, rather than a midlife issue, helps explain why his professional identity as a psychoanalyst was so precious and necessary for him. Had Erikson lived to the present day, he would probably have found a larger, more sympathetic audience receptive to his ideas and attitudes about Jesus, and a way of articulating them more precisely. As things stood then, however, his unwillingness (or inability) to do so, rooted in the circumstances of his upbringing, was experienced and interpreted by many as evidence of evasiveness or insincerity rather than as an expression of unwavering loyalty to *all* his significant others. The inclusive-yet-indistinct kind of piety this produced provoked more anger and incomprehension among Jews than among Christians because, historically speaking, the Christian emphasis on the singularity of Jesus as the Son of God often entails a corollary belief in the collective guilt or culpability of the entire Jewish people in slaying God; a belief that was not formally repudiated by mainstream Christian churches until the Second Vatican Council in 1965 (Reuther 1997). It is this belief, which John Dominic Crossan has called "the oldest lie," that furnished the pretext for anti-Semitic persecution and prejudice in the West (Crossan 1996). And as the controversy over Mel Gibson's movie *The Passion of the Christ* demonstrates, this belief persists in many corners of the world, and in many Christian denominations, to this very day (Burston 2005a).

Had he not been so devastated by the attacks on his integrity that plagued him in the 1970s as a result of all this, Erikson might have produced a body of work that probed the overlapping yet divergent frameworks for Jewish and Christian identities more thoughtfully. And again, perhaps not. By then he was quite elderly and probably overwhelmed at the complexity of the debates in the fields of theology, biblical archeology, and interfaith dialogue.

CONSCIENCE, AGGRESSION, AND CIVIL DISOBEDIENCE

Meanwhile, more trouble was brewing with Anna Freud and her circle. In 1964 Erikson produced a book of essays on psychoanalysis and ethics titled *Insight and Responsibility*, which he dedicated to Anna Freud and which she (once again) professed not to understand. Then in 1969 Erikson published a lengthy psychobiography of Mohandas K. Gandhi. Unlike *Young Man Luther*, which was a prolonged meditation on adolescence and the identity crisis, *Gandhi's Truth* was a meditation on middle age and the ripening of conscience and care beyond the house-holding or child-rearing phase of life.

Though never stated in so many words, Erikson's challenge to Freudian orthodoxy here lay in his evolving approach to the subject of conscience, which Erikson linked thematically to the study of militant nonviolence and civil disobedience. Classical Freudianism explains conscience by reference to two "intrapsychic agencies," the ego ideal and the superego. The superego consists of primarily negative injunctions and prohibitions that are internalized (or introjected) toward the end of the Oedipal stage, while the ego ideal is the result of a deepening identification with an idealized image of the parent of the same sex or some other idealized (older) figure—incidentally, perhaps the only instance when Freud refers to processes of intergenerational identification.

In any case, while the superego is punitive, punishing any transgressions of prevailing cultural codes with feelings of guilt, the ego ideal is normative and engenders feelings of shame when the person fails to live up to his self-chosen standards of decency, courage, creativity, and compassion. Conversely, however, when they do live up to their ideals, people enjoy the riches of a "good conscience." Initially, Freud was inclined to view the ego ideal and the superego as two distinct entities, the former being a derivative (but growth-enhancing) offshoot of the individual's narcissism, the latter being a sublimation of the death instinct—a basically destructive force that is harnessed in the service of civilization, deflecting aggression away from external targets and turning it inward on the ego.

Though it played an important part in his reflections on social psychology (Freud 1921), with the passage of time Freud became less and less interested in the ego ideal and tended to subsume it increasingly under the superego— an issue we return to in chapter 7. The more important point, at present, is that whether the ego ideal and the superego are two distinct entities with disparate sources of "instinctual" energy, or two aspects of the self-same psychic system, as Freud sometimes appeared to believe, the fact remains that according to Freud, conscience is constituted in early childhood during the resolution of the Oedipus complex and does not change or develop appreciably after that point.

Perhaps the first theorist of note in analytic circles to openly challenge this developmental itinerary was Melanie Klein, who located the origins of the superego in the (pre-Oedipal) oral phase (Segal 1964). Erikson, by contrast, took things in the opposite direction, and instead of situating its origins earlier, argued that the Oedipal superego is merely the first installment in a life-long developmental process in which conscience changes in response to stage-specific needs and conflicts all the way through late middle age. Moreover, according to Erikson, the full unfolding of conscience does not simply embellish on early introjections or identification with the father imago, but embraces specifically maternal sensibility that is inclusive and nonviolent, rather than a strict, wrathful, and paternal. Indeed, in his psychohistorical explorations, Erikson used Gandhi's identification with his mother to illustrate the ways in which the maternal principle can be harnessed in the service of sanctifying life, and affirming extralegal ethical principles that necessitate civil disobedience in certain circumstances.

The clinical roots and ramifications of these dramatic changes in perspective, which we address later, are somewhat beside the point here. The more pertinent consideration (from a biographical standpoint) is that by the early to mid-sixties Erikson felt the manifest inadequacy of Freud's theory of conscience acutely and was increasingly irritated by Freud's more complacent and conformist followers, who construed the widespread disenchantment of youth as a collective expression of failure to resolve their Oedipal antipathy toward their elders. Though he was slow to warm to this theme in print and criticize his colleagues directly, Erikson was appalled by this reductionistic, self-serving appraisal, and was preparing for a confrontation of sorts.

So whatever else it was, *Gandhi's Truth*, like *Young Man Luther*, was a ve-
hicle that gave Erikson an opportunity to wax ambivalent about his own profession, or, more precisely, about the outdated theories still embraced by the
majority of his colleagues. In the course of his reflections, Erikson developed a
thoughtful critique of the psychoanalytic theory of aggression and the ethological ideas of Konrad Lorenz (1965), which lent credence to Freud's theory of
the death instinct. At the risk of oversimplifying somewhat, Erikson said that
the "death instinct" theory is completely misguided (Evans 1967), and it is instructive to note that his reflections on this point vividly anticipate Erich
Fromm's reply to Freud and Lorenz in *The Anatomy of Human Destructiveness*,
published in 1973. The difference—and it is a striking one, on reflection—is
that Erikson anticipated (and probably influenced) Fromm in this case, rather
than vice versa; further proof of the deep affinities between them.

In any case, by 1969 Erikson felt the time was ripe for a thorough reconsideration of the concept of aggression. In the midst of the Vietnam War, the
Cold War, and widespread civil disobedience that bordered, at times, on civil
war, the intuitive truths of yesteryear had become worn-out clichés. Having
written with great perceptiveness about the conflict between the generations,
the psychosocial ravages of racism, and the problems of technological culture,
Erikson probably feared that sticking stubbornly with the old conceptual
schemata in the name of fidelity to Freud was sterile and otiose, and might
doom his profession to irrelevance, socially and scientifically speaking. And
even if we leave the urgency and complexity of the prevailing social unrest entirely to one side, the fact remains that the "sell by" date on the biological underpinnings of Freudian theory had long since expired. Though others' efforts
to revamp them—John Bowlby's, for example—had already met with derision
and official disapproval from Anna Freud and her circle, Erikson brought this
passionate conviction with him to the Congress of the International Psychoanalytic Association in Vienna in 1971, where, as *Time* magazine reported on August 9, he "warned the congress against an abstract use of the term aggression
and accused the delegates of treating the topic too theoretically. He asked that
it no longer be discussed in decades-old formulations."

But at the end of the congress, *Time* continued,

> "Anna Freud . . . tried to smooth over the previous speakers differences and con-
> ceded that psychoanalysts still had a "clouded vision" on aggression. Then,
> sounding like a reincarnation of her father, she added: 'But who else should ar-
> rive at valid results if not we?'" (p. 66)

As was often the case with Anna Freud's efforts at diplomacy, there was a
barb in it—a "meta-communication"—that betrayed her real feelings on this
score. On the one hand, while not actually acknowledging that the theoretical

framework was grossly inadequate, she conceded that the orthodox theory of aggression was "clouded." On the other, she expressed confidence in psychoanalysis, as it was presently constituted, to discern the truth. In effect, she was trying to placate Erikson, who was dissenting openly from the majority, and arguing forcefully for change, while intimating to those whom he criticized that his objections and concerns were actually quite overwrought. In short, she was trivializing his concerns. And what was the upshot of this curious exchange? Precisely what one would expect in the circumstances: "Everybody applauded. But nothing had really been settled. Psychoanalysis, which has survived two great schisms provoked by Jung and Adler, seemed headed for a new and challenging schism" (p. 66).

Actually, as we know with hindsight, there was no schism. But though the prediction proved false, *Time*'s overall characterization of the mood that prevailed at the Vienna Congress was probably quite accurate. This unsatisfactory state of affairs was doubtless quite painful for Erikson, who, after all, was almost seventy now, and had earned the right to publicly criticize colleagues for their smug backwardness. But this prompts the reflection that, unlike Martin Luther, whose courage he admired, Erikson never did break away from his "church," even when his efforts to bring about internal reform were deflected, defeated, or diluted. To understand Erikson personally, we must ask ourselves what deterred this elder statesman, who had a vast and adoring following at the time, from striking out on his own. It was not allegiance to the pope—or rather, to Anna Freud. On the contrary, it was his loyalty to the movement's founder, Anna's father, that enabled him to contain (though certainly not to repress) his anger and disappointment at her rigidity.

Obviously, this somewhat contrived analogy puts Sigmund Freud, a Jewish atheist, in the role of Jesus—a curious, and, to some, deeply distasteful comparison. But while it may be a misleading analogy in other instances, it was quite apt where Erikson is concerned. With the exception of Luther, Gandhi, and Jesus, no man evoked the same sense of reverence in Erikson that Freud did. Indeed, despite the striking oddity of the exercise, Erikson did not even shrink from comparing Jesus' practice of laying on of hands with certain features of analytic technique (Erikson 1981). So for Erikson, if not for the rest of us, Jesus, Luther, Gandhi, and Freud were all kindred spirits. And Freud was the only member of this curious fraternity of the mind with whom Erikson had enjoyed personal contact, had actually seen and spoken to. So despite a deepening antipathy toward Anna and her style of leadership, Erikson's loyalty to Sigmund Freud anchored him eternally in the IPA.

While Erikson never left the fold, however, he sublimated his rebellious impulses into the creation of a new discipline called *psychohistory*. Ostensibly a judicious extension of psychoanalysis into the domain of historical scholarship, the psychohistory movement was actually a pseudo-schism, since aspiring psychohistorians did not need to have an orthodox training analysis in order to work in comfort in Erikson's circle. On the contrary, most of Erikson's colleagues in this new field were historians, anthropologists, philosophers, political scientists, and/or literary types of Robert Lifton's generation, including H. Stuart Hughes, Bruce Mazlish, Kenneth Keniston and Robert Coles. Moreover, most of their meetings were at Lifton's home in Wellfleet, Massachusetts. Working closely with this younger crowd on a series of influential publications, Erikson reveled in the collegiality and open-endedness of it all, welcoming practitioners of all the human sciences into their midst, and all on more or less equal terms.

ON ABLATION: THE BERMAN EPISODE

Gandhi's Truth, published in 1969, was followed by *Dimensions of a New Identity: The Jefferson Lectures* in 1974. Though Erikson was intrigued with Thomas Jefferson's views on Jesus and organized Christianity, which resembled his own, it was not a strong or successful book because of Erikson's unwillingness to reckon with the somewhat sordid and hypocritical sides of Jefferson's character and conduct, especially with respect to slavery. In January of 1975 Kai Erikson published a lengthy conversation between his father and the Black Panther leader Huey Newton in *In Search of Common Ground* (Erikson 1975). The conversation, which took place in 1971, was a candid and animated exchange. Both participants obviously enjoyed it. But during the course of this conversation, Erikson likened Newton to a follower of Gandhi—a Satyagrahi. As a matter of fact, however, Gandhi had coined the term *Satyagrahi* to describe a militant practitioner of ahimsa, or nonviolence. In view of Newton's refusal to rule out armed insurrection and his open embrace of a doctrinaire Marxist-Leninist line that was comparable, in all essentials, to that of the totalitarian brainwashers that Erikson's friend Robert Lifton had subjected to such searching psychological analysis a decade previously (Lifton 1961), this statement was odd, to say the least. Erikson had conjured with some dubious comparisons before, but this one was so wooly and off the mark that it suggested he was loosing his grip.

Though the conversation occurred four years before it appeared in 1975, many of his associates date the beginning of Erikson's long decline to that year. And, as Friedman points out, many friends and relations reported that Erikson, who had retired to Tiburon, California, now had difficulty concentrating and was increasingly dependent on family and friends to help edit and organize the many articles, books, chapters, and anthologies that still flowed from his pen. As Erikson's health deteriorated, he experienced a heightened desire to safeguard his privacy. Just prior to retirement he had been interviewed extensively by Richard Evans (Evans 1967), been the subject of an adoring and influential study by Robert Coles (Coles 1970), won many awards, appeared on countless magazine covers, and so on. But in many ways, he still felt profoundly misunderstood, even by ardent admirers, and feared being turned into an icon whose real message was lost in the midst of all the publicity. So after retirement Erikson was decidedly wary of the media and all the hype that still surrounded him. And though he had never formally been baptized, he now attended a local Episcopal church with Joan on a semi-regular basis, cultivating a close relationship with their minister, John Thornton.

Then, late in March of 1975, Marshall Berman, a political scientist at City University of New York, launched a scathing attack on Erikson. It appeared in a review of *Life History and the Historical Moment* in the *New York Times Book Review* (Berman 1975), and it was a very harsh appraisal, with a strong ad hominem flavor. Berman's critique was not unprecedented. Left-wing psychoanalysts like Erich Fromm and Joel Kovel had already criticized Erikson severely (Fromm 1970; Kovel 1974), as did many feminists (Janeway 1971; Strouse 1974), many of whom misunderstood or misconstrued his meaning.

While Kovel's critique of the previous March had been scathing, Berman's critique was more devastating, questioning Erikson's personal and intellectual integrity in a way that was profoundly unsettling for Erikson and his readers. Why? Ever since the publication of *Young Man Luther*, Erikson had been ruminating publicly about the nature of authenticity and the meaning of "meaning it." As a lifelong admirer of Kierkegaard, Erikson came by this preoccupation honestly, of course. But by now, the explicit emphasis on finding one's "voice" (which once informed his portrait of Luther) colored most of his psychohistorical books and essays, including his recent (and extremely flawed) book on Thomas Jefferson. Indeed, much of his charisma hinged on people's perception of him as being a playful, profound, and yet utterly sincere man—an "honest broker" in the roiling conflicts between generations and ethnicities, who did not sell anyone short.

Berman, a rising journalistic star was widely perceived as an "expert" on authenticity as well. His first book, *The Politics of Authenticity: Radical Individualism and the Emergence of Modern Society* (Berman 1970), covered an impressive range of themes and thinkers on this issue very competently, and gave Erikson full credit for being genuinely engaged in his biography of Gandhi. But five years later, reviewing *Life History and the Historical Moment*, he reversed himself completely, arguing that this public perception of Erikson— which he once shared—was at variance with the facts. By his current estimate, said Berman, Erikson was a posturing phony: a self-invented man. He had concealed his Jewishness by changing his last name from Homberger to Erikson, displaying "cosmic chutzpah" by claiming, in effect, to be his own son. The seeming universality of his message, said Berman, was achieved only by denying his ethnic particularity—a kind of ontic insincerity that placed the value of his whole perspective in doubt.

Having thoroughly impugned Erikson's integrity, Berman then trashed *Life History and the Historical Moment* as being vague, stale, and unfocused, when in fact it was an extremely stimulating—if somewhat disorganized and heterogeneous—volume. He also reproached Erikson for completely neglecting the issue of Jewish identity, betraying an uneven familiarity with Erikson's previous work. (After all, Erikson had earlier addressed the issue of Jewish identity in Europe quite perceptively in chapter 9 of *Childhood and Society*.)

Berman's charges had a special resonance for Jewish and psychoanalytically oriented readers, who knew that denial of the father and the fantasy of being or becoming one's own father is Oedipal in nature or derivation—at least according to Freud. Whether he intended it specifically in that way or not, Berman's critique read like a veiled accusation that Erikson was still acting out his unresolved Oedipal issues. No doubt many readers interpreted it that way. In retrospect, however, this appraisal, which is based on Berman's fragmentary knowledge of Erikson's childhood, lacks realism and generosity. As an illegitimate child stranded, so to speak, between two fathers—one who was palpably ambivalent toward him and one who rejected him before he was born—Erikson could not be expected to have had anything remotely resembling a "normal" Oedipus complex. Indeed, his uncertain parentage placed him at the (often hostile and mistrustful) intersection between two faiths, and his failure to embrace—or reject—either one wholeheartedly, under the circumstances, is not surprising. Indeed, it speaks well for him. But these facts, which Erikson guarded jealously until old age, came to light only in the wake of the Berman controversy and Friedman's meticulous and illuminating biography. In the meantime, however, even some of Erikson's colleagues, like historian Bruce Mazlish, found Berman's harsh and misleading appraisal illuminating and persuasive.

Berman's assault left Erikson and his family reeling. He never responded to it publicly, but instead wrote a series of memoranda that were circulated to friends and followers between 1975 and 1979, detailing the inaccuracies in Berman's critique. Some found Erikson's reply to Berman adequate and persuasive. Some did not. But the lack of a public response left Erikson vulnerable, and book sales plummeted as a result. Of all the letters Erikson composed during that period, perhaps the most revealing was not even couched as a rebuttal to Berman, but was presented as a personal note to Hope Curfman from the Montview Presbyterian Church in Denver, composed after Christmas in 1976. In it, Erikson said that Jesus "was most assuredly a Jew, if one of a new kind," and acknowledged his own determination "to live on the shadowy borderline of the denominational ambiguities . . . into which I seem to have been born." And while acknowledging his fondness for eminent Christians like Saint Francis of Assisi, Martin Luther, and others, he also pointed out that "nobody who has grown up in a Jewish environment can ever be a non-Jew" (Friedman 1999, 454–55).

Berman's attack was followed swiftly by a more charitable assessment from another celebrated psychoanalyst, Charles Rycroft, in an article entitled "Freud and the Imagination," which appeared in the *New York Review of Books* on April 3, 1975. Rycroft did not mind (or even mention) Erikson's blurry religious affiliations. But echoing Yankelovich and Barrett (1971), Rycroft—who agreed with most of what Erikson said—insisted that Erikson had exaggerated his own originality, minimizing his differences with Freud. In his own words:

> [P]sychoanalysis, to the extent that it remains attached to Freud's ideal of a scientific psychology, can have nothing to say about value. Erik Erikson, the psychoanalyst who has most concerned himself with problems of meaning, value and ethics—even to the extent of introducing the word "virtue" into his psychoanalytical vocabulary—has, as Yankelovich and Barrett point out, been more engaged in "rediscovering prescientific truths" and absorbing them into the psychoanalytical theory than in extending psychoanalytical theory so that it can contribute anything new to history, literature and moral philosophy. And, as Yankelovich and Barrett also pointed out, Erikson has consistently "blurred the extent of his divergence from the psychoanalytical movement" and the extent of his dependence of a philosophy at odds with that of Freud. (Rycroft 1985b, 275–76)

The following year, Rycroft's friend and frequent correspondent, Paul Roazen, published *Erik Erikson: The Power and Limits of a Vision* (1976). Metaphorically speaking, it is tempting to place his appraisal somewhere on a continuum between Rycroft's and Berman's. According to Roazen, Erikson simply lacked the clarity or the courage to think his positions through to their ultimate logical conclusions. Moreover, though hidden in carefully crafted, artfully rendered phrases, there was an elusive, ambiguous, or frankly silly quality to some of Erikson's formulations and assertions that disguised a conservative agenda—witness his introduction of the term *virtue* into analytic discourse, a development Rycroft merely found telling, but that Roazen viewed with evident mistrust.

Meanwhile, however, Roazen's charge of a conservative subtext resonated with the objections of many feminist critics at the time, who pointed to the masculine root of the Latin word *virtus*, from which the word virtue is derived. And as we shall see, there were some grounds for these misgivings. Like many feminist and profeminist theorists of the day, Erikson was quite critical of Freud's patriarchal bias, telling Richard Evans that it had warped his image of womanhood, which he termed the "weakest part" of his theory (Evans 1967, 43–45). But in practically the same breath, Erikson confided that in his own estimation, "a woman's identity develops out of the very way in which she looks around and selects the person with whose budding identity she can polarize her own. Her selection is already an expression of her identity, even if she seems to become totally absorbed in someone else's life" (49).

Depending on your perspective, this passage can be read either as (1) a tacit endorsement of traditional sex roles, which confine women to the domestic sphere, or (2) a reminder that even in more traditional cultures, a woman's identity formation in some sense precedes (and is therefore expressed in) her choice of a mate, and that the relationship that ensues may polarize her own identity development further, even when it appears to have been subsumed in her husband's (à la Joan Erikson, perhaps). In instances like these, when the tone of his statements was somewhat ambiguous and open to more than one interpretation, feminist critics invariably put the worst possible construction on Erikson's words, to make it seem as if Erikson was merely supporting the status quo, or pathologizing women's strivings to achieve an autonomous identity (Janeway 1971; Strouse 1974). The real truth was more complex.

In any case, viewed through the prism of Berman's critique, Erikson's real or imaginary failings were the results not of trauma or ambivalence, but of insincerity, opportunism, and hype. Viewed from Roazen's more balanced perspective, Erikson's opacity was chiefly the result of a peculiar combination of timidity, grandiosity, and a tendency to self-deception. And while Berman's avowedly Marxist orientation probably colored his dismissal of Erikson, Roazen merely deplored the fact that Erikson concealed his conservative agenda rather than owning up to it more candidly. A political scientist who had studied social conservative thought in great depth and detail, Roazen allowed that being conservative, or more conservative than he let on, does not invalidate Erikson's work as a whole, nor does it justify the kind of sweeping dismissals feminist and left-wing critics subjected him to.

Unfortunately, despite his determination to give Erikson his due, Roazen's book hurt Erikson, too. So in 1977 Erikson quietly submitted a brief to the Freud Archives in the Library of Congress detailing three factual errors in Roazen's account of his relationship with Freud. But privately, Erikson was most distressed that Roazen had found Berman's objections to Erikson's name change (and his ostensible denial of his Jewishness) persuasive. As Roazen later remarked to Friedman, he had received one of the circular letters Erikson sent, but did not think it addressed the issues at hand. Indeed, on October 23, 1976, Roazen wrote to Rycroft about the Berman controversy, and on November 10 Rycroft replied:

> Some years ago I wrote a paper . . . in which I described a group of patients who attempted to disown their pasts entirely, who denied that their parents had had any effect on them whatsoever, and who, if they were drawn to analysis as they often seemed to be, dated their lives from the moment they started analysis and regarded their true parent [*sic*] as having been their analysts, and their true ancestry his or her analytic lineage. Such people, I said, aspired to be self-made in the most literal sense of the word or, if they couldn't achieve that, to have parents whom they themselves chose. When I read this paper to a group of analysts, I was embarrassed to discover that my thesis applied too well to many analysts; most of the examples I had chosen were people who aspired unsuccessfully to become analysts, but my paper gave the impression of being a roman à clef about actual analysts. It sounds as though Erikson exemplifies my thesis up to a point, though I certainly did not have him in mind when I wrote it. (Dufresne 1997b, 290–91)

As it turns out, Rycroft's paper was finally published in *Psychoanalysis and Beyond* (Rycroft 1985a). On close inspection, it has an almost uncanny bearing on the whole Berman controversy, and on important parallels between Rycroft's and Erikson's ideas that neither was fully conscious of, which go well beyond the contents of the Roazen-Rycroft exchange.

In the introduction to "On Ablation of the Parental Images, or the Illusion of Having Created Oneself" (1985a), Rycroft remarked that the first draft of this paper was offered to the *International Journal of Psychoanalysis* and the International Psychoanalytic Library in 1965, but was turned down "because it was thought to be impolitic to publish an essay which discussed some of the psychopathological reasons which lead many people to become psychoanalysts" (214).

And what were these reasons, according to Rycroft? Chiefly, the pervasive desire to invent or acquire a new identity, and to deny the existence, or, less aggressively, the importance of one's own parents in one's upbringing and character formation. Tendencies toward the ablation of parental images have a paradoxical effect on the character and destiny of those who harbor them. Indeed, Rycroft noted that for someone "for whom it is not totally catastrophic, ablation of the parental images may be at one and the same time imaginatively liberating in a way that can be creative and also productive of an element of falsity and dishonesty of character which throws suspicion on the value of their creativity" (220).

Why? Because

> [i]f the natural parents are disowned, the patient acquires an illusion of choice
> about precisely those aspects of himself that are given and unalterable; his
> parentage, his identity, his physical and mental constitutional endowment. If his
> parents are psychologically dead to him, he can choose other parents and there-
> fore his identity. Or he can deny that he ever had parents and claim to be self-
> made in the most absolute sense imaginable. Or he can arrogate to himself at-
> tributes which he claims to derive from parents who he himself claims to have
> discovered. This last possibility is, short of delusion, only open to people with
> considerable intellectual development, who can then claim that their only really
> significant ancestors are the philosophers, prophets, mystics or psychoanalysts
> whom they themselves have discovered. (220)

For many, perhaps, it is tempting to apply the label "ablator" to Erikson
without qualification or delay. But before leaping to conclusions, let us examine the defining features of the ablator type more carefully, using actual
examples to provide us with a basis for comparison.

One vivid and serviceable example of the ablation of parental images can
be culled from Erikson's own case notes. In "The Problem of Ego Identity"
(1956a), under the heading of "The Choice of the Negative Identity" (section
5), Erikson described an American high school girl

> of middle European descent who secretly kept company with Scottish immi-
> grants, carefully studying and easily assimilating their dialect and social habits.
> With the help of history books and travel guides she reconstructed for herself a
> childhood in a given milieu in an actual township in Scotland, apparently con-
> vincing enough to some descendents of that country. Prevailed upon to discuss
> her future with me, she spoke of her (American-born) parents as "the people
> who brought me over here," and told me of her childhood "over there" in im-
> pressive detail. I went along with the story, implying that it had more inner
> truth than reality to it. The bit of reality was, as I surmised, the girl's attach-
> ment, in early childhood, to a woman neighbor who had come from the British
> Isles: the force behind the near-delusional "truth" was the paranoid form of a
> powerful death wish (latent in all identity crises) against her parents. The semi-
> deliberateness of the delusion was indicated when I finally asked her how she
> had managed to marshal all the details of life in Scotland. "Bless you, sir," she
> said in a pleading Scottish brogue, "I needed a past." (Cited in Wallerstein &
> Goldberger 1998, 205–6.)

This case is interesting, among other reasons, because it demonstrates both
the astonishing creativity and the dishonesty of ablators, and the poignancy of
the needs and conflicts that give rise to their efforts. This girl not only loathed
her parents, she "needed a past." Here, as elsewhere, Erikson plays artfully on

the ambiguity of language. On the one hand, his patient was saying that she "needed a past" as a cover story to sustain a pretense that passed for delusion among her relatives. And that was doubtless what she consciously intended to convey. On the other hand, without saying so in quite so many words, she was also saying, in effect: "I am ashamed of my parents, as they were of theirs. I lack a past that I can identify proudly with."

Unfortunately, in stressing the death wish toward the parents—"latent in all identity crises"—Erikson oversimplified the issue somewhat. After all, judging from his own account, this troubled lassie did not just repudiate her parents, but all of America as well. Or, more to the point, she did not just reinvent herself as another kind of American—a Southerner, Westerner, or the like—but returned (in fantasy) back across the Atlantic to model herself on a new immigrant who is still proud and conscious of her ethnic origins. Though Erikson himself did not say so, in so many words, her ablating fantasies were probably a response to the anonymity and uprootedness of her parents' lifestyle.

As Erikson noted repeatedly, uprootedness is endemic to America, where, for hordes of immigrants, the ability to assume or acquire an American identity hinges largely on erasing or effacing as far as possible the language, customs, and allegiances of the "old country," in abandoning or repudiating all earlier ties and identifications, thereby shattering the intergenerational nexus and the capacity for "intergenerational identification" that Erikson prized so highly and thought indispensable to the consolidation of ego strength in adolescence and early adulthood. In its place, as Erikson noted, they were given the consolation of belonging to a world of "self-made" men. In other words, American culture commended and rewarded them for uprooting themselves, thereby transforming passive into active, engendering a sense of mastery and pride instead of the humiliation and confusion that usually overtakes those who passively acquiesce to being uprooted because they simply have no choice.

Judging from the evidence to date, neither Erikson nor Rycroft were aware of the strong convergence in their respective approaches to this matter, because they approached these phenomena from different, though complementary, perspectives. Erikson's reflections on displaced and marginalized Native Americans, and on European (and especially Jewish) refugees in America thematized the debilitating inner conflicts of people whose uprootedness was completely involuntary, due to conquest, persecution, and exile (Erikson 1964c). In all such instances, Erikson viewed individual cases as microcosmic reflections of the culture at large, and pointed to the way in which involuntary uprootedness shatters the individual's sense of cosmic coherence. Similarly, his reflections on the lingering aftereffects of the frontier mentality and the restless mobility of the American populace addressed a mode of self-uprooting that facilitates (rather than impedes) adaptation to prevailing cultural norms and expectations, and therefore constitutes what Fromm called a "socially patterned defect" characteristic of American culture. Either way, in Erikson's account, individual psychodynamics were rooted in prevailing cultural trends.

Rycroft approached the same phenomenon the other way around, seeing cultural patterns as instances of psychopathology writ large. Rycroft was struck with the peculiarities of a certain class of what Helene Deutsch called "As If" personalities: people whose proclivities toward self-invention were so vivid and at variance with the truth that they deserved a special label. And to his apparent consternation, Rycroft also found that an extremely large percentage of such patients sought a training analysis, hoping to use their prospective professional identities as ways of denying their own roots. In due course, however, Rycroft realized that "people who exemplify this tendency are common in all social movements which repudiate the past and claim that it is possible to start again and afresh from scratch" (1985a, 215) by ignoring the experience and the wisdom of previous generations. He even reproached R. D. Laing, one of his own analysands, for catering to such attitudes in the "counterculture."

Before returning to Erikson, let us acknowledge the element of truth in Rycroft's characterization of the counterculture, and of Laing as well (Burston 2000). But as a description of Erikson, the "ablator" profile is much less fitting, on the whole. In contrast to Laing, who often urged the young to distrust their elders, Erikson cultivated young people's hunger for meaningful connection. He encouraged them to wrestle with and remake their ethnic and religious traditions, rather than reject them in sweeping, angry gestures that robbed their lives, and those of their children, of their deeper historical foundations. Besides, on reflection, the real ablator in Erikson's family drama was his biological father, who tried to ablate the image of his child, not vice versa. Rather than denying his father's existence, Erikson was constantly trying to discover who his real father was, and in naming himself "Erik Erikson," paid tribute to the culture of the man who had fathered and abandoned him—affirming the existence of an enduring bond in the face of its manifest denial. Is this data consistent with the "ablator" profile? I think not.

Though he did not use Rycroft's terminology, of course, it is fair to say that Berman successfully summed up Erikson as an ablator in the minds of his contemporaries. And the reproach hurt deeply. Close friends have remarked that the Berman controversy haunted him until the end of his days. While he rallied sufficiently in the coming years to write "The Galilean Sayings and the Sense of 'I'" (1981) and claimed to have embarked on an important new project, efforts to turn this intriguing paper into a book proved fruitless. Despite ample support from friends and a steady influx of books and articles about Jesus and his environment, the writing would not flow. While physical infirmity and failing vision had something to do with it, the Berman episode and its lingering aftermath probably transformed a dual loyalty that was a source of creative tension back into a source of neurotic disability. When he and Joan finally made an ill-advised return to Cambridge in 1987, Erikson was visibly frail. Apart from his lengthy (and extremely gratifying) collaboration with Stephen Schlein, the psychologist who edited *Erik Erikson: A Way of Looking at Things* (Schlein 1987), which was a notable success, efforts to keep him vital and engaged were increasingly unsuccessful. After a series of sad and slightly bizarre misadventures involving the joint purchase of a house with a lesbian couple Joan had befriended, Joan and Erik finally moved to Harwich, Massachusetts, where Erik died in a nursing home on March 12, 1994.

In retrospect, it is tempting to view the elderly Erikson's ordeal as an instance of what Jung termed *enantiodromia* in the collective psyche. In other words, we could speculate that Erikson's reputation had been somewhat inflated, and that the abrupt deflation brought about by Berman's scathing attack set the stage for the more balanced and realistic appraisal that was soon to follow. And at the time, no doubt, his stock was inflated. Even Erikson thought so. Unfortunately, however, with a few notable exceptions, the sweeping and mean-spirited denunciations he endured in later life did not give way to much ongoing reflection or to balanced efforts to apply and deepen his insights, whether in- or outside of psychoanalytic circles.

Having said that, it is also tempting to view the elderly Erikson's ordeal in specifically Eriksonian terms, as a search for integrity in the face of despair, occasioned by a process of internal life review. For, as Friedman points out, Erikson's probing reflections on Isak Borg in *Wild Strawberries* betrayed a strong measure of identification with Bergman's protagonist, indicating that Erikson had already embarked on this stage of his life at Harvard. Friedman's assessment of the elderly Erikson's dilemma is both candid and balanced. Beginning in the late fifties, there was a process of image building around Erikson that created a public impression of a man who was much less shy and diffident than he actually was. The gap between the public image and the private man is evidenced (among other things) in the fact that the man who interpreted children's play so engagingly, and who connected so deeply with other people's children, had serious difficulties with two of his own—not counting Neil, of course. Despite the exalted public image, Erikson never achieved the full measure of integrity and wisdom called for by his own developmental theory.

A more illuminating interpretation is suggested by Patrick Mahoney's article "Freud's World of Work" (Mahoney 1998). Mahoney notes that Freud's "self-analysis" was not a talking cure at all, but a "writing cure," indeed, a "publishing cure" (39). In Mahoney's estimation, writing, for Freud, was "more than just a working medium," it was both personally and professionally, an "organizing and creative experience" (ibid.) Nevertheless, Mahoney observes, Freud's self-cure was "only partial," though he does not spell out why this was the case. Fortunately, it is apparent from context that by "writing out" his inner demons Freud developed a public persona, a devoted following, and a stable, comfortable livelihood that helped him manage his demons more effectively, rather than exorcise them completely.

The same may be said of Erikson. While there is far less self-analysis and/or disguised autobiography in Erikson's clinical "specimens" and case histories than there is in Freud, his clinical vocabulary and the concepts of basic trust, identity crisis, generativity crisis, and so on were all rooted deeply in personal experience, and he had hoped to effect a "self-cure" by exploring these issues more clearly with his patients than his own analysis had permitted him to do. So while his analysis with Anna Freud left many of his deeper conflicts relatively untouched, Anna and Sigmund Freud did confer on him a professional role and a methodology that helped him organize and direct—or, in their words, to sublimate—his inner conflicts into creative efforts that benefited others, and still warrant sustained attention and admiration.

Finally, if we bracket his various failings and idiosyncrasies, and set other petty concerns aside, the tragic element to Erikson's life—which warrants our sympathy and respect—finally comes into view. Because of the pervasive shame and ostracism elicited by his childhood upbringing, because of his artistic temperament, his inability to complete a college education, and so on, Erikson's professional identity as a psychoanalyst was absolutely central to his whole adult existence and afforded him many coveted opportunities for self-expression, recognition, and financial prosperity. But though he worked hard to gain their trust, he was never really trusted by Anna Freud and her circle. Moreover, when he did depart from Freud's ideas to broaden the horizons of psychoanalysis, many of his worthwhile contributions were ignored, misinterpreted, or absorbed into the analytic mainstream without due acknowledgment.

Second, Erikson came to America without much hope of success, only to be swept up in enthusiasm for his new home. Even when his enthusiasm waned, as it did in later years, he hoped to give something back to America, and to help Americans to see themselves in a more realistic light—not to lose their optimism and sense of humor or ignore their precious gifts and freedoms, but, by the same token, not to minimize the adverse and unforeseen consequences of their brash new cultural experiment, with its core commitments to individualism, competition, and ceaseless technological innovation. But despite the tact and the meticulous craftsmanship he put into packaging his message, at the end of day—or, less figuratively, of his life—he was deemed a total phony in one of the nation's most prestigious journals, and he watched that charge gain currency even among some academic stars he had taught or mentored, some of whom rose to prominence on the new tide of Erikson bashing.

Finally, when Erikson's family dramas came to light in Friedman's biography, and again in an article by his daughter, it did nothing to enhance Erikson's faltering hold on posterity. So the final tragedy that beset him is that in the minds of many, his personal problems and failings overshadow his substantive contributions. This is deeply unfair, a sorry reflection of how trivial and twisted intellectual discourse has become in our time. The way some people talk about Erikson nowadays, one gets the impression that his ill-fated relationship with Anna Freud and her inner circle and his public humiliation by a posse of mean-spirited detractors in academia are either irrelevant, insignificant, or his just reward for his familial failings and frailties. That kind of trite dismissal spares us the effort of really having to think about what Erikson said in a critical and historical context. And perhaps that is just how we want our waning icons served up today: "Just the dish, please, with nothing on it."

Why is the prevailing level of discussion of Erikson's ideas so low? There is no simple answer to this question. If one wished to trade in clichés, we could say that envy, Oedipal father hatred, and/or projection were at work here—all, no doubt, with some justification. But while they are very handy explanatory devices in circumstances like these, generic dynamisms of this sort lack specificity and fail to address the concrete historicity of the situation. That being so, let us bracket interpretations like these for the moment, and recall that psychoanalysts and their followers among the intelligentsia were always wary of name changes and shifts in religious orientation because they frequently accompanied the adoption of "revisionist" views. For example, Alfred Aladar (1870–1937) was a Hungarian Jew who became Alfred Adler on arriving in Vienna. He joined Freud's circle in 1902 and converted to Lutheranism in 1909, as his differences with Freud came to a head. His name change and conversion were not prompted by any animosity toward his father, as far as I can judge—though, like Erikson, Adler disliked the exclusivity of the Chosen People ideology, and these outward changes probably promoted his assimilation into the mainstream of the Austro-Hungarian Empire (Ellenberger, 1970).

Or take Otto Rosenfeld (1884–1939), who detested his abusive, alcoholic father, and who changed his last name to Rank shortly before his "adoption" as Freud's protégé. Freud was so intrigued with this gifted young man that he actually paid for Rank's education at the University of Vienna, and in repayment evidently expected a lifetime of loyal service. And he very nearly got it. Rank was the diligent secretary of the fledging Vienna Psychoanalytic Society, and coeditor (with Hanns Sachs) of *Imago*, after Jung's "defection." Despite his youth, he was also a trusted member of Freud's inner circle and a proud bearer of Freud's famous ring. In due course, however, Rank was accused of a Jungian deviation and, rather than succumb to the strictures of orthodoxy, resolved to go his own way (Burston 2002b). Though he never renounced Judaism formally, Rank's last book, *Beyond Psychology*, bristled with denunciations of the Mosaic mentality of Freud and his followers, which he contrasted unfavorably with the more "artistic" outlook of Saint Paul, whose spiritual rebirth supposedly afforded him a genuine understanding of psychological renewal (Rank 1941). So at the end of his journey, poor Rank repudiated his father, his analytic "stepfather," and the religion of their respective forefathers—which is not an enviable place to be in.

These events transpired before World War II, but the sheer horror of the war did nothing diminish the stubborn sectarianism of the psychoanalytic movement. Indeed, it compounded the problem, as the memory of the Shoah somehow blended with these earlier events, increasing the potential stigma associated with changing one's name or faith, even for nominal Jews like Adler, Rank, and Erikson. Besides, as Roazen frequently points out, there were vivid strains of heresy running through Erikson's work. His second psychosocial stage of autonomy (versus doubt and shame) puts a manifestly Adlerian spin on Freud's anal phase, by situating the problem of overcoming the inferiority complex squarely in the developmental itinerary of childhood, thereby rendering it universal. And by the same token, Erikson's musings on the prospective side of human psychology, on the issue of self-authorship and the identity crisis in adolescence, have a distinctly Rankian feel to them, undercutting the traditional Freudian determinism of early childhood experience.

Given his obvious—and, in my view, quite commendable—willingness to smuggle dissident trends into his epigenetic theory, Erikson became a victim of guilt by association. As a result of Berman's attack and others like it, he was forced into a mold that was not of his own making that did not reflect his real character or achievement. And there was enough lingering suspicion and animosity toward the earlier dissidents to make Berman's case seem plausible at the time. Indeed, after Berman, one did not even have to make a case against Erikson explicitly. In many liberal and left-leaning intellectuals, one could rely on encountering a mood of inarticulate and inchoate mistrust of Erikson to shape discussion and carry the day. And so, in the minds of many, Erikson's ablating and revisionist tendencies were all of a piece.

My argument, in a nutshell, is that while Erikson was indeed a revisionist, he was not much of an ablator, appearances notwithstanding. If one searches Friedman's biography, for example, one finds evidence of ambivalence toward Judaism and of mild ablating tendencies, but not the deep, programmatic dishonesty or self-invention that disfigured the life and work of another famous psychoanalyst, Bruno Bettelheim (Pollack 1997). Besides, had Rycroft paused to reflect a little longer, he would have found reasons to revise his opinion. After all, in another remarkable essay entitled "On Selfhood and Self-Awareness" (1991), Rycroft conceded that one could "emigrate, change one's name, one's profession, one's religion, one's political opinions and still be true to oneself," and, conversely, that one could "maintain the same position and opinions throughout life and be untrue to oneself" (151). True indeed, and as pertinent to Erikson's life and work, and his struggles with orthodox Freudianism, as Rycroft's earlier paper "On the Ablation of Parental Images" (1985a). Whatever else he was, Erikson was also one of those who could not be completely consistent and maintain the same opinions and yet still remain true to himself. But this begs the question: Can one be true to oneself while altering all these "externals"—one's nationality, name, religion, and so forth—and avoid being called a traitor or a sham? Obviously not—even in America, of all places. What a sad, strange fate.

4

Situating Erikson

BEYOND EGO PSYCHOLOGY

One frequent criticism of Erikson's work is that his concept of identity is vague and ambiguous, subject to striking shifts in emphasis (Friedman 1999; Fromm 1970; Kovel 1974; Roazen 1976). Though these criticisms have merit, no doubt there is also a lucid, intelligible core to Erikson's work, and from the perspective of a non-psychoanalyst the tendency to single Erikson out for censure on this score is puzzling, to say the least. After all, to a seasoned skeptic—or anyone who values clarity and consistency—the whole analytic lexicon is so fraught with ambiguity that the meaning of the most basic concepts still seems to be up for grabs.

Take the ego, for example. If we pause to think about it, the ego is alleged to be or to do various things that, on the face of it, are completely incompatible with one another. Freud says that the ego is governed by the "reality principle," and is the locus of the "perceptual-consciousness system," or of memory, judgment, and other cognitive functions that collectively comprise our "reality testing apparatus" (Freud, 1911, 1923, 1932). That much we can manage. But we are also told that the ego is (1) the differentiated portion of an undifferentiated, alogical id, and (2) a precipitate of abandoned object cathexes, built up by incremental processes of identification and introjection, which is (3) charged with the deployment of various defense mechanisms that distort rather than enhance our grasp of existential actualities. In short, we are told that consciousness and our reality-testing apparatus are nestled in the midst of a largely unconscious entity that, for all its Apollonian pretensions, is both a product and a source of irrational (or at least a-rational) processes that obscure or override the "reality principle" somewhat (Freud 1921, 1923).

To make matters worse, Freud adds that despite our subjective sense of self-mastery, our fragile ego is really the abject servant of the id, the super-ego, and the constraints and demands of external reality (Freud 1923). And then, later, Freud reverses himself somewhat and accords more autonomy and power to the ego opening the door for the even more masterful ego of Heinz Hartmann (Hartmann 1951; Weiner 1966).

And so, at last reckoning, the Freudian ego is conscious and unconscious, rational and irrational, servile and masterful. Really, what next? One thinks of Freud's celebrated essay "The Antithetical Sense of Primal Words" (1910b). But then no simple or singular binary opposition is connoted here. This ego is a veritable three-ring circus, a cornucopia of sliding signifiers, an identity crisis in the making. An entity this protean conjures up the image of some mythological or heraldic beast, with a lion's head, a serpentine torso, a bat's wings, and a fish's tail. Or perhaps a more serviceable analogy would be a ge-nie in a bottle, an obliging shapeshifter who effortlessly transforms himself into whatever form circumstances (or our whims!) require.

Erikson never acknowledged, much less addressed, the various obscurities in the psychoanalytic theory of the ego. And though linked to Hartmann and Rapaport, and ego psychology in general, as Roazen pointed out, Erikson's "ego" is really much more indebted to the ideas of Paul Federn and Victor Tausk (Roazen 1971). In a celebrated posthumous paper "The Origin of the 'The Influencing Machine' in Schizophrenia" (1919), Tausk first made refer-ence to disturbances of "identity," speculating that the problem for schizo-phrenics is not one of being overwhelmed by the intensity of the drives, as it is for neurotics, but of inner fragmentation and deficiency, a want of internal organization brought about by ego weakness. From this point view, the goal of therapy would presumably be to foster ego strength. Subsequently, for Fed-ern, who embellished on Tausk's ideas, the ego became concerned with main-taining an inner sense of coherence and continuity, with preserving bound-aries, which is precisely what is was for Erikson (Roazen 1971, 1986).

Another feature of Erikson's work that is indebted to Tausk and Federn is his emphasis on elucidating the sources of health, rather than morbidity. Af-ter all, notes Roazen, a deep faith in the recuperative powers of the patient prompted Tausk and Federn to ignore Freud's strictures and to analyze psy-chotics. A similar faith is found in Erikson's remarks on the prognosis for war veterans and disturbed adolescents. According to Erikson, the vividness of symptoms and the apparent depth or severity of regression must not blind us to the possibilities of reorganization and renewal conferred by a newly emerg-ing sense of identity.

Though he never met or cited Tausk, Roazen continues, Erikson knew and admired Federn. When pressed, however, he said could not remember distinctly whether or not he had heard the idea of identity bandied around in Federn's seminars. It hardly matters. As Roazen points out, there is little doubt that Federn's seminars provided considerable stimulation for this germinal idea, and that Erikson's "ego" is rooted in a slightly heterodox tradition of analytic theory that was geared to the treatment of psychotics, at least in the first instance.

But while some Eriksonian ideas and objectives become intelligible this way, Erikson's subsequent introduction of the epigenetic and ethological perspectives on the roots of ego strength, or, in simpler terms, mental health, imparted new dimensions to this discussion that warrant scrutiny. And putting these in historical perspective requires that we step back even further, and review the ideas of Freud and followers in a little more detail.

Freud's classic statement on the ego appears in *The Ego and the Id* (Freud 1923). According to Freud, the ego—*das ich*—is the entity engaged in all conscious mental functions such as language, logic, memory, perception, self-awareness, motility, and social judgment. Its operations are only partly conscious, however, since the mental processes that support these vital functions are normally unavailable to conscious introspection. The ego is weak or nonexistent at birth but grows stronger with each successive psychosexual phase. Even so, however, in Freud's estimation, the ego remains a relatively powerless and vulnerable entity, which must answer to "three tyrannical masters": (1) the requirements of adaptation to external reality, (2) the id's insistent demands for pleasure, and (3) the superego requirement to keep the processes of adaptation and instinctual satisfaction within the bounds of acceptable conduct.

Freud groped for metaphors to describe the ego's relative helplessness. Taking his cue from Plato, he likened it to a rider of a horse—*the Id*—who is much weaker than the animal he ostensibly controls, which sometimes ignores the rider's directives. Freud also likened the ego to a *slave* of the id, who is entirely dependent on it for direction and energy. On reflection, a more fitting metaphor for the ego (as Freud depicted it, anyway) might be a shuttling diplomat or negotiator who is constantly employed in negotiating workable compromises between three antagonistic powers. In this scenario, the diplomat, though clever, has little power of his own to use as leverage, and little to gain by his own activity beyond ensuring that the conflicts between these powerful entities does not descend into total war or chaos, lest his own small territory, wedged between them, get engulfed as well. Furthermore, as with most diplomacy, most of the "negotiating"—between the instincts, the requirements of adaptation, and the prompting of conscience—goes on behind closed doors, that is to say, beneath the threshold of consciousness. In this way, the ego performs what Freud called a silent synthesizing function that integrates the workings of the various personality components so that they appear to function in unison.

In striking contrast to the ego, said Freud, the id—*das es*—lacks structure, realism, and restraint, and is therefore conducive to anarchy and chaos. Initially, Freud defined psychoanalysis as a psychology of the id and its effects on the ego, and it was only later in his career that he started to look more carefully at the ego. This led many to the mistaken conclusion that Freud's ideas about the ego were a kind of afterthought.

In 1954, however, the world discovered an unpublished article of Freud's, preserved for posterity by Princess Marie Bonaparte very much against Freud's own wishes, as Erikson himself observed. Written in 1895, it foreshadowed many of his later ideas about the ego and the id, and demonstrates where they came from. As Freud told Wilhelm Fliess, the Berlin physician for whom this piece was written, he was anxious to give the ideas he was gleaning from his work a firm scientific foundation, so he attempted to explain the processes of repression, anxiety, pleasure and unpleasure, and all the ego functions—memory, perception, self-awareness—in terms of neurological processes. He called this ambitious undertaking a "Project for a Scientific Psychology" (Freud 1954).

In retrospect, it transpires that Freud's turn-of-the-century neurology and his mistaken ideas on neuronal functioning led him to depict the ego as a brain mechanism that lacks its own intrinsic energies and seeks to maintain a dynamic equilibrium in the brain by reducing internal tension to the lowest possible level (Gustav Fechner's *constancy principle*). Ego psychologists like Heinz Hartmann, David Rapaport, and others who befriended Erikson challenged Freud's formulation, however. They accepted Freud's definition of basic ego functions, and of the various "defense mechanisms" enumerated by Freud's daughter, Anna, which also operate unconsciously, for the most part. But they maintained that the ego is more than a clever negotiator brokering compromises between foreign powers. In a manner of speaking, it is a power to be reckoned with in its own right, with motives and interests of its own, which seeks to expand its territory by appropriating as much energy as possible for its own purposes (Hartmann 1951; Weiner 1966).

This reassessment of the ego's role changed the balance of power in the person's overall psychic structure, leaving the individual more scope for autonomous choice and activity than he had in classical psychoanalysis. Prior to ego psychology, the ego was seen as a reactive creature, responding to the problems and pressures that the instincts, the superego, and external reality posed for it, and dependent on the id for its basic energy, aims, and pleasure. However, according to ego psychology, the ego is not merely a reactive entity. It has energies, aims and problems of its own, and its own sources of satisfaction (through mastery or a sense of efficacy) that are different from that of the instincts.

Leaving theory aside, from a therapeutic perspective, the categorical imperative of psychoanalysis—"Where the id is, the ego shall be"—is quite unaffected by this dramatic shift in emphasis. From both the classical and ego psychology perspectives, the chief goal of therapy is to strengthen the ego at the expense of the id. And there are other themes shared by the classical mentality and ego psychology, like the idea that the ego develops more with each new psychosexual phase, or that in the event of neurotic disturbance the redeployment of specific quantities of psychic energy wrested from repression and their (more or less conscious) consecration to specific purposes is necessary to restore health. Indeed, the attempt to systematize these ideas about the "economics of the libido" led Hartmann and Rapaport to develop a very speculative model of the mind, involving hypothetical quantities of hypothetical energies, the so-called bound and/or decathected (free-floating) desexualized libido, and so forth.

For better or worse, however, Erikson was not a systematic thinker, and was mercifully free of this kind of closet metaphysics. In fact, though he did not dismiss the notion completely, he said very little about the "economics of the libido." Moreover, Erikson understood the relationship between the ego and the instincts in a dramatically different manner than Freud and Hartmann—one that is consonant with the work of ethologists like Konrad Lorenz and Julian Huxley. After all, if you pause to think about it, Freud's contention that instincts—and their "derivatives" in dreams and symptoms—lack realism and restraint, hamper the organism's efforts to adapt to reality, makes no sense from an ethological standpoint and is at variance with observable realities. By maintaining a homeostatic equilibrium within the organism, and between organism and environment, instincts are designed—or, more accurately, selected—to enhance adaptation, not to obstruct it. As Erikson pointed out:

> What we do not ascribe to animals, and are usually surprised to find in reports and in moving pictures made in their natural habitat, is a certain built in balance, a restraint and discipline within their ecological niche of survival and activity. For an analogy to what we call ego, we may have to contemplate a certain chaste restraint and selective discipline in even the "wildest" animals; a built-in regulator which prevents (or "inhibits") carnivorous excess, inappropriate sexuality, useless rage, and damaging panic, and which permits rest and play along with the readiness to attack when hungry or intruded on. Similarly, different species of animals share environments with a minimum of mutual interference or distraction, each minding its own section of the environment unless, and until, vital interests prove to intersect. Thus, the state of the adapted animal is defined

by what we might call ecological integrity; a combination of mutual regulation and reciprocal avoidance which safeguards adaptation within the characteristic environment and with other species sharing it. (1964b, 150–51)

Erikson was tactful enough not to say so, perhaps, but these remarks render Freud's Hobbesian worries about the dangers inherent in returning to a "state of nature" (Freud 1930) utterly specious. Whatever else it may be, a state of nature is *not* one of incessant strife and competition, a war of each against all, since competition both with and between species is *normally* subject to multiple instinctual/ecological checks and balances. The idea that aggression is unchecked in nature, or that restraints on competition and aggression are all a product of "civilization," as Freud contended, is actually a civilized conceit. The more likely scenario, as the elderly Erikson suggested, is that many of the aggressive tendencies that the later Freud ascribed to the "death instinct" aren't instinctive at all, but are rather a product of faulty or excessive socialization.

In any case, by contrast with Erikson, who was receptive to ideas and observations gleaned from outside the analytic setting, Hartmann et al. merely echoed Freud and downplayed the tragic and supposedly insuperable conflicts between instinctual endowment and the demands of civilization. On the whole, ego psychologists were either not equipped or not motivated to critique Freud's theory of instincts, and so built upon it, deepening the speculative trend in Freud's philosophical anthropology.

Unlike the ego psychologists, Erikson had the sense to heed ethological findings and to insist that the animal equivalent to the human ego *is* instinct. Indeed, he reserved the term *instinctive* for adaptive or life-enhancing behaviors that promote the interests of the species. By contrast, he used the term *instinctual* for libidinous or aggressive drives that are prone to be excessive, irrational, or potentially injurious to the person and/or the enveloping community precisely because they are *divorced* from instinctive patterning. Impulsive behavior of this kind, which Freud assigned to the id, does not resemble animal instinct, properly so called. It instead resembles the kind of erratic behavior that occurs when encroaching threats or environment degradation or change threatens the species in question, and the cyclical dance between successive generations begins to unravel, placing its future in jeopardy.

In light of the preceding, Erikson also felt called upon to reconsider the role of ritual in human behavior. In classical psychoanalysis, ritual is interpreted as a neurotic and/or compensatory form of behavior whose primary function is to give expression to magical thinking and/or an irrational ambivalence through symbolization, and to prevent the "return of the repressed" or the emergence of antisocial trends. But when Konrad Lorenz and Nikolaas Tinbergen refer to the "rituals" performed by various species, they mean highly synchronized behavioral repertoires involving at least two animals that serve an adaptive function, not a pathological one (Lorenz 1965; Tinbergen 1953, 1954). With rare exceptions, Erikson's reflections on human ritual (Erikson 1958b, 1966a) adhere more closely to the ethological model than the psychoanalytic one, which he reserved for plainly pathological cases, that is, an arid or obsessive *ritualism* rather than a life affirming *ritualization*. By Erikson's reckoning, the relative absence of instinctive programming in the human species dictates that culture must devise meaningful rituals that regulate the commerce between the sexes and cement the bond between generations, to provide meaningful templates for *intergenerational identification* and a sense of continuity that bolsters ego strength.

Finally, no summary of Erikson's relationship to ego psychology would be complete without some mention of his work on play. As Erikson understood it, play is a basic human need, and involves activeness, imagination, role-playing, and symbolization. Apart from his eloquent reflections on how play mediates the experience, expression, and resolution of conflicts during childhood, Erikson accorded deep significance to play as a humanizing factor *throughout the life cycle*—one that is neglected not just by ego psychologists, but by mental professionals of all shades and stripes (Erikson 1964b). Despite the studious neglect of the experts, most of us can still distinguish between a tiresome "childishness," which is atavistic, and the trait of "childlikeness," a desirable trait that connotes enduring qualities of innocence, hopefulness, openness, and an ability to see things in an unconventional light. Playfulness as a dimension of adult development confers elasticity, imagination, and zest in living (Erikson 1982b), and features strongly in Erikson's psychohistorical reflections on Luther, Gandhi, Freud, Einstein, and George Bernard Shaw. While we do not dwell on this theme in the chapter devoted to psychohistory, Erikson hit on something absolutely vital here.

Indirectly, Erikson's reconsideration of instinct, ritual, and play raises another issue, namely, his emphasis on the specificity of cultures. Beyond stipulating the need for a "conflict free sphere of ego operations" and the provision of "an average expectable environment" in which the ego gradually unfolds (Hartmann 1951), Hartmann and associates had said little about the specific needs or environmental supports the ego requires to gain strength, sophistication, and resilience. Though he took his time in doing so, by the late 1960s Erikson chided ego psychologists for their lack of cultural sophistication and made the viability of culture and the intactness of ego functioning contingent on a number of interrelated factors that are entirely outside the purview of most ego psychologists, including universal human needs for recognition, for ritualization, for play, and for intergenerational identification—needs which, by Erikson's reckoning, are not simply stage specific, and which transcend gender, class, and culture as well (1968, 1975).

In addition to stressing the specificity of different cultures and the existence of generic human needs, Erikson deviated from Hartmann and Rapaport on two critical dimensions as regards mental health. First, like Freud, Hartmann and his followers assumed that the ego grew in strength and sophistication with each successive psychosexual phase, assessing ego strength chiefly through quantitative criteria, for instance, how much libido the ego possesses or deploys independently of the id. This sounds quite impressive and scientific, until it dawns on us that what is really at issue here are intangible quantities of a purely hypothetical energy. Besides, from the standpoint of classical Freudianism and ego psychology alike, even an intact infantile ego is deemed weak, because it is still poorly cathected with energy. In other words, we are dealing with a variant of the old phallocentric fantasy/fallacy that "bigger is better." Erikson objected vigorously to this way of thinking. In his own words:

> If the newborn infant brings with him . . . the pervasive quality that insures what is waiting for him (and relying on him) in the needs and drives of individual women, in the traditions and generations of mothers, and in universal institutions of motherhood, does it really make sense to speak of an infant's rudimentary ego being "weak," and to liken it to what is weak in an isolated adult's neurotic dependence? Why burden infancy with the prototype of a weak ego and adulthood with a utopia of a strong one? It is here that our traditional concept of reality fails to account for the fundamental fact that the infant, while not able to test what we call our reality, is competent in his actuality. True, all beginnings are characterized by vulnerability, but as long as vulnerability is accompanied by active adaptation to protective conditions, it is not a state of weakness. (1964d, 176)

In other words, ego strength is relative to the stage of development in question. Each stage has its own specific modes of competence, which are best assessed by *qualitative* criteria, and the tendency to judge earlier stages as deficient relative to later ones is a silly, outmoded prejudice that invariably warps our judgment. Borrowing from ethology again, Erikson said that the chief criterion of ego strength is a capacity for (and responsiveness to) processes of *mutual activation* between the generations, that is, the capacity to elicit and sustain in one's parent or child, teacher or student, the optimal degree of confidence and competence that circumstances allow. Indeed, he continued, behind most stubborn transferences and libidinal imbalances lies an experience of "missed mutuality" that occurred at a crucial point in the person's development. By stressing the role of reciprocity and mutual facilitation between the generations, rather than intrinsic or endopsychic sources of ego strength, Erikson moved the ego directly out into the interpersonal field, and away from the internalized, almost closed systems that Freudian and ego psychological models of the mind often threaten to become.

Erikson's second major "deviation" on the subject of ego strength concerns the place of inner conflict in a healthy psyche. By Hartmann's reckoning, the absence of inner conflict, or the ability to bracket or compartmentalize it, are the definitive criteria of mental health. For Erikson, by contrast, inner conflict is a vital prerequisite for maturity and an ever-present possibility in human development. It is not as if, having achieved a certain level of maturity, inner conflict is likely to disappear—not in Erikson's view, anyway. Despite his rejection of Freud's instinct theory, and his warm personal relations with Hartmann and Rapaport, Erikson never predicated health or maturity on the existence of a "conflict-free ego sphere." Indeed, his theory of psychosocial stages is predicated on the assumption that growth is only accomplished through the successful resolution of a series of protracted crises or inner conflicts.

In sum, ego psychology was a departure from Freud in several important respects. And though placed in that category by friends and critics alike, Erikson made significant departures from ego psychology, refusing institutional pressures toward systematization, questioning the Freudian view of instinct and of ego strength, stressing the ubiquity of inner conflict, and delineating various (nonsexual) needs and processes that he deemed vital to ego development—needs for recognition, play, ritual, and so forth—that completely escaped the notice of his contemporaries. And though it may seem like a trivial point, at first glance, Erikson did not reify his constructs the way Hartmann and Rapaport did. He saw the tripartite division of the psyche into the id, ego, and superego as a splendid heuristic schema and nothing more. So while he pursued his theorizing about the ego and identity vigorously, he never believed in the literal existence of the id, ego, or superego the way "true believers" do.

INNOVATION AND FIDELITY TO FREUD IN ERIKSON, KLEIN, FROMM, WINNICOTT, AND LACAN

Finally, beginning in the early 1960s Erikson tried to bring about a rapprochement between psychoanalysis and ethics and to demonstrate that religious experiences and strivings are not necessarily pathological, that is, that they partake of the instinctive as well as the instinctual. In this respect, he deviated very far from Freud and Hartmann, who argued that psychoanalysis is "value free" (Hartmann 1960). In some ways, his reflections on psychoanalysis and ethics resemble those of Erich Fromm, a forthright revisionist who took Freud to task for his positivism, parochialism, sexism, and so on (Fromm 1947, 1959). But unlike Fromm, who did not mince words, Erikson placated his more orthodox critics by making his theoretical and clinical innovations appear like logical or necessary extensions of Freud's own work. This marks him as what I term a *crypto-revisionist* (Burston 1991). This label is not intended pejoratively and is not based on intellectual merit, or indeed the lack of it, but on a theorist's *emotional* stance toward Freud personally, and the way he or she defines his or her identity vis-à-vis the first psychoanalyst.

To put this label into historical perspective, consider that during the twentieth century the psychoanalytic movement really spawned four basic types of influential theorists. The *orthodox* were movement conservatives whose unwavering loyalty to Freud often made them rigid, doctrinaire, and incapable of being critical of Freud. With few notable exceptions, they treated cogent criticism of Freud as evidence of "unconscious resistance" to psychoanalysis, and deviation from Freud or the mainstream among movement insiders as evidence of mental illness. As everyone knows, orthodox Freudians are now a dwindling minority, quite literally a dying breed, but in Erikson's day they still held the reins of power in the most prestigious training institutes.

The *crypto-revisionists*, a more diverse group theoretically speaking, also idealized Freud, but disguised their departures from "the master" as logical or necessary extensions of his theory, much as Erikson, Klein, Lacan, and Donald Winnicott were wont to do. In effect, they behaved like religious reformers who attributed new cosmological or ethical ideas to older, traditional sources, resulting in curious and contestable intellectual pedigrees for their ideas, and new ways of reading and/or appropriating old texts and ideas, both for good and for ill. They tended to curry favor with the orthodox when they could, but, if forced to, would go their own way, invoking Freud's name in support of their heresies, as Klein and Lacan did, for example.

A third group, Freud's loyal opposition, were analysts who make a candid avowal of their revisionist intentions but tried to reconcile a certain degree of fidelity to Freud with openness to other ideas and influences, for example, Ludwig Binswanger, Paul Schilder, Ronald Fairbairn and most of the British "Middle School," and, last but not least, Erich Fromm. Finally, there was the dissident fringe composed of analysts who openly broke with Freud, like Adler, Jung, Rank, Reich, and Horney, and thoughtful critics like Ian Suttie whose ideas were assimilated by others active in the loyal opposition, for example, Fairbairn and John Sutherland.

If Erich Fromm and R. D. Laing epitomize Freud's loyal opposition and the dissident fringe, respectively, Erik Erikson is a splendid example of a *crypto-revisionist*, albeit a deeply creative one. But as we have seen from the preceding chapters, to understand Erikson's desire to maintain an unwavering fidelity to Freud requires more than an understanding of psychoanalytic theory. It requires some knowledge of his life and of the intimate interrelationships between life experience, identity formation, and creative work—a field of study that Erikson himself created, almost single-handedly, in the form of psychohistory. Erikson's innovations here took some courage to sustain, because indirectly, and as discreetly as possible, they called attention to the fact that the history, theory, and practice of psychoanalysis are densely intertwined with mythology and collective amnesia of one sort or another.

Consider the following example. Psychoanalysts generally imagine that the models of psychopathology they employ are derived from the neutral, objective (or, alternatively, empathic) observation of anomalies of memory, perception, or affect encountered in the clinical setting. These behavioral oddities furnish the basis for further inquiries into the structure and origins of the mind, using free association dream interpretation and the analysis of transference/countertransference to formulate and test hypotheses. While each case is a little different from every other, the cumulative results of empirical/clinical inquiry supposedly yield generalizations about development that suggest recurrent patterns and/or a series of mental stages, each with their own peculiar conflicts and developmental tasks. The failure to negotiate any of them successfully, and the temptation to regress to an earlier developmental phase in the wake of loss, trauma, or unbearable privation is supposedly the chief source of mental disorder. Therefore, psychoanalysis or analytic psychotherapy consists in putting development "back on track."

So by this account, the sequence of events that leads to theory formation is basically as follows: The first step consists in the dispassionate observation of some behavioral anomaly in the other person (i.e., the patient). The second consists in formulating some hypotheses to account for this or that specific phenomenon. Third, these hypotheses are carefully weighed and tested in light of evidence emerging from the patient's unconscious. Fourth, if remedial interventions (interpretation of resistances, of the transference, etc.) prove effective, a therapist/theorist may tentatively venture some conjectures on more generic processes or mechanisms that may give rise to disturbances of this kind. Fifth, the accumulation of data from comparable cases allows the therapist cum theorist ample opportunity to sharpen, modify, or discard features of her initial formulation as she discerns the central or dominant tendencies in cases like these and differentiates them from purely individual variations. In this way, empirical generalizations about the mentality and development of hysterical, obsessional, depressive, paranoid, schizoid, and narcissistic types becomes possible. Empirical generalizations like these are not merely possible, but vitally necessary so that, sixth and finally, clinicians can pool their observations to help future practitioners anticipate, investigate, and manage the range of variations that are likely to emerge on these basic themes.

This is the conventional wisdom about how psychoanalytic research and theory formation works. And among other things, it assumes that there is slow but steady progress in the analytic field. Well, perhaps. But as Erikson himself pointed out in "On the Dream Specimen of Psychoanalysis" (Erikson 1954), by midcentury, the art of dream interpretation among mainstream psychoanalysts was rapidly disappearing, to be displaced by the use of transference and countertransference interpretation, which now lacked this earlier (and potentially invaluable) source of evidence and insight. Is this progress? Erikson thought not. Though he did not say so in quite so many words, he evidently experienced it as a tactical retreat—and an ill-advised one at that. But even more importantly, for our purposes, Erikson warned against the tendency among psychoanalysts to reify their guiding metaphors and bend the data gleaned from the clinical setting to conform with their ingrained preconceptions, thus bringing the progress of the discipline (on supposedly empirical grounds) to a grinding halt. Commenting on the use of the topographical, structural, dynamic, genetic, and adaptive viewpoints for describing and assessing unconscious mental processes in "On the Nature of Clinical Evidence" (1958a), Erikson said:

> [T]he fate of the "points of view" was preordained; since on their medical home ground they were based on visible facts such as organs and functions, in the study of the mind they sooner or later served improper reifications, as though libido or the death instinct or the ego really existed. Freud was sovereignly aware of this danger, but always willing to learn by giving a mode of thought free reign to see where it might lead. He also had the courage, the authority, and the inner consistency to reverse such a direction when it became useless or absurd. Generations of clinical practitioners cannot be expected to be equally detached or authoritative. Thus it cannot be denied that *in much of the clinical literature the clinical evidence secured with the help of inferences based on Freud's theories has been increasingly used and slanted to verify the original theories.* (77; emphasis added)

Bending the data to suit the theory is a very serious offense. But for our purposes, the most important drawback to the conventional wisdom is that it leaves the culture, personality, and experiences of the various theorists involved entirely out of account. Indeed, it deliberately subtracts their bias and subjectivity from the whole process of theory formation, which it depicts as occurring in a kind of cultural and historical vacuum. The resulting mystification can only do mischief. Erikson knew this and, as if in rebuttal to prevailing mythology, always attempted to situate Freud in his cultural and historical context rather than turn his ideas into articles of a dogmatic faith. And instead of perfect neutrality, which is what the Freudian faithful enjoined, he called for "disciplined subjectivity" as the preferred therapeutic stance.

Finally, we cannot fail to notice that the conventional wisdom ignores the fact that psychoanalysis did not simply originate in Freud's dispassionate observation and treatment of his patients. On the contrary, Freud's self-analysis was an indispensable element in the creative, turbulent process that engendered *The Interpretation of Dreams* (1900), which is widely acknowledged as the basis of all subsequent developments in the analytic field (Blechner 2001; Grinstein 1980; Lippmann 2000). And only the most naive or disingenuous person will maintain that a self-analysis can be perfectly neutral or objective, or that it lacks an autobiographical dimension in the literal sense of writing one's own history.

And so to the heart of the matter. Many hard-nosed scientists distrust or disparage analytic theory because they suspect an autobiographical dimension behind or beneath many psychoanalytic constructs. And their suspicions are well warranted, since many influential theories abroad today are at least partly autobiographical in nature and derivation (Erikson 1975, chap. 1). Obviously, if you are an empiricist, or merely mindful of cultural differences, this fact raises vexing questions as to the generalizability of analytic constructs. For example, is the Oedipus complex unearthed in the course of Freud's self-analysis a universal phenomenon, a necessary rite of passage for normal development? Or was Freud generalizing indiscriminately from his own experience when he construed it as the "core complex," as he did in *Totem and Taboo* (1913)?

All through the twenties and thirties prominent anthropologists like Franz Boas, Alfred Kroeber, Bronislaw Malinowski, and Paul Radin disputed the universality of the Oedipus complex. (So did Ruth Benedict and Margaret Mead, pupils of Boaz who influenced Erikson.) With the exception of Wilhelm Reich, Erich Fromm, and a handful of others, most analysts before World War II were basically unmoved by their arguments. Curiously, however, recent trends in analytic theory show a dramatic shift in their direction. Nowadays, only a tiny minority of analysts keep Oedipal issues in the foreground and argue for their centrality. Most are siding with former "heretics" like Otto Rank (1929), Melanie Klein (Segal 1964), or Erich Fromm (1959), who maintained that Oedipal issues are not psychological bedrock, but the by-product of pre-Oedipal disturbances of one kind or another (Burston 1989).

Erikson would not have gone that far, of course. For example, in his first book, *Childhood and Society* (1950), Erikson, who did fieldwork with Kroeber, befriended Mead, and so on, demonstrated a deep and sympathetic acquaintance with cultural anthropology and a corresponding appreciation of the variability and specificity of child-rearing practices in other cultures. But he did so, significantly, without disputing the universality of the Oedipus complex. And yet oddly enough, in retrospect, Erikson's evolving developmental theory put much more emphasis on pre-Oedipal and post-Oedipal issues than on Oedipal ones. Indeed, his concepts of *basic trust* in infancy and the *identity crisis* in adolescence become the chief source of his fame and popularity.

With old Oedipus dethroned, so to speak, what became of the Freudian superego, which supposedly crystallizes in the aftermath of the Oedipal conflict? As we will see presently, Erikson's trajectory for the development of conscience does not stop in childhood or adolescence, but stretches all the way into middle age, and unlike the Freudian superego, which has a predominantly punitive and paternal quality, Erikson's notion of mature conscience has a distinctly *maternal* feel to it.

How can we account for these subtle but profound changes in Erikson's work? Following Erich Fromm, let us differentiate between *matricentric* and *patricentric* mentalities, or those that are shaped predominantly by attachment to and identification with the mother and those that bespeak greater emotional involvement—positive and negative—with the father (Burston 1989, 1991). Fromm originally intended this typology to account for elective affinities between religious doctrines and political movements, and different styles of leadership. So, for example, by Fromm's reckoning, Martin Luther, who minimized the role of maternal imago in Christian devotion and was embroiled in resolute defiance of (and unconscious compliance with) diverse forms of paternal authority, was a decidedly patricentric type—a characterization amply borne out in Erikson's psychohistorical study, as we shall see in the following chapter. And conversely, Gandhi, whose maternal attitudes and attributes baffled or repulsed many Westerners, but endeared him to his followers, was a matricentric type of leader.

Without disputing its usefulness in classifying religious and political leaders, I submit that Fromm's matricentric/patricentric typology is also extremely useful as a way of classifying analytic theorists. Thus Freud, who attempted to trace the origins of Western civilization to the lingering reverberations of a primal parricide and its guilty aftermath, was a patricentric theorist; while Jung's emphasis on the "Great Mother" and his leanings toward J. J. Bachofen were decidedly matricentric in orientation (Neumann 1963; Hogenson 1983). Similarly, among crypto-revisionists in the IPA, Jacques Lacan's preoccupation with the "name of the father" was a typically patricentric trope, while Klein, Winnicott, and Erikson explored more maternally focused themes.

Having said that, however, let me also hasten to add that our ability to differentiate matricentric from patricentric theorists among the crypto-revisionists does not detract from (and should therefore not obscure) some overriding similarities, which may be more salient in the final analysis. All of them, without exception, made fidelity to Freud a cornerstone of their personal and professional identities, no matter how far they deviated from or embellished on his ideas. For example, Lacan bridled at the suggestion that he was a Lacanian and maintained to his dying day that he was simply a Freudian. Indeed, he predicated his entire life's work on an ostensible "return to Freud," despite the fact that, like Erikson, he abandoned Freud's militant atheism and professed great respect for organized religion (Schneiderman 1984; Dufresne 1997a).

Nowadays, of course, most people contend that unwavering fidelity to Freud, or protestations to that effect, are not a criterion of probity or profundity, or of anything other than a childish idolatry. I share that view. However, for those of us living in a post-Freudian era, it is important to remember that some of the best and brightest minds of the twentieth century came up that way, and we cannot simply dismiss them all on that account. Even so, I remain utterly baffled by Lacan, who professed unwavering fidelity to Freud but vigorously proscribed many of his major works, including *Totem and Taboo, The Ego and the Id, The Future of an Illusion*, and *Civilization and Its Discontents*. Lacan's peculiar dismissal of many major texts (trumpeting his superior fidelity to "the master" all the while) rendered his aggressive courtship of the orthodox utterly ineffectual and deepened his reputation for eccentricity and self-aggrandizement.

Though he steered clear of *The Future of an Illusion*, Erikson never suggested that any of Freud's books were not kosher, or were irrelevant to what Freud was "really" trying to do. No doubt his more conventional brand of Freudian piety was part of Erikson's recipe for success—a success Lacan envied, or perhaps feared. After all, Lacan pronounced Erikson's books anathema, too, because he was supposedly the most subtle and persuasive—and therefore the most dangerous—of all the ego psychologists (Roazen 2000a).

Though Erikson and Lacan both made fidelity to Freud the cornerstone of their personal and professional identities, and therefore did not—and perhaps could not—make a candid avowal of their revisionist intentions, Erikson's way of keeping faith with Freud is more persuasive to my mind. However, it is still quite problematic, and there were many instances when staying within the fold required some fancy footwork and skillful rhetoric. For example, consider Erikson's views on the processes of self-authorship or self-creation entailed in his theory of identity formation. For Erikson, identity is not something that is passively incorporated or merely handed down by tradition. Individual identity is actively constructed or created by and for the person within the context and constraints provided by tradition. Though rooted in tradition, it is nonetheless uniquely personal. And if it is not unique, the developing individual has failed in some sense, or else society has utterly failed him. Erikson's emphasis on self-authorship attests to a certain kinship with revisionists like Otto Rank, Erich Fromm, and Ernest Becker, among others, and it took a good deal of effort and goodwill on the part of Heinz Hartmann and David Rapaport not to notice this and to see it as a practical extension of Freud's own work.

Having said all that, there is one area where Lacan's passion for fidelity to Freud surpassed Erikson's, namely, in the dogged patricentricity of his theory, which provided French feminists like Julia Kristeva, Luce Irigaray, and Hélène Cixous a superb platform from which to launch their own careers (Dufresne 1997a). Like Freud, Lacan simply could not credit the maternal imago with the numinous power to inspire awe, reverence, and dread. In Lacan's estimation, the law of the father stands at the portals of culture, barring the way to those who maintain any previous loyalties. And in a similar spirit, Lacan maintained that unconscious fantasy invariably conjures up the phallus as the universal object of desire for both sexes. In effect, then, Lacan reasserted the primacy and universality of the Oedipus complex by transposing it out of its Lamarckian-evolutionary setting in *Totem and Taboo* into an equally questionable theory of structural linguistics. In either case, the effect is the same: to ontologize the Oedipus complex, or to render the law of the father gender and culture constitutive—a veritable "core complex," as Freud said, though Lacan never actually used that term specifically, to my knowledge (Burston 1989).

By contrast with Lacan, Erikson used the term *core complex* frequently, albeit usually in the plural. Instead of referring to single core complex, as Freud did, Erikson referred to an ongoing series of core complexes, totaling eight in all. While Erikson conceded the universality of the Oedipal conflict—rightly or wrongly, depending on your point of view—he never insisted on the *primacy* of the Oedipal complex. If anything, he emphasized the struggle between basic trust and distrust in the *pre-Oedipal* domain. And the virtue that springs from the successful resolution of this phase, namely, hope, carries the indelible imprint of the mother's welcoming and sustaining smile, of the enveloping warmth of her embrace, as all his writings attest.

The matricentric emphasis in Erikson accounts for his affinities with another famous crypto-revisionist, Donald Winnicott. Like Erikson, Winnicott had a vivid appreciation of the newborn's search for recognition in the eyes and face of its mother as it constructs its first tentative sense of self intersubjectively, in and through its deepening awareness the mother's devoted or delighted gaze (Winnicott 1989b). That being so, it is scarcely surprising that Winnicott's references to Erikson are invariably respectful, though they suggest that he understood Erikson's work in an imperfect and idiosyncratic fashion, much as he interpreted Freud quite creatively to suit his own purposes (Winnicott 1989a). But Freud tended to equate the ego with the self (Meyer and Bauer 2002). Winnicott, like Jung, tended to equate the ego with a false self, a persona developed in the struggle to adapt to adverse circumstances, rather than the true self. Erikson's views on the ego fall somewhere between Freud's and Winnicott's. Like Jung and Winnicott—and unlike Freud—Erikson clearly differentiated between the ego and the self, but, like Freud and the egopsychologists, he predicated mental health on robust ego functioning.

In any case, we have established that Erikson was a crypto-revisionist who made substantive alterations to classical Freudianism and to ego psychology, yet contrived to make them appear as logical or necessary extensions of Freud's own thought. In so doing, he minimized, magnified, and obfuscated things somewhat to defend and authenticate his intellectual pedigree, which he prized dearly. Erikson was also a decidedly matricentric theorist, one who made peace, rather than waged war, with American ego psychology.

Leaving the clinical rationale for his theories aside, the reasons for Erikson's matricentric orientation are easy to discern from his biography. An illegitimate child who bonded strongly with his mother, yet for various reasons identified ambivalently with his stepfather, was not likely to overestimate the father's importance in the child's psychological development. Having said that, however, the roots of his excessive Freudian piety suddenly become more opaque. After all, was Freud not his father surrogate?

Well, almost. Perhaps "stepfather surrogate" would be a more accurate description. As Erikson himself acknowledged, he became Freud's symbolic stepson because his *previous* efforts (with Theodor Homberger, his real stepfather) had proved unsatisfactory, and because Freud supplied this itinerant artist with a vocation that enabled him to combine his creative sensibilities with the healing mission pressed on him earlier by Homberger, who grew to respect Erik's new vocation. So if Erikson exaggerated his fidelity to Freud, more than hero worship, self-protective or opportunistic motives were at work. In addition to helping him reconcile with his stepfather, in a manner of speaking, the psychoanalytic movement became Erikson's extended family, and he used the status and economic stability it conferred on him to play the role of Joseph and to save his hitherto-estranged kin from the horror that engulfed Europe. This is not a trivial consideration for a talented and sensitive boy born out of wedlock, a youth who teetered on the brink of madness, and a man who narrowly escaped the genocidal ravages of National Socialism. After all, in this way he could mitigate and atone for all anger and disappointment he both experienced and engendered while he was growing up.

5

Psychohistory—Luther and Gandhi

HISTORY AND PSYCHOHISTORY

Psychohistory is a ticklish business, which requires some patience and acumen to sort out. To begin with, as Charles Rycroft pointed out, we must always remember that on some level "psychoanalytic studies of the dead are spurious, since they involve making interpretations about people who are not present to confirm or reject them, and making inferences about precisely those aspects of their lives which there is the least likelihood of finding documentary confirmation" (1985b, 229).

Of course, this fact did not deter Freud from "analyzing" Leonardo da Vinci (1910a) or Moses (Yershalmi 1991), and Erikson got around Rycroft's objection by assuming that the central conflicts of his protagonists were really the conflicts of Everyman, which animated and bedeviled the hero's whole cultural landscape. In other words, by Erikson's reckoning, Luther's struggle with his father was not only typical but, in a deeper sense, thoroughly representative of a widespread ambivalence toward paternal authority characteristic of the age, while Gandhi's deep identification with his mother was congruent with the deeply matricentric quality of Indian culture. By embracing and addressing these features of the collective psyche, said Erikson, Luther and Gandhi forged new cultural ideologies and new spiritual identities to go along with them. Quoting Jawaharlal Nehru, Erikson observed that Gandhi's impact on India was "a psychological change, almost as if some expert in psychoanalytic methods had probed deep into the patient's past, found out the origins of his complexes, exposed them to his view, and thus rid him of that burden" (1969, 265).

However, said Erikson, Gandhi could not have achieved such salutary effects within the framework of existing intellectual and devotional norms and, like Luther before him, had to break with tradition somewhat in order to renew and revitalize it. But the moment of truth, the proverbial leap of faith that heralded the emerging new synthesis could occur only after a profound inner crisis. To illustrate this point, Erikson adapted an old rhetorical device that made the life of his subject seem to pivot around an "event" or combination of events that starkly revealed the latent tensions and contradictions that tormented his protagonist, the inner and external resolution of which committed him—always a "him," for Erikson—to a new course of action, a new (or dramatically renewed) system of belief and a scale of values, and that irrevocably. This, said Erikson, is the crucible of "greatness": how Luther became Luther, Gandhi became Gandhi, and so on.

Whether this approach to writing history is valid, or whether the selectivity involved in composing a narrative this way misrepresents the seamless flow of events is a useful debate for historians, to be sure. But that it is effective as drama and as a way of focusing the mind on specific features of a subject's life that are integral to their identity—whether in their own minds or in ours—is not really subject to doubt. Why? Because the pivotal events that Erikson describes with such deft artistry—Luther's fit in the choir, Gandhi's fateful train ride to Durban in 1893—had the effect of turning a fate suffered passively (and the conflicts accrued in the process) into an identity forged and embraced through active decision. The "patient" becomes an "agent," and an effective—and risk-taking—one at that. We all respond to this kind of epic storytelling, whether accurate or not.

Unfortunately, a riveting tale is often told in a manner that is closer to myth that to historical truth. And for reasons of their own, as Erikson was the first to concede, psychiatrists and psychoanalysts confound the errors of ordinary mortals by a kind of "reverse mythologizing." Instead of demythologizing, as they claim to do, mental health professionals frequently misjudge historical figures without the faintest inkling of how silly or presumptuous they are being (Heschel 1969a). These errors in judgment are the result of a tendency to pathologize ways of thinking and of being that are foreign to the clinician's own cultural perspective.

To illustrate the perils of pathologizing difference, I am reminded of a story told to me by Dr. Leon Redler, who was a psychiatric resident at Metropolitan Hospital in New York City in 1964. Redler was baffled by the vague and ambiguous criteria his teachers employed when diagnosing someone schizophrenic. The consulting psychiatrist assured him that his perplexity was baseless; anyone whose speech was incomprehensible to the attending clinician should earn the label "schizophrenic." Redler replied that he was reading

Hegel at the time, and found him impossible to fathom. Would the senior psychiatrist, in his position, diagnose Hegel as schizophrenic, he asked. "I most certainly would," was the prompt reply.

Admittedly, this exchange was harmless, as it merely elicited a frank expression of a professional bias. So what? The point of this story is that clinicians are trained to assess and interpret behavior and speech in terms of psychopathological categories and processes that describe the disturbances of their contemporaries, and not in light of the categories and experiences characteristic of the people they are analyzing, who inhabit different cultural universes. And when they lack the incentive or the judgment to tackle their subject's situation in all its concrete historicity, in a constructive and sympathetic fashion, and get caught in the act, they often disguise their ignorance handily behind a *new* diagnosis.

Among the first to draw attention to this state of affairs was Albert Schweitzer, whose doctoral thesis, *The Psychiatric Study of Jesus*, demolished three attempts to turn Jesus into a case study by psychiatrists Dr. George Lomer, a German; Dr. Charles Binet-Sangle, a Frenchman; and Dr. William Hirsch, an American, who all deemed Jesus to be "paranoid" for one reason or another (Schweitzer 1911). Schweitzer's rebuttal to these would-be psychohistorians was so cogent and compelling that he felt no need to speculate about the motives and misconceptions that gave rise to these smug, self-serving "diagnoses," which disguised a massive ignorance of Jesus' cultural and historical setting. And yet, strangely enough, there is no mention of Schweitzer's thesis in *Young Man Luther*, though Erikson wrestled with some equally tendentious and one-dimensional appraisals of Luther. Stranger still, Schweitzer's thesis was not mentioned in "The Galilean Sayings and the Sense of 'I'" (1981), and we have no way of knowing whether Erikson simply took its existence for granted or was actually unaware of it.

In any case, since the late nineteenth century there has been deep distrust among historians toward the pretensions of psychiatrists or other amateurs who boldly rush in where seasoned professionals tread tentatively at the best of times. The term *panclinicism*, often invoked in this context, refers to the widespread tendency to impute or infer the existence of psychopathological traits or processes as a cover for profound ignorance of the subject's cultural context. And though guilty of this sin on very rare occasions, in all fairness, this was not Erikson's style. If anything, he erred in the *opposite* direction by idealizing his subjects excessively.

Unlike most clinicians who study the lives of historical figures, Erikson was more interested in identifying the sources of health than of illness and was more apt to see redeeming features and recuperative potential in acute crises than the vast majority of his peers. It is for this reason that Erikson chastised Dr. Paul Reiter, a Danish psychiatrist who summed Luther up as "manic-depressive." According to Erikson, Reiter's two-dimensional diagnosis entailed a repressive notion of normality, according to which the person must habitually exhibit "an inner balance, a simple enjoyment of life and an ordinary decency and decided direction of effort" (Erikson 1958b, 34). To his credit, Erikson doubted whether this kind of "inner harmony" really is normal, statistically speaking, and added that if this sort of normality really does exist, "I would expect it least of all in such a sensitive, passionate and ambitious individual as Luther" (ibid). On the contrary, as he said: "[W]e have come to take it for granted that any greatness harbors massive conflict" (245).

Though it was never intended in this fashion, of course, Erikson's critique of Reiter's Kraepelinian bias could also be construed as an oblique commentary on the limitations of contemporary ego psychology, with which Erikson himself was closely associated when he wrote *Young Man Luther*. Heinz Hartmann predicated maturity and mental health on the growth and consolidation of a "conflict-free sphere of ego operations." But Erikson's treatment of Luther suggested that in instances of "greatness," at any rate, real maturity and deep conviction are born only of profound and protracted inner conflict. Nowhere is this more apparent than in Erikson's reflections on the masculine and feminine polarities in Luther's character, and the way his theological development mediated and reconciled the innately bisexual disposition that, by Freud's reckoning, anyway, is common to us all. Had he adopted the more orthodox approach, Erikson would have dwelt extensively on the passive-homosexual aspects of Luther's devotional attitude and used this to disparage or dismiss him—to "explain away" his experience of transcendence, to trivialize his search for certainty and wholeness. As it is, however, Erikson took the high road, acknowledging the existence of these tendencies, but dwelling on the constructive aspects of Luther's reflections on religious experience and the relation of the soul to God.

But while discarding the sweeping panclinicism of his more orthodox colleagues, Erikson was unable to break with orthodoxy entirely. Accordingly, Erikson insisted that Luther had an Oedipus complex—and had to have one, to develop ego strength. To be fair, if we read this assertion in light of his remarks on the Oedipus complex in *Gandhi's Truth* (1969) or *Life History and the Historical Moment* (1975), this assertion carries some authority. Erikson's reflections on the Oedipus conflict as an early intimation of death and mortality, written in the late sixties, had a profundity that warrants sympathetic attention, whether we give it credence or not. However, *Gandhi's Truth* was eleven more years in the making, and in the meantime, Erikson's discussion of Luther's Oedipal issues is the weakest, most formulaic section in *Young Man Luther*. It entails no real, concrete analysis of Luther's personality, but rather a lot of psychoanalytic boilerplate. Indeed, one cannot entirely escape the impression that this material was self-consciously woven into the book to ward off incipient charges of "deviance," and I will wager that most readers of *Young Man Luther* promptly forgot about Luther's (real or alleged) Oedipus complex, but were vividly impressed by Erikson's handling of Luther's identity crisis and his stubborn anality, which was also featured prominently in the more or less contemporaneous discussion of Luther in Norman O. Brown's book, *Life against Death* (1960).

Meanwhile, these instructive and deepening differences between Erikson and his more orthodox colleagues, which were obvious to insiders, were ignored by the general public, and, with a few notable exceptions like Bruce Mazlish (1974), Frank Manuel (1976), and Peter Gay (1988), Erikson's repeated avowals of fidelity to Freud did not serve him well among professional historians, who often dismissed him as just another Freudian. Why? Because despite his attempt to transcend the characteristic defects of Freudian historical writing, there was still a tendentious quality to *Young Man Luther*. After all—and by his own admission—Erikson *was* searching Luther's life for evidence to justify and to illustrate his evolving theories of identity and the life cycle. Therefore, he was reproached with trying to make the evidence fit a preconceived theoretical schema, as all analysts are wont to do.

Much as we deplore the dismissive tone of Erikson's severest critics, their biases existed for a reason. For if we pause to think about it, the terms *psychohistory* and *psychobiography*, which Erikson brought into the public domain, were bound to arouse some suspicion. Whether she knows it or not, every biographer is already a psychologist of sorts, even if she deliberately confines herself to elucidating her subject's *conscious* experiences and intentions. A biography is, by definition, the chronicle of a life, but it is seldom simply a chronological recitation of actions and utterances observed from the outside, so to speak. To make a biography lively and convincing, the author must re-create the subject's life as it was lived from the inside out, as it were. To do so effectively, the author must elucidate at least some of the implicit meanings and motives that informed and animated the subject's actions and utterances in diverse circumstances. And to account for certain trends in the subject's development and attitudes, the author must invoke some notion of personality formation, whether tacit or explicit.

Erikson was well aware of this, and called attention to the "implicit psychology that underlies so much anti-psychology" in the field of biography and historical scholarship, and rightly so. Nevertheless, for this very reason, perhaps, the term *psychobiography* is already a bit redundant and, being a neologism, vaguely portentous. By affixing *psycho* in front of *history* or *biography*, an author may intend to convey that he elucidates his subject matter more astutely than an "ordinary" biographer could through his masterful use of psychoanalytic theory, or some specific version of it. But good biographers have always understood the lived meanings and tacit motives that animate their subjects' behavior, and the fact that they do so does not commit them to a psychoanalytic perspective, however broadly conceived. Besides, what many critics say is perfectly true. The appearance of sophistication and depth achieved by some psychohistorians disguises a narrow parochialism, a polemical agenda, and/or profound ignorance of the historical record.

In fairness to Erikson, he was well aware of these dangers. In a foreword to *New Directions in Psychohistory* (Albin 1980), he wrote:

> [N]ew fields defined by hyphens can all too easily lack some of the rigor of the traditional fields. To a psycho-historian, for example, it might seem unnecessary to define what history was and is. Before long, then, his work may fuse with trends that may just as well be called psycho-journalism or psycho-politics— and this is one of the less savory connotations of these words. . . .
>
> The "psycho" aspect of our work is grounded in psychoanalysis, a field that grew out of clinical work and had to develop some Hippocratic rules of its own. We, too, must be on our guard that our eagerness to heal and to change will not involve us in diagnoses and prescriptions that are the province of, say, an ever renewed political science.
>
> Luckily, our very methods can help us from going off too many deep ends. First, they will force us, as we go along, to subject our own motivation to a combination of psychological and historical analysis, each tempering the other. And then, we may come to affirm that rather than being a separate field, we are really part of a great trend that strives for a wholeness of perspective in all fields concerned with human fate and therefore cultivates a complementarity of developing methods. (lx)

When Erikson wrote these lines, he was already seventy-nine years old, so one should read this passage with the proverbial grain of salt, and in a charitable frame of mind. The caution against premature "diagnoses and prescriptions" is salutary, of course, even if the assertion that they are really the province of "an ever renewed political science" is a bit odd. But to a seasoned skeptic, the suggestion that psychohistory obliges practitioners to dwell reflexively on their own motives for pursuing a subject, and therefore precludes "going off too many deep ends," sounds a bit complacent. It begs the question: When is a practitioner's analysis of his own motivation deep or detached enough to eliminate gross shortcomings? And how many "deep ends" is "too many"? And how will the practitioner discover when he has lost his bearings and is plummeting headlong into the vortex of his own projections? The only built-in constraint Erikson hints at here is that if his self-analysis fails him, the psychohistorian comes across facts that fly in the face of his theory and will have the realism and decency to abandon it. Admittedly, he doesn't actually say so. But he alludes to it in his usual elliptical fashion.

In fairness to Erikson, it must be said that the judicious and "disciplined subjectivity" he sought to bring to bear on historical research is not universally deplored among historians. After all, in some respects what he was after was strikingly reminiscent of the approach of Edward Gibbon. In the words of Roy Porter:

> Gibbon advocated impartiality. By this we must not understand any speciously scientistic notion of neutrality, but rather an endeavor, through cultivating self-awareness, to rise above partisanship towards the pinnacle of the "philosophical observer." There was no "solution" to the problem of bias. Gibbon coped with bias by revealing it; by exposing the prejudice of his sources, and presenting, rather than suppressing, the personality of "the historian of the Roman Empire." Impartiality arose not out of a fetishism of facts but from the operations of the mind, from analysis, imagination, wit and a capacity to hold judgment in suspense. . . . Not the least element of Gibbon's craft of history is to include, indeed to implicate, the reader within his theatre of the world. The reader seems to be a missing person in so much history-writing nowadays, presumably because academic historians have lost all sense of writing for a public. Gibbon, by contrast, enters into a compact with his audience, often directly addressing them. (1988, 163)

A comparison of Gibbon and Erikson, though perhaps hazardous, may be instructive. To begin with the last point first, Erikson always spoke in the first person and was always quite candid about his conscious agenda. That being so, Gibbon's ideal of impartiality, like Erikson's concepts of judiciousness and "disciplined subjectivity," eschews "a fetishism of facts" and is tempered in the process of "cultivating self-awareness." Erikson's ability to address readers personally and draw them into his "theater of the world" was as impressive as Gibbon's, though the mode of address, the technique of persuasion, was different. Gibbon was blunt, eloquent, hilarious, and scathing. Erikson was as eloquent and as funny as Gibbon, when circumstances required, but had a gentle, more elusive presence. His gift for indirect communication, his powers of observation, allusion, and the crafting of clever analogies, evoked a completely different kind of authorial persona, one with a stronger feminine polarity. Nevertheless, when Erikson is in good form, his authorial voice wafts off of the page just as palpably, and makes him an arresting writer who earns our interest and sympathy, even when he finally fails to persuade.

Unfortunately, Erikson's stylistic strengths sometimes enabled him to disguise or overlook instances when his tendency to idealize and/or identify with his subjects colored his characterization of things, suggesting that a little more self-analysis might have helped things along a little. As we explore

Young Man Luther, for example, we find psychohistory rebounding on its author in surprising and unexpected ways.

WHY LUTHER?

Before we examine the text itself, let us ask ourselves: Why did Erikson write this book in the first place? According to Erikson, the main reason was to elucidate the concept of the adolescent identity crisis he had first outlined in *Childhood and Society*—a concept that, in his estimation, was still widely misunderstood by many of his professional colleagues. For some time now, Erikson had been saying that adolescents had particularly strong (and apparently contradictory) needs for objects of repudiation and devotion, and therefore deserved a "psychosocial moratorium" to find an ideology (and, in due course, another person) to embrace and commit themselves to. All right, then, but why choose Luther specifically to illustrate the dynamics of the identity crisis? Why not someone else?

One reason Erikson chose Luther for his first full-length "psychobiography" was that Luther experienced and expressed all the torments of adolescence in a particularly vivid and protracted way. Another, more obvious (though unmentioned) reason is that Luther was not at all an obscure figure. He was what Hegel termed a *world-historical individual*, whose writings, utterances, and deeds transformed the world irrevocably, for good and for ill. His illustrious contemporaries included Nicolaus Copernicus, Desiderius Erasmus, Thomas More, François Rabelais, and Niccolo Machiavelli—the last of the medievals or the first of the moderns, depending on how you juggle your historical schemata. Erikson was keenly attuned to generational dynamics and to what sociologists term *cohort effects*. Looking backward, it is hard to think of a generation that had more impact on modernity than they. And with the possible exception of Copernicus, Luther was the most influential of them all.

Moreover, Luther was an absolutely *intriguing* character. He was a religious radical intent on toppling the ecclesiastical hierarchy and resurrecting "the priesthood of all believers" enjoined on the faithful in the Hebrew Bible. But he was also a social conservative who vilified anyone opposed to the secular authorities. He attacked the selling of indulgences and cult of saintly relics with a clarity and indignation worthy of Voltaire. But to the end of his days, Luther was also deeply superstitious, a firm believer in witchcraft and celestial portents who claimed to literally "see" demons and evil spirits lurking about the Prussian landscape.

Does this sum him up? No, not nearly. As a good medieval cleric must, Luther dutifully reviled "the flesh," echoing centuries of Christian tradition.

But he was bitterly opposed to priestly celibacy, spoke frankly of conjugal pleasures, took pride in his children, and, in later years, ate and drank with deliberate abandon to "mock the devil" or to chase away bouts of anxiety and depression. A man of great vigor and industry, who survived three epidemics of Bubonic plague and lived to the age of sixty-three—a remarkable accomplishment in those days—Luther was also prone to legendary bouts of constipation, dizziness, and other diffuse ailments. Finally, Luther began his religious vocation as a humble monk who was utterly convinced of his own worthlessness. But after finding his voice, as Erikson put it, he became an aggressive preacher who harbored a megalomaniacal identification with Christ and who claimed to know precisely what scripture meant and what God intended, even (or especially) if more learned doctors of the church did not. What analyst-cum-biographer could resist addressing a subject this colorful and contradictory?

But there were other, more personal determinants involved in Erikson's choice of a subject. As we gathered earlier, Erik's mother, Karla, kept a kosher house but was a devoted reader of Kierkegaard. She frequently reminded Erik that his maternal ancestors included both the chief rabbi of Stockholm and a prominent church historian. Evidently, Karla hoped that Erik would embrace her own religious sensibility, which was Jewish, but leavened with a deep familiarity and respect for what Erikson called "the existential core" of Christian teaching. And significantly, as far as I can judge, she never expected this spiritual openness from her other children.

Had he been more welcome and accepted in the Jewish community, had he and Theodor Homberger bonded sooner, perhaps the middle-aged Erikson might have followed in the footsteps of the chief rabbi and ended up doing a study on the identity crisis of Maimonides or the Ba'al Shem Tov, or of Kafka, Herzl or Achad ha'Am—assuming the idea of an identity crisis even *occurred* to him in those circumstances. In choosing Luther as his subject, Erikson was clearly discarding the rabbinic identity fragment in favor of the church historian, because of the lingering pain and conflict associated with his Jewish upbringing. He was also affirming a tie to his unknown father, who by all accounts was a Danish artist, and therefore a Lutheran by birth.

Moreover, in choosing Luther, Erikson selected a subject with a strong (though ambivalent) sense of the continuity between the Jewish and Christian traditions—a theme that resurfaced in his later reflections on Jesus. While many elements of Lutheran theology have vivid antecedents in Christian theology, and above all, in Saint Augustine and William of Ockham, Luther's views on human sexuality were decidedly Hebraic. And in terms of leadership, his style was prophetic rather than saintly.

Why does this matter?

Without belaboring the issue, let us simply say that a saint is someone who emulates and identifies with God—one who, by dint of dedication and effort, achieves a degree of spiritual perfection and inner harmony that ordinary mortals do not. He guides by example and by appeals to self-mastery, and is usually *not* vigorously opposed to the powers that be, or an advocate for the disenfranchised and dispossessed. But as Richard Marius points out, the medieval notion of *imitatio Dei* that underscores the Catholic concept of sainthood is basically incompatible with Lutheran theology because of Luther's emphasis on our innate depravity and the futility of attempting to change or transform ourselves by our own effort (Marius 1999). Luther doesn't rule out a prophetic sensibility, however. Unlike the Christian saint, who pursues self-transformation and self-transcendence through identification with Christ, the Hebrew (or Christian) prophet is much more concerned with redressing social injustice, and often starts out as a marginal or deeply tormented figure who may come to the service of the Lord rather reluctantly and who readily expresses anger and disappointment with others, and may even cherish openly ambivalent feelings toward the Almighty (Heschel 1969a, 1969b). That is Luther in a nutshell.

Another reason Erikson chose Luther was the existence of some uncanny parallels between Luther's life and his own. For example, Luther's father, Hans, moved from Eisleben, where Martin was born, to Mansfeld, where Martin was raised, because of a scandal that no one in the family, least of all Luther's mother, dared discuss—possibly a homicide, thought Erikson. Erikson then went on to discuss the developmental impact of family secrets and parental deception on an extremely sensitive and intelligent young boy, and the way they strengthened propensities to basic mistrust. Though it was not apparent at the time, perhaps, we know now that Erikson spoke from personal experience and that he had issues with his mother's secretive and deceptive manner and the anguish that she and his stepfather experienced over his illegitimacy. In a similar vein, Luther disappointed his father by choosing the monastery over the legal profession, much as Erikson disappointed his stepfather by choosing art over a medical career. Once in the monastery, Luther took seven years to find himself, by Erikson's reckoning, while Erikson wandered through Europe for about seven years before finally settling down at Dorothy Burlingham's school in Vienna. Finally, says Erikson, Luther's psychosocial moratorium took a protracted adolescent struggle well into early adulthood. He finally found his own voice and the courage of his convictions through his work, and, above all, through his writings, which he invested with great artistry and care. The same could be said of Erikson, of course, though Erikson's break with orthodoxy was never as loud or explicit as Luther's was. While Luther aimed for rupture, rejection, and polarization when his efforts at internal reform where stifled by Rome, Erikson aimed at creating and conserving consensus, and fostering a consciousness of continuity—though not always, or at all costs.

So, for example, while acknowledging his debt to Anna Freud in *Young Man Luther*, Erikson also took issue with her characterization of the heated religious and political debates that are—or at any rate, were—so common among teenagers and young adults. Indeed, he gently reproached her for depicting them as little more than defensive strategies young people use to disguise their underlying instinctual motives and conflicts from themselves and others. In effect, though not in so many words, Anna Freud had implied that intense verbal and intellectual exchanges at this time of life are largely dress rehearsals for the rivalry and preening that constitute the prelude to the more intimate phases of courtship and coupling.

If you pause to think about it, there is something quite condescending in this appraisal. The implicit suggestion here is that ideological debates of youth are the products of repression, sublimation, or displacement, that is, that they serve a chiefly *defensive* function to prevent the embarrassment or mishap that would presumably occur if immature minds were overwhelmed by the strength of their own passions. By Erikson's reckoning, however, such discussions in adolescence and early adulthood are indicative of a search for what Erich Fromm, in another context, called a framework of orientation and devotion (Fromm 1955). They are attempts to clarify and defend the young person's fundamental choices. In short, they articulate basic value commitments and, by implication, a future direction in life, and help to develop a kind of cognitive self-world schema that is firm but flexible enough to sustain continued growth into adulthood.

At the same time, while they borrow from and embellish on elements of the traditions they share, youthful controversies also attest to young people's need to reject, repudiate, and perhaps ridicule the past, to define their identity negatively by emphasizing dramatically what they are not. As tedious or excessive as these spirited discussions may seem in retrospect, said Erikson, the task of deepening and transforming tradition, of remaking it so that it is relevant and accessible, now and in the future, is carried out in this way by each successive generation. In other words, it is vital to the development of ego strength and the anchoring of the individual in society. And, conversely, it is vital to the well-being of society that adolescents and young adults embrace this task with vigor.

Though the wariness of historians toward Erikson's Freudian tendencies is understandable, one wishes that they would address themselves more sympathetically to a theory of tradition that describes the dynamics of cultural change and conservation in terms of both universal and age-specific developmental needs. After all, tradition addresses urgent psychic needs for the creation of shared meanings and communal modes of life. And whether we know it or not, we need tradition to sustain psychic growth and maintain our psychic equilibrium, just as we need innovation and change when existing cultural forms have outlived their relevance or usefulness. Periods of history in which tradition is straining to survive or adapt, and new cultural forms are emerging, engender virtual epidemics of psychopathology. This fact is extremely well known, even to historians who treat the mental health professions with suspicion or downright contempt. So, like it or not, the study of history and the concepts of identity and tradition converge and overlap on this issue. On this level, then, Luther and the Reformation really were superb subjects for Erikson. The question we posed earlier is: Was he aware of his identification with his subject? And if so, was his reflexive awareness of his own motivation sufficient to keep him from going "off the deep end," as he himself put it?

Judging from the available evidence, Erikson was partly aware of his personal identification with Luther. In *Gandhi's Truth* Erikson observed that "the psycho-historian's choice of subject often originates in early ideals and identifications" (1969, p. 56), and there are many instances on record of Erikson consciously identifying with Luther, which Freidman draws to our attention. But *unconscious* identification is another matter, and one that is apt to falsify judgment. For example, Erikson depicted Luther as a humanist and a revolutionary, though in truth he was neither. Let us take these characterizations one at a time.

LUTHER IN CONTEXT

In *Martin Luther: The Christian Between God and Death*, Richard Marius points out that like Erasmus in *In Praise of Folly* (1511), Luther condemned the absurdity of most scholastic disputation, the sale of indulgences, and the cult of the Virgin. And as a result, Luther enjoyed the friendship and support of Erasmus for a time. But tensions between them were brewing from 1518 onward, and the final break was precipitated by Thomas More's condemnation of Luther, which Erasmus, who was More's friend, felt obliged to take seriously (Marius 1999). In 1525 Luther broke angrily with Erasmus and the humanists on the issue of free will, branding them all heretics. Erikson acknowledged the existence of a rupture between Luther and Erasmus, but attributed it to Luther's loathing for Erasmus's alleged "intellectuality," rather than to deep doctrinal differences. The tacit implication of this remark is that Luther's piety was grounded in feeling, and that he experienced Erasmus as some sort of effete intellectual and saw himself as a full-blooded man of faith—an early exponent of Charles Kingsley's "muscular Christianity," perhaps.

There is a grain of truth in this assertion. Erasmus and Luther were men of different temperaments (Green 1964). Erasmus was a keen linguist and historian, and a great admirer of Saint Jerome, whom Luther heartily detested. Erasmus was also given to irony and understatement, and reveled in ambiguity when it suited his purpose. Though there is occasionally some ambiguity in Luther, of course, it was never deliberate, and irony was too subtle for his taste. Luther favored a blunt, unequivocal style, and found Erasmus slippery and evasive, calling him an "eel." Significantly, however, his use of this unflattering epithet did not deter Luther from relying on the second edition of Erasmus's translation of the New Testament (1519) in composing his own— a fact that Erikson takes as evidence of their enduring affinity.

Having said that, Erikson's attempt to explain the rupture between Erasmus and Luther in terms of Erasmus's alleged "intellectualism" falters when we consider that the piety expressed in Erasmus's *Enchiridion militis christiani* (1501) was as profoundly heart centered as Luther's, notwithstanding the eloquent opacity and elusiveness in the later works and correspondence that Luther found so maddening and that Erasmus employed freely when he needed cover from the forces of intolerance—among whom he eventually numbered Luther (Marius 1999). For much as he deplored the arid disputations of scholastic theologians, Erasmus resembled Aristotle and Saint Thomas in having some faith in our innate sociability, our ability to govern ourselves, and in the efficacy of good works, carried out in the proper spirit, to ennoble and edify the human spirit (Green 1964). Some humanists and their fellow travelers, the Unitarians, even allowed for the possibility that Jews, Muslims, and Hindus, if they conducted their lives in a Christian spirit, could commend themselves to God, and be welcomed into heaven in the hereafter.

"Heresy!" thundered Luther. Salvation is always an unmerited gift of God. There is nothing we can do in this world to really merit salvation. Luther argued that works without faith are of no avail, and indeed, are idolatry, and that only those who embrace Jesus Christ as their personal savior will enter the kingdom of heaven. So temperament, though important, is not sufficient to explain the dissolution of the friendship between Luther and Erasmus. Philipp Melancthon, Luther's close friend and ally, was also man of very different temperament. But Luther and Melancthon saw eye to eye on doctrine. Finally, as W. H. H. Green demonstrates in considerable detail in *Luther and the Reformation*, the temperamental differences between Erasmus and Luther did not hinge simply on this matter of "feeling." The fact is that Erasmus deplored violence and spotted Luther's tendencies in that direction early on. He was a different kind of reformer than Luther was, and, reflecting on their disparate agendas, once said: "I laid a hen's egg; Luther hatched a bird of quite a different breed" (Green 1964, 164).

That being so, Erikson's attempt to depict Luther as some sort of humanist, without really addressing the doctrinal differences between Erasmus and Luther, comes across as quite glib. And it is doubly glib in light of the fact that another psychoanalyst, Erich Fromm, had summed these doctrinal differences up admirably almost two decades earlier in *Escape from Freedom* (1941), a book Erikson was quite familiar with. The issues that split Luther and Erasmus centered on the importance of tolerance and the relationship between "grace" and "works." Another issue that divided Luther from Erasmus and his circle was that the humanists interpreted scripture allegorically, for the most part, and made ample allowance for the existence of more than one valid interpretation of a text. They also acknowledged the wisdom of many pagan poets and philosophers, arguing that they were perfectly compatible with a Christian way of life. In short, they were averse to a rigid or doctrinaire attitude toward religious faith. Not so Luther. Though he put a selective emphasis on certain biblical texts and deliberately ignored others, Luther maintained that the Bible is the literal and infallible word of God. He also claimed to know precisely what the Bible meant in any given instance, even if the text itself was deeply obscure to other learned commentators who were more well-versed in Hebrew and Greek—like Erasmus, for example.

Another problem with Erikson's portrait of Luther is his fanciful claim that "Luther left the heavens to science and restricted himself to what he could know of his own suffering and faith, that is, to what he could mean" (Erikson 1958b, 213). Fiddlesticks! Luther meddled in science as freely as he did in politics, and heaped abuse on Copernicus on the grounds that the heliocentric theory contradicted scripture (Bush 1967). After all, said Luther, at the battle of Jericho God commanded the sun to cease its revolutions, indicating that the sun circles the earth, and not vice versa. (Fortunately for posterity, Melancthon, who condemned Copernicus as well, nevertheless saw to it that the Copernican theorem was taught in Lutheran schools, giving Lutheran communities an edge over Catholic ones in terms of the advancement of science.)

In short, there was a literalistic and, by implication, fundamentalist attitude in Luther that was at variance with the spirit of Catholic humanism *and* the emerging scientific worldview. What is less commonly appreciated among scientific historians is that it also clashed with traditional medieval sensibilities. As any church historian will tell you, Saint Augustine interpreted the first six "days" of Genesis allegorically, and thereby set the tone for subsequent commentary of this matter in both the Catholic and Orthodox churches.

In addition to the untenable claim that Luther was a humanist of sorts, Erikson claimed that Luther was a revolutionary. Erikson carefully qualified this characterization by saying that Luther also harbored deep reactionary tendencies, arguing that *all* great revolutionaries conceal reactionary attitudes in their unconscious as well. Well, perhaps. But for the average historian, a more parsimonious interpretation would dispense with hypothetical "unconscious" motives and simply declare that Luther was an opportunist, who supported insurrection when it proved expedient and opposed it when he returned, in due course, to his real agenda.

In all likelihood, I suspect, both positions are partly true. Initially, Luther posed as a revolutionary in order to win sympathy and support and to unsettle his powerful opponents, and mixed conscious and deliberate machinations of this variety with an unconscious agenda that surfaced only later. But to call that agenda "revolutionary," as Erikson did, is to fuse or confuse two mentalities that are only sometimes intertwined—that of the radical religious reformer and that of the revolutionary political activist.

Luther was indeed a religious radical who opposed Rome because he believed that *all* men should read the Bible and pray in their own tongue. Moreover, said Luther, any believer can be a priest and give the sacraments, provided he knows the word of God and that the community elects him to office. In short, clerical authority comes from the community, and since the mass should be delivered in the vernacular, rather than in Latin, there is no need for the authorization of priests from Rome.

But there was an important caveat attached to these reforms, namely, that the state must *ratify* the community's decision to endorse a priest. If not, the priest is just not kosher, so to speak. So in Luther's universe, the state controls the church, rather than vice versa, and the clergy, in turn, advise their flock that it is their religious duty to obey their lords and masters. Say what you will, this is not a revolutionary platform. In terms of social and political power, Luther merely rendered unto Caesar what was formerly Saint Peter's, if I may put it that way (Marcuse 1973).

As historians of the Reformation point out, this doctrinal shift endeared Luther to fractious princes and the indigent rabble eager to regain their livelihoods by appropriating church lands. It also fostered the emergence of national churches and, indeed, of nationalism generally. Finally, the Reformation created an urgent need for public education, so that all men could read and reflect on scripture—an idea unheard of in feudal times and later promoted by the Enlightenment, albeit for different reasons. But while it hastened the advent of modernity and the dissolution of the feudal order, Luther's religious "revolution" also enjoined strict obedience to secular authority—even for those thrust to the brink of destitution and beyond (Green 1964).

Oddly enough, Erikson's American readers usually overlooked this fact, though it was not lost on Erikson's fellow émigrés in the Frankfurt Institute for Social Research. Writing mostly in German in the thirties, Max Horkheimer, Theodor Adorno, and Herbert Marcuse all drew attention to two other traits in Luther's character that were minimized in Erikson's portrait: his extreme patriarchalism and his anti-Semitism. Marcuse's reflections on Luther were available to Erikson in a volume called *Studies on Authority*, published in German 1936 by Felix Alcan in Paris, and later reprinted in *Studies in Critical Philosophy* (Marcuse 1973). And in 1941 Horkheimer and Adorno drew clear links between Luther's anti-Semitic statements and then-current Nazi propaganda in a report on their "Research Project on Anti-Semitism" (Horkheimer and Adorno 1941). The Frankfurt School construed Luther's patriarchalism as an early and indirect expression of an emerging bourgeoisie starting to flex its muscles, because it was linked, in their minds, to Roman law, which Luther had studied before his flight to the monastery. Roman law was severely patriarchal, and the revival of Roman law and its adaptation and application to extant conditions of trade, industry, and civic government were used extensively by the burghers of Luther's era to undermine the power of the church.

Though he scarcely acknowledged the existence of the Frankfurt School, Erikson acknowledged the element of truth in their characterization, noting that entrepreneurial ambition and distrust of the clergy were probably the principle reasons why Hans Luther, a peasant turned entrepreneur, pushed his son Martin toward the legal profession and deplored his pursuit of a monastic vocation. Having said that, however, Erikson also argued that the exigencies of the class struggle, while scarcely irrelevant in this context, imposes too narrow and reductionistic a framework to grasp the depth and complexity of Luther's inner life. And though he did not dwell on it much, Erikson also noted Luther's antipathy to the cult of the Virgin and indeed any view of Mary as intercessor, dispenser of grace, and so on.

But whereas Erikson made a sensible allowance for the role of broad political and economic factors in Luther's life and times, when it came to addressing Luther's attitude toward the maternal imago and its relation to the sacred, he underestimated the significance of his data. He did offer some interesting conjectures about the biographical origins of Luther's antipathy to the Virgin, for example, his (real or alleged) experience of his mother as unavailable, weak, unreliable, and so on, and the way these experiences were probably linked to male domination. But if Luther's antipathy to Mariolatry had some diffuse or indirect social determinants like these, it also had very direct social and political consequences from which Erikson averted his gaze. Luther's so-called priesthood of all believers was a purely male fraternity. Women may have faith, profess Christ as their savior, and be saved on the

Day of Judgment, but they are still second-class citizens in the kingdom of heaven. In Luther's view, women lacked the Christlike qualities of males and must meekly submit to their husbands, just as their husbands must submit to the civic authorities in all circumstances. Whether we construe Luther's patriarchalism as a belated expression of ancient male prejudice, Roman legalism, or an emergent class consciousness, there is no doubt that women's second-class status in the devotional sphere sanctioned male domination, promoting or at least tacitly encouraging witch burning and all manner of domestic violence. Had Luther's Reformation floundered and Erasmus and the humanists prevailed instead, the women's movement would have emerged much earlier, with who knows what consequences for the history of European civilization.

Finally, there is the issue of Luther's anti-Semitism. Initially, in his more charitable moods, Luther explained the Jews' refusal to convert as rooted in a sensible loathing for the papacy and wariness toward the pagan elements Catholicism had introduced into Christian teaching. For a few years he even deluded himself into thinking that once he had purged the Christian faith of these sordid accretions the Jews would convert en masse. However, after many abortive efforts to convert local Jewry, in 1543, at age sixty, Luther exhorted his contemporaries as follows:

First, to set fire to their synagogues or schools.

Second, I advise that their houses also be razed and destroyed.

Third, I advise that all their prayer books and Talmudic writings, in which such adultery, lies, cursing and blasphemy are taught, be taken from them.

Fourth, I advise that their rabbis be forbidden to teach henceforth on pain of loss of life and limb.

Fifth, I advise that safe-conduct on the highways be abolished completely for Jews.

Sixth, I advise that . . . all cash and treasure of silver and gold be taken from them.

Seventh . . . Let whomsoever can, throw brimstone and pitch upon them, so much the better . . . and if this be not enough, let them be driven like mad dogs from the land. (Berke 1996, 345)

This inflammatory speech was not an isolated incident. As Richard Marius points out, Luther's last sermon, delivered three days before his death, was another attack upon Jews. Surely this signifies something. In fairness to Erikson, of course, this was old man Luther, not young man Luther, speaking. Still, in terms of moral geography Luther the elder landed squarely on *Kristallnacht*, which was scheduled quite consciously by the Nazi leadership to occur on November 9–10, 1938, to overlap with Luther's birthday. This fact was well known to men of Erikson's generation, so we can only surmise that Erikson was loath to acknowledge the depth or extent of Luther's anti-Semitism. He treated Luther's anti-Semitic outbursts as the result of injured pride and frustrated evangelical zeal, tinged with some of the murderous hatred he presumably inherited from his father—nothing more, nothing less. While vehement and troubling, he conceded, they were never really intended as a program of action or as a spirited endorsement for pogroms.

That is just possible, of course. But in view of how his incendiary words were taken up subsequently by the German people, one wonders at the calm conviction that underscores Erikson's disclaimer. After all, Luther's utterances were often read in Protestant churches during the Nazi era to incite and legitimate the various abuses that culminated in the Holocaust. And as C. G. Jung pointed out in *Aion*, many members of the Nazi elite persuaded themselves that they were merely "finishing Luther's work" (1959, 102). And Jung was in a position to know, having worked closely with the Nazi brass for several years before he rejected National Socialism (Ellwood 1999).

How can we account for all these oversights and omissions? Faulty scholarship? Perhaps that is part of it. But as Lawrence Freidman points out, Erikson was warned *explicitly* by Erich Fromm not to overlook Luther's anti-Semitism long before he completed his book (Freidman 1999, 273). The real reason Erikson minimized or obscured the truth on these issues was not faulty scholarship, but the fact that he had a strong need to *idealize* Luther. And the reason this is so strange—and so tragic, finally—is that in many respects Luther was really the antithesis of everything Erikson stood for. Though no revolutionary, Erikson certainly was a humanist, whose religious sensibilities were catholic, with a small *c*. He deplored anti-Semitism in all its forms. Moreover, unlike Luther, who tried to rob the maternal imago of any awe-inspiring or numinous significance, Erikson traced the experience of the numinous back to the joyous reciprocity of the mother-infant bond, rather than to remorse over some (real or imaginary) primal parricide, as Freud did. (If anything, Erikson could be accused of slighting the numinous significance of the father imago, rather than the reverse.)

So on reflection, we have a very peculiar situation on our hands. Though he approached Luther with admirable insight and restraint, in some respects Erikson himself was opposed, with every fiber of his being, to the intolerance, the virulent sexism, and the anti-Semitism that the older Luther embodied and expressed. Why, then, did Erikson idealize Luther? Perhaps the curious parallels between Luther's life and his own prompted him to identify with Luther as a young man. This tendency was reinforced by the fact that his wife, Joan, exerted a subtle but strong influence on him to join her in her devotions. With the wisdom of hindsight, we might say that his slow but steady migration toward Christianity as his spiritual home would have faced intractable difficulties had he broached Luther's anti-Semitism openly. For though the American Lutheran Church has publicly repented and repudiated the anti-Semitism of its founder in recent years, it was in no mood to address these issues at the time.

WHY GANDHI?

Erikson fared better in his biography of Gandhi, which contains far more reliable information about this subject's childhood and is much less encumbered by idealizing tendencies. Though he described Gandhi's saintlier moods and moments in reverential tones, Erikson readily acknowledged Gandhi's shrewd practicality, his skills as a negotiator, and his frequent pettiness and cruelty toward members of his own family. Indeed, once discovered, Gandhi's troubled family life gave Erikson pause, and prompted a long "letter" to the Mahatma to clarify the reasons for his anger and disappointment. Entitled "A Personal Word," and addressed to "Mahatmaji," this section of *Gandhi's Truth* is twenty-five pages long and furnishes the first chapter in part 3, concerning the textile workers strike at Ahmedabad, which Erikson claimed is the core of his book. Erikson's "letter" is a frank and illuminating confession that says at least as much about Erikson as it does about his subject.

Why Gandhi? As was the case with Luther, a multitude of motives probably prompted Erikson's interest. One was a desire to revisit his own youthful past. As a teenager, Erikson had discussed Gandhi with Edwin Blos and, in all probability, had read Romain Rolland's biography of Gandhi when it first appeared in 1924. Indeed, on page 2 of *Gandhi's Truth*, Erikson recalled his youthful conviction regarding the affinity between "that Galilean," or "Him who had the gift to speak to fisherman in a manner to be remembered through the ages," and "the skinny Indian leader enshrined in Delhi," which is entirely in keeping with Rolland's characterization (1926, 20).

Another reason was that Gandhi was admired by the followers of Martin Luther King Jr., who sought to transform American society by eliminating racism and "pseudospeciation." Henry David Thoreau had addressed the issue of civil disobedience for an earlier generation of Americans and had even gone to jail briefly to voice his opposition to slavery. But at this juncture in American history, when violent reprisals against civil rights activists were common, the risks entailed were much higher than they had been for Thoreau. Thoreau had risked his liberty and his reputation when he went to jail, and considered whatever losses he suffered well worth the bargain. And rightly so. But Gandhi and his followers, like King and his supporters, frequently risked their very lives in their defiance of the civic authorities. Erikson admired their courage and sought to articulate a psychoanalytic rationale for militant nonviolence that would dispel the smug, disparaging appraisals of many of his analytic colleagues who characterized nonviolent protest among young people as nothing more than Oedipal "acting out."

Another reason Erikson embraced Gandhi was that, like Luther, Gandhi was a religious reformer of great courage and conviction who attempted to remake religious tradition in ways that would promote general emancipation. By calling attention to his success, Erikson hoped to encourage younger people not to be dismissive of their own cultural traditions—not to become "ablators," in Rycroft's terms. That being so, it is instructive to note that Erikson's portraits of Luther and Gandhi converge in their sympathetic portrayal of these budding orators as stubborn, somewhat self-absorbed young men at odds with the legal profession, wrestling with internal contradictions and restless inner compulsions that issued in a series of humiliating failures before they finally found their way, and their own distinctive "voice."

But strangely enough, despite these striking parallels, if you scour the text of *Gandhi's Truth*, you find that *explicit* comparisons between Luther and Gandhi—as monks, orators, and politicians—are few and far between. Indeed, it is not until the end of *Gandhi's Truth*, on page 398, that Erikson actually credits Gandhi with embracing the heart of Luther's "religious actualism." In what does "religious actualism" consist? According to Erikson, it begins with a candid confrontation (at an early age) with the naked actuality of death and a precocious awareness of our inevitable finitude, followed by a paradoxical, life-affirming ability to wrest an abundance of meaning and zest from the jaws of fate, and a simultaneous willingness to risk one's life for the sake of one's principles and beliefs.

In other words, Erikson's notion of a religious actualist corresponds to what other people call a religious *existentialist*. And if his reflections on this point are any indication, Erikson seemed to think that this fact justified treating Luther and Gandhi as kindred spirits. But if you look at the lives of Luther and Gandhi more closely, it turns out that this characterization goes only so far. Indeed, the more we think about Luther and Gandhi as embodiments of trends or types *other* than Erikson's beloved *homo religiosis*, the more Erikson's belated comparisons seem contrived to avoid reflecting on their enormous differences.

Consider the following: Luther and Gandhi were both lawyers who overcame deep inhibitions to assume their mature vocations, and both considered themselves latter-day disciples of "that Galilean." But Luther advocated violence against Jews and, before that, against starving, disenfranchised peasants who rioted against their feudal lords in the desperate hope of wresting a bit of dignity and self-determination from impossibly oppressive circumstances. Gandhi, a disciple of John Ruskin and Leo Tolstoy, redefined the ancient Jain concept of ahimsa, or nonviolence, and led a nonviolent worker's strike against the captains of industry in Ahmedabad. Luther was profoundly intolerant of other faiths, while Gandhi preached the underlying unity of the world's great religions. Finally, as Erikson himself points out, Luther married late but was a tender husband and a proud, devoted father, for the most part, who poured out his hatred and disappointment on the pope or the infidel, while Gandhi espoused a disinterested love of all humanity, yet was quite cruel to his own wife and children, and above all to his eldest son, Harilal.

This last observation addresses the ways in which Luther and Gandhi channeled or deflected their aggressive impulses. And for a psychoanalyst concerned with the roots of violence, as Erikson was, this striking difference in their respective modus operandi is not a trivial concern. As Erikson often pointed out, "militant" nonviolence requires that its adherents have a good deal of discipline and "fight" in them, and Gandhi often used warrior metaphors in speeches and exhortations to his followers. By not seizing directly on this comparison and exploring its manifold implications, Erikson passed up a splendid opportunity to embellish on the revisions to Freud's theory of infantile sexuality he had tendered in *Childhood and Society* some two decades before.

As Erikson pointed out in *Childhood and Society*, Freudian theory seeks to discern the roots of human aggression to three consecutive psychosexual phases or "erotogenic zones" that are ideally subsumed under "genital primacy"—oral, anal, and phallic. Moreover, Freudian theory was apt to differentiate qualitatively and quantitatively between different "styles" of aggression according to the locus and degree of libidinal fixation that presumably gives rise to them. In *Childhood and Society*, Erikson broke these Freudian stages down into a series of substages, paying special attention to retentive and eliminative issues and the development and use of the musculature for defensive and aggressive purposes. That being so, he was oddly inattentive to the fact that the middle-aged Luther fairly gorged himself at every opportunity, and suffered from severe constipation, while Gandhi fasted for weeks at a time, and used an enema daily to "purify" his body (Koestler 1959).

In other words, when you address minute particulars rather than indulge in broad generalizations, these two "religious actualists" were as different as night and day, even by very conventional criteria. If their modes of aggression are not sufficiently instructive, are their attitudes to food and sex, which are not controversial, not deeply illuminating from a *psychological* point of view? Besides, from a Freudian standpoint, doesn't an unusual or excessive preoccupation with these modes of incorporation, elimination, retention, and so on have any bearing on the way people manage their aggressive inclinations?

Rightly or wrongly, Freud thought so, and a more orthodox appraisal of
Gandhi's life and character would have dwelt at greater length on this issue.
The paucity of reflection on this theme is a telling indication of how far Erikson had drifted from orthodoxy in the interval between *Childhood and Society*
and *Gandhi's Truth*.

SEX AND AGGRESSION IN LUTHER AND GANDHI

Having said that, however, *Gandhi's Truth* did dwell thoughtfully on the themes
of "mature" or genital sexuality and the problem of guilt, and in ways that are
still consonant with a fairly orthodox perspective. This was unavoidable, since
sexual desire becomes a pressing issue in connection with the shocking suicide
of Gandhi's eldest son, Harilal, which perturbed Erikson deeply. Against his father's wishes, Harilal married, drank alcohol, and eventually converted to Islam
before he took his own life at age forty-one. By that time, father and son had
been profoundly estranged for many years, and Gandhi had actually disowned
him. As Erikson pointed out, Gandhi cherished the belief that a child's disposition is indelibly inscribed in its psyche by the attitude and disposition of his parents at the moment of conception. Moreover, he regarded his lustful feelings for
his own wife, Kasturba, when Harilal was conceived as being thoroughly de-
praved, and did not hesitate to say so to Harilal in admonitory moods. Finally,
Erikson notes, Gandhi regarded his own father's attitude to his mother, Putali
Ba, in a similar light. In short, the intergenerational "curse" that afflicted
Gandhi and his offspring wove the experiences of sex and guilt together in an
intricately interconnected web that enveloped them at birth or before.

   As Erikson himself points out, Indian culture is a study in stark contrasts,
and no more so than in its appraisals of sexuality. Sensuousness is celebrated
in painting and sculpture, and cultivated, intensified, and refined in Tantric
yoga, where it is associated with the sacred. And yet at the same time, sex is
shunned by the male sadhu, or ascetic, who prefers celibacy and sees the dis-
charge of any seminal fluid as a loss of "vital force." So here it must be said
that while he was deeply rooted in his own native soil, Gandhi showed no
affinity for the sensuous side of Indian culture. Indeed, when asked by a
Protestant minister if he believed in original sin, Gandhi promptly answered
in the affirmative (Erikson 1969, 249). And while his notion of original sin
may not have conformed to all the specifications of Christian doctrine, his belief in the intergenerational curse handed down from father to son as a result
of sexual sin, our innate depravity, and so on, are highly analogous beliefs.

   That being so, it is instructive to note that though raised as a Jain of the
Vaishnava sect by his mother, Gandhi was also thoroughly Westernized dur-

ing his twenties. Indeed, as Gandhi himself relates in his *Autobiography*, he did not even read the Bhagavad Gita until his arrival in London at age twenty-one (Gandhi 1993). Meanwhile, once in London, he was profoundly influenced by Ruskin and Tolstoy, whose attitudes to sexuality were profoundly similar to his own.

The reference to original sin in *Gandhi's Truth* prompts another question that Erikson neglected to ask: What would Luther have made of Gandhi's attitude toward sex? In all probability he would have found it quite morbid and argued that sex within marriage is blessed, even if it is frequent, vigorous, and enjoyed chiefly for its own sake. But strangely enough, Erikson didn't even mention Luther until part 2 of *Gandhi's Truth*, where he finally reminds readers of his first effort to modify the standard psychoanalytic "traumatology" to illumine Luther's life and work, and stoutly declares: "I consider any attempt to reduce a leader of Gandhi's stature to earlier as well as bigger and better childhood traumata both wrong in method and evil in influence" (99).

Fair enough. That is true, as far as it goes. But it does not alter the fact that Erikson paid far more attention to anal themes in Luther's life and work than he did in Gandhi's. In fairness to Erikson, perhaps, that may have been unavoidable. After all, Luther's tirades against the pope are infused with such ferocious scatological humor and invective that his anal streak *cannot* be ignored, even by conventional historians (Green 1964). If anything, Erikson overplayed his hand here, because he interpreted a disputed passage in Luther's *Table Talk* to mean that Luther's epiphany took place while he was evacuating his bowels—an idea echoed by Norman O. Brown two years later, in *Life against Death* (1960). Erikson reasoned that for someone who suffers from chronic constipation, having a splendid bowel movement could easily engender a "religious" experience. But on reflection, most religious virtuosi find God in moments of rapture and exaltation on mountains, in deserts, in caves, in silent meditation, or deep in prayer. If Erikson was right, Luther was the first (and perhaps *only*) specimen of *homo religiosis* to have his crucial revelation during the act of defecation.

Erikson had plenty of religious admirers in the 1960s and 1970s, and it must be said that their collective reticence on this point is most impressive, and may attest to the reality of divine intervention in human affairs. For it is a miracle that some of the Protestants who read this particular conjecture didn't lynch Erikson, and that Catholics didn't beatify him for it.

Strangely enough, W. H. Auden actually *welcomed* Erikson's interpretation. According to Auden:

> That this revelation should have come to him in the privy is fascinating but not, I think, surprising. There must be many people to whom religious, intellectual

or artistic insights have come in the same place, for excretion is both the primal creative act—every child is the mother of its own feces—and the primal act of revolt and repudiation of the past—what was once good food has become bad dirt and must be gotten rid of. From then on, Luther's fate became his own. (1960, 17)

Well, perhaps. But if many people have vivid insights while defecating, as Auden claimed, *very few actually report them*. Indeed, if pressed, I doubt that Auden himself could have furnished us with another instance of an epiphany of this kind—excluding one of his own, perhaps.

This does not categorically rule out Erikson's interpretation, of course. As Erikson points out, one of Luther's intimates—a certain Rohrer—interpreted the passage in question in precisely the same way. But no one before or since Luther has reported an insight of earth-shattering significance while relieving his bowels. So the question becomes: *Why* did Luther have this experience? Or more to the point: Did he, really? Or is there a problem with Erikson's interpretation of the text?

We may never know for certain, of course, but in all likelihood, Luther's epiphany did *not* occur in the way Erikson and Brown described it. Vivian Green and Richard Marius both insist that Luther's account of his epiphany is worded more ambiguously than Erikson acknowledges, and could simply be construed as saying that the blessed event occurred in meditation cells *adjacent to* the monastery's privy, which is probably what Luther intended to convey (Green 1964; Marius 1999). So what of Erikson's interpretation, if these scholars are right and things did not happen as he claimed they *must* have happened? Suddenly, all the interpretations based on this alleged "event" are rendered specious, the data marshaled in their support are open to new interpretations, and the whole proverbial house of cards collapses. Moreover, given his obvious discomfort with the harshness of Gandhi's attitude toward sex, Erikson really ought to have said something about another instructive contrast between these two religious reformers. Luther was celibate until the age of forty-one, when he married Katie von Bora, and his *Table Talk* contains many frank celebrations of conjugal love (Green 1964). Gandhi, by contrast, married at thirteen and, by his own account, was highly sexed—though he embraced celibacy at age thirty-one and reviled "the flesh" for the remainder of his life. Even to a naive or nonpsychoanalytic reader, their adult lives describe opposing trajectories as regards genitality: from celibacy to marriage (Luther), and from marriage to celibacy (Gandhi).

What renders this contrast more intriguing is that Erikson could have said much more about it in light of his own theories, which are quite serviceable here. Basically, Freud's developmental schemata grind to a halt at the point where the person starts to have offspring. However, Freud also noted that the process of raising a family requires much cooperation and fellowship with other members of the community that calls for new libidinal investments of a more diffuse, "aim-inhibited," or sublimated variety. Though he eschewed the economics of the libido, on this point, Erikson acknowledged that the familial and communal phase of "householding" roots the individual in a particular community, and went on to point out that the kinds of ego supports afforded to adults by communal integration often promote parochial identification with the interests and perspectives of the cultural enclave he or she happens to inhabit. The process of "setting down roots," while necessary for subsequent development, may also inhibit or preclude the eventual emergence of a panhuman identity, and promote what Erikson called *pseudospeciation*, or the tribal tendency to exalt one's own cultural group, and disparage or disdain outsiders, often as a pretext for violent acts or attitudes.

Though Erikson did not emphasize this fact, by his own admission Luther, who started his family late in life, was far more prone to pseudospeciation and violence than Gandhi was. He was also markedly *antiascetic*. By contrast, Erikson points out, "To be an ascetic in the Hindu sense of *Brahmacharya* is not just a matter of not being active sexually or of cutting off one's masculinity; it is a matter of stepping outside of the daily consolidation and maintenance of what two sexes create and take care of together" (1969, 400).

Moreover, he reminds us "how deeply at times Gandhi minded having to become a householder" (399) and points out that "true saints are those who transfer the state of householdership to the house of God, becoming father and mother, brother and sister, son and daughter, to all creation, rather than to their own issue. But they do this in established 'orders,' and they create or partake in rituals which will envelop and give peace to those who must live in transitory reality" (399–400).

In effect, Gandhi tried to do just this in the prime of his life, while his whole family was still comparatively young. This caused him and his loved ones no end of anguish. But in his own mind, at any rate, the vows of poverty and celibacy he embraced were absolutely necessary to promote the courage and self-sacrifice required to bring an end to racial discrimination and the caste system (Gandhi, 1993, 192). Whether this is true or not is somewhat beside the point. The point at issue is that, seen in context, Gandhi's embrace of celibacy was not merely prompted by a flight from "real life," nor was it merely a symptom of neurotic guilt, Oedipal or otherwise. Erikson was right. Among other things, perhaps Gandhi's voluntary celibacy represented a culturally congruent and life-affirming discipline that he deemed necessary to the repudiation of pseudospeciation, or to the affirmation of a panhuman identity.

Erikson is also persuasive in his illuminating discussion of the elderly Gandhi's odd habit of sleeping beside young virgins. Gandhi started this unusual practice at age seventy-seven to stop the fits of shivering that interrupted his sleep, and which nothing else could allay. If reproached by others for this practice, he would sometimes reply that this practice not only dispelled the ungovernable chills, but was also a salutary test of his virtue!

In the interests of dispelling any ethnocentric prejudices, Erikson recalls a passage from the book of Kings in which the elderly King David, finding himself in a similar predicament, employs comely Abishag the Shunammite to warm his brittle old bones (1 Kings 1:3–4). Thenceforth, says Erikson, this practice was known as *shunamitism*. Meanwhile, however, in *Unsecular Man*, Andrew Greeley points out that cohabitation and bed sharing were quite common among celibate men and women in Christian orders until the sixth century (Greeley, 1972). The Irish were the last to give up *agapetism*, as these chaste intimacies were then called. According to legend, says Greeley, Saint Brendan the Navigator reproached a monk named Scuthin for this practice, of which Rome heartily disapproved. Undeterred, Scuthin recommended it to Brendan as a method for testing his virtue. Apparently intrigued, Brendan resolved to spend a night sleeping beside a virgin, but cut the experiment short when he found himself utterly unable sleep. What he said or did afterward is not recorded. Evidently, Scuthin had made his point! (187–88).

Erikson did not mention Saint Brendan or "agapetism" here, but we are probably justified in supposing that poor Gandhi's situation was closer to that of King David than of Saint Brendan, and that he probably slept more, rather than less, beside his younger female companions. The real reason Gandhi slept beside young women, said Erikson, was to gratify a deeply repressed desire for "contact comfort," or, less figuratively, for a comforting maternal embrace. And to this we may add what Erikson clearly implies without actually saying so—that by rationalizing this practice as a test of his virtue, Gandhi could minimize the extent of his own dependency needs while indirectly calling attention to his continuing virility, thereby augmenting his reputation as a spiritual virtuoso—an ascetic's version of the Latin male's *machismo*, perhaps.

Of course, if that were all there was to it, we could write off Gandhi's shunamitic episodes as an amusing and probably harmless conceit in a stubborn but enfeebled old man—a species of denial, mixed with mourning for lost opportunities. But in truth, the stakes were much higher than this limited appraisal suggests. Gandhi started to shiver uncontrollably only when his last, most spectacular and nearly fatal fast failed to avert the imminent partition of India and Pakistan, and when the horrifying sectarian violence that accompanied this process had reached a fever pitch. Gandhi had always stood for a unified and nonsectarian India in which Hindus and Muslims lived peaceably together with members of other faiths. So though India was finally achieving independence, the way in which this process was unfolding robbed him of any sense of accomplishment and hope for the future. Indeed, Gandhi remarked, "If I can master this," that is, practice his agapetism diligently, "I can still beat Jinnah!"—Jinnah being a Muslim leader who was among Gandhi's earliest supporters but later spearheaded the partition of Pakistan (Erikson 1969, 404).

Evidently, then, Gandhi had hoped that a belated upsurge of libido, if properly sublimated into spiritual energy, would give him the requisite authority and charisma to turn back the tide of sectarian strife. Despite its delusional aspect, says Erikson, seen in context Gandhi's odd behavior was less a reflection of vanity or belated regrets than of despair brought on by watching the dreams and efforts of a lifetime becoming so hopelessly perverted that they were no longer recognizable. I couldn't agree more. But I hasten to add that Luther was not deeply dismayed at the prospect of sectarian violence between Protestants and Catholics. Had Luther predicted the length and intensity of the sectarian struggles that engulfed Europe in the wake of the Reformation, which claimed millions of lives, he may have demurred, of course. And then again, perhaps not. In any case, he did little to discourage it, and he said and did many things that incited, rather than contained, the violence, which continues to this very day in Northern Ireland.

MOTHER- AND FATHER-CENTERED DEVOTIONAL TYPES

Thus far we have dwelt upon oral, anal, and genital themes in Erikson's psychobiographies. But another striking feature of Erikson's characterizations of Luther and Gandhi is the way in which their youthful neuroses bespoke an emotional overinvolvement with one parent. In Luther's case, a stark ambivalence toward his father permeated his entire life, creating alternating currents of defiance and compliance toward authority. The cyclical (or perhaps spiraling) character of these conflicts prompted him to *defy* his father by leaving the legal profession and entering the monastery, then to *comply* with his father's expectations (unconsciously) by failing as a monk. However, snatching victory from the jaws of defeat, he overturned his father's verdict by excelling at self-abasement, becoming a successful priest-theologian before defying the "father" of the church in the name of his "heavenly Father," and so on.

In Luther's case, said Erikson, ambivalence toward the father was mostly unconscious, because the deep feelings of hatred and the thirst for revenge he cherished toward his father were as deeply repressed as his identification with him. But in Gandhi's case, said Erikson, the overarching motif is of a deep identification with the mother, which prompted the development of an almost androgynous persona. While Gandhi's maternal identification prompted him to repress his own desires for tender, maternal care, says Erikson, his positive identification with his mother was thoroughly conscious and never disavowed. On the contrary, as Gandhi said several times, he aspired to be as maternal as possible.

Other evidence of a strong matricentric orientation is furnished by the fact that, like his mother, Gandhi fasted frequently, for very long periods. Moreover, as an adult he took up the spinning of cloth—a traditionally female occupation in India—and enjoined it on *all* his followers, ostensibly in the interests of promoting economic self-reliance. Further evidence of Gandhi's matricentricity is that on the eve of her death, his wife, Kasturba, made Gandhi promise to care for an orphaned relative named Manu, who later wrote a memoir entitled "Bapu, My Mother." But the most revealing (and hilarious) evidence Erikson adduced for Gandhi's maternal identification is an episode from his sojourn in London, where he went as a young man to qualify for the bar. On the eve of his return to India, Gandhi gave a sumptuous party for all his vegetarian friends and attempted to amuse them by reciting the story about an MP named Addison, who was giving his maiden speech in the House of Commons. Addison began with the words "I conceive . . . ," became flustered, repeated the words twice more, then sat down, mortified. A parliamentary colleague arose and explained, "The gentleman has conceived thrice, but has produced nothing," and the whole parliamentary assembly erupted in laughter. Gandhi, notes Erikson, was so identified with poor Mr. Addison that he became flustered in the retelling of this well-known tale and couldn't finish it. In fact, he had to sit down himself, as awkwardly as Addison himself had done (150).

Though Erikson did not say so in so many words, it is likely that the neurotic difficulties young Gandhi experienced as a consequence of his maternal identification abated considerably when he left London, and that he finally abandoned what was left of his desire for Westernization during his twenty-year stay in South Africa. After all, says Erikson, Gandhi's maternal identification was not a merely personal idiosyncrasy. On the contrary, claimed Erikson, "a primitive mother religion is probably the deepest, the most pervasive, and the most unifying substratum of Indian religiosity" (402). And this fact, presumably, constituted a formidable challenge for Gandhi's leadership. After all, said Erikson:

"Father Time" in India is a Mother. The World is an Inner Space; and if Freud gently chided Romain Roland for his "oceanic feeling," a sense of being enveloped, embedded and carried by the world—that feeling is what made Roland (and also Herman Hesse) a Western spokesman for the more self-conscious Indian's sense of time and space. Now every man's inner life is a composite of the modern and the archaic, the logical and the non-rational, the proper and the passionate. But Indians, I believe, live in more centuries at the same time than most other peoples; and every Indian, be he ever so well-educated and pragmatic, lives in a feminine space time that is deep inside a HERE and in the very center of a NOW, not so much an observer of a continuum of means and ends but a participant in a flux marked by the intensity of confluence. . . .

Historically, all this *may* be related to an ancient and stubborn trend to preserve the India of the mother goddesses against all the conquerors, their father gods, and their historical logic. The power of the mother goddesses probably has also given India that basic bisexuality which, at least to her British conquerors, appeared contemptible and yet also uncanny and irresistible in every sense of the word. Gandhi, so it seems, tried to make himself a representative of that bisexuality in a combination of autocratic malehood and enveloping maternalism. He may thus have succeeded in gathering in what was at loose ends in the lives of his followers, and indeed, of the masses. Against all this, I began to realize, Gandhi had tried to erect a bulwark based on radical factualness, obsessive punctuality and absolute responsibility—all within a meaningful flux he called truth. (43–44)

These passages warrant careful attention. Without referring to them by name, for some reason, Erikson alluded here to the matriarchal theories of J. J. Bachofen and Robert Briffault, who speculated that in many cultures, the advent and ascendancy of father gods was preceded by a period in which mother deities prevailed. Often enough, they observed, a male-dominated pantheon is imposed on a people by foreign conquerors, and evidence of lingering allegiance to or nostalgia for the old faith assumes a quaint mythological guise that is often hidden from the uninitiated. According to Erikson, however, Indian culture remained more loyal than most to the maternal deities that presided at its birth. Moreover, he speculated that this fact may account for two of its distinctive features, namely, the lived sense of time and the difficulties this indefinite dwelling-in-the-present engendered for the process of modernization. Gandhi's self-appointed task, said Erikson, was to drag India kicking and screaming into the modern world, while selectively reinterpreting and reshaping its cultural traditions—abolishing caste but embracing vegetarianism, celibacy, and the like—to engender a distinctively Indian kind of ego strength that draws equally on the maternal and paternal imago.

Though he did not cite scholarly sources to support his claim regarding the "primitive mother religion" that is the oldest substratum of Indian religion, Erikson probably culled this impression from reading Rolland's biography of

Sri Ramakrishna (Rolland 1929). Prior to his training in Advaita Vedanta, Ramakrishna was a devotee of Kali, the Hindu Mother Goddess, and at one
point in his religious training spent six months dressed as a woman in a traditional Hindu rite called Madhurva Bhava, during which time he apparently
lost all consciousness of being male (Wulff 1997, 324). Alternatively, Erikson's references to the stubborn matricentricity of Hindu religion may have
been gleaned, or perhaps merely reinforced, by reading Erich Neumann's
book *The Great Mother* (Neumann 1963) or Heinrich Zimmer's article "The
Indian World Mother" in the *Eranos Yearbooks* (Zimmer 1968). I cannot
prove this, of course, but Erikson's reluctance to acknowledge Jungian
sources for his ideas has already been clearly established.

That said, it is also intriguing to note that Erikson's reflections on the matricentric character of early Indian religion (and its attendant obstacles to
modernization) bear a striking resemblance to remarks made by Erich Fromm
and Michael Maccoby in *Social Character in a Mexican Village*, published
one year later in 1970 (Fromm and Maccoby 1970). Fromm and Maccoby
made a very thorough study of indigenous Mexican culture and concluded
that strong matricentric tendencies were in evidence among many Mexican
peasants who lacked the industry, the discipline, and the hopefulness needed
to innovate that marks successful entrepreneurs. Conversely, those peasants
who had a more patricentric mentality were more apt to persist and to thrive
in the capitalist economy that was slowly making inroads on the formerly feudal Mexican countryside.

Fortunately for Fromm and Maccoby, their perspective on matricentric and
patricentric types in the Mexican countryside did not hinge on historical conjectures about a primitive matriarchy, and were supported with more than one
hundred deep and extensive interview protocols; impressive anthropological,
historical, and sociological data; and standardized psychological tests of various kinds. This is not to say that Fromm did not dabble in the theories of Bachofen and Briffault. As a matter of fact, he did (Burston 1991). But Fromm
was also prudent enough to ground his theories of matricentric and patricentric mentalities in a theory of object relations, and dwelt perceptively on the
way these characteristic orientations are reinforced by prevailing cultural and
economic trends, thus freeing himself from reliance on obscure historical conjectures like these (Burston 1989). Though their pioneering study has never received its due, the fact that Fromm and Maccoby were able to buttress their interpretations with rigorous empirical and statistical methodologies gave their
reflections on the problems of modernization in Mexico a good deal more
rigor and authority than Erikson's easygoing pastiche of ideas.

Meanwhile, on a slightly different note, *Gandhi's Truth* contains some
oblique indications that Erikson was a little squeamish about certain features

of Gandhi's "enveloping maternalism," and his "bisexual" disposition. Reflecting on the pleasures, the pressures, and the problems of the joint family system in which Gandhi was raised, Erikson observed that if Gandhi's older siblings "learned 'to live for, as well as in, mankind'—a felicitous phrase well applicable to the style of life Gandhi would later try to institute in his ashram—they did not learn it only from the mother. The father, Kaba Gandhi, had to look after every member of his clan, whether they were ready to get married, settle down, or assume jobs. He is even said to have helped Putali Ba (Gandhi's mother) in household work" (1969, 105).

Erikson then goes on to quote one of Gandhi's Indian biographers, Pyarelal, to the effect that Kaba Gandhi, a high-ranking civil servant, was frequently observed peeling vegetables for his wife's kitchen while discussing affairs of state with local dignitaries, adding, "The total image is one in which it is difficult to allocate masculine and feminine identifications" (105).

On the face of it, this last comment seems like a dispassionate clinical observation until one realizes that the alleged difficulty in allocating "masculine and feminine identifications" rests principally on the fact that Kaba Gandhi was *frequently observed peeling vegetables.* (Good gracious! What next?) Professor C. K. Raju, a prominent Indian academic who is well acquainted with Gandhi's home province of Gujarat, concedes that the sight of a senior government official peeling vegetables during office hours would be somewhat unusual in this milieu. But he also hastened to add that it does not betoken or even hint at the dramatic "role reversal" that Erikson imagined was in play (Raju, personal communication). Our misgivings on this score are redoubled by the fact that the ostensible confusion of gender roles that enveloped the future Mahatma is supposedly a *normal* accompaniment to the adolescent identity crisis, according to Erikson's own theory of development. So though he would probably have denied it, perhaps Erikson was hinting that Indian culture institutionalized a permanent adolescent identity crisis—for males, anyway.

Having said that, one cannot help wondering if this is the same Erik Erikson who gave us such a lucid and heartfelt critique of the thoughtless (and incipiently racist) application of the "masculinity-femininity" scale of the Minnesota Multiphasic Personality Inventory to the study of African American males, whose soulful emotional responses or desire to be singers prompted Thomas Pettigrew to conclude that the majority of them suffered from an impaired sense of masculinity. As we saw previously, Erikson countered that the MMPI, which was standardized on a group of middle-class Minnesotans in the thirties, cannot generate norms that are valid for all humanity—that in Naples, in Harlem, or indeed in Bombay, one is apt to find young men who admire soulful singers as exemplary role models for adult masculinity.

Looking back at Erikson's critique of Pettigrew and the vivid sense of satisfaction and relief I felt on reading it many years ago, I realize that Erikson provided people of my generation with a role model for responsible, evenhanded criticism in the mental health professions, which eschews rhetorical and ideological extremes but speaks truth to power all the same. The beauty and novelty of Erikson's approach was that it channeled his palpable anger at the parochialism and stupidity of uncritical practitioners of "objective" psychological testing into a clear, constructive critique of the invisible impact of racist prejudices.

However, in the present instance, Erikson's impressionistic style clearly led him astray. Peeling vegetables is not an exemplary masculine trait. But neither is it an intrinsically feminine one—even in India. Many men, myself included, peel vegetables nearly every day of their lives, and do not feel their manhood is compromised as a result. And while we are seldom privileged to engage in earnest discussions of public affairs while doing so, unless I am sadly mistaken, there is nothing in the nature of coordinating these two activities regularly in this manner that warrants clinical scrutiny or interpretation.

So once again, though no one noticed it at the time, Erikson was out on a limb. And while a paucity of empirical, anthropological, and historical study contributed to the "squishy" character of his interpretations, here and there, cultural and personal biases played into them as well. For example, take his remarks on Kaba Gandhi, and the implied antithesis between masculine identity and domestic work. Where did this idea come from? It was common enough in his own environment, to be sure. Theodor Homberger, his stepfather, was a workhorse by all accounts, but left all the housework to Erik's mother, Karla. And Freud, his "scientific" stepfather, worked very long hours, but did no housework either. Indeed, considered as a vocation and a style of life, rather than a therapeutic procedure, psychoanalysis is imbued with a heroic work ethic, which Erikson's admirer David Riesman deemed "Protestant" (Riesman 1950) but which is actually based on an absurd (if often unconscious) tendency among analysts to pattern their habits and attitudes on Freud's example. This fanatical devotion to one's career (and/or making money) may not have any adverse effects on unmarried or childless psychoanalysts. But those married with children, as Erikson was, might profit from his experience and think twice before imitating Freud's example. Indeed, they would actually do better to emulate Kaba Gandhi and cultivate skillful techniques of harmonizing the demands of their professions with the needs of their family.

Erikson's aversion to child care and domestic labor of any kind have already been discussed by Lawrence Friedman and Sue Bloland-Erikson. In light of what they have said, it seems that Erikson felt overwhelmed, demeaned, or compromised by the performance of such duties, and that the strong identification with Freud to which I have just called attention merely intensified a preexisting reluctance. In light of his remarks about Kaba Gandhi, I strongly suspect that the prospect of peeling vegetables (and so forth) may have threatened to revive the memory of his own gender identity issues or his own protracted adolescent identity crisis. In short, his illegitimacy; his inability to identify with his distant, demanding stepfather; and the lingering consequences of these early childhood experiences, coupled with his idealization of Freud, colored the mind of Gandhi's biographer, reinforcing conventional sex role stereotypes.

GANDHI AS PROPHET

Gandhi's Truth is deficient in another important respect, namely, in its failure to address the prophetic element in Gandhi. One of the hallmarks of the prophetic tradition is the conviction that all human beings, without exception, are created in the image and likeness of God. Another is the injunction to love truth and to practice justice and mercy. Taken together, these elements produced a kind of leveling, democratic sensibility that enabled the prophets of old to challenge authority and convention, often at great personal risk. Throughout the Hebrew Bible we find them cutting the pretensions of kings and princes down to size, and scorning the empty, ritualistic piety of wealthy priests and patrons of the temple who oppressed the widow, the orphan, and the stranger at every opportunity (Heschel 1969a).

Meanwhile, the prophetic insistence that all of us are equal in the eyes of God, regardless of our worldly station, runs directly counter to the ethos of the caste system that Gandhi so vigorously opposed. This is not to say that disbelief in the caste system was unprecedented in India. As Professor Raju points out, both Buddhism and Advaita Vedanta pronounced the nullity of caste distinctions long before, cautioning adherents not to be fooled by them. But at the end of the day, the thrust of their critique was primarily epistemological or cognitive in character, aimed at liberating the mind from self-imposed fetters. While they did not accord it any ontological validity, neither Buddhism nor Advaita Vedanta made the active and utter dismantling of the caste system a vital prerequisite for individual and collective emancipation. Gandhi did. Nor did they link the pursuit of individual liberation with collective emancipation, as Gandhi did. Why?

Like his friend and admirer Rabindranath Tagore, Gandhi was deeply committed to the project of decolonizing India and of enabling colonized people all across the world to engage with their former colonial masters as equals. Perhaps, as Erikson suggests, Gandhi realized that the project of promoting equality and mutual recognition among Asian and African peoples and the great European powers lacked power and moral authority as long as they oppressed one another, and made invidious distinctions within their own ranks. And perhaps the roots of Gandhi's urgent insistence on dismantling the caste system did not stem from this adult insight, but instead derive from some features of the Jain religion.

Then again, it is instructive to note Gandhi was exposed to the prophetic temper in John Ruskin's book *Unto This Last*, which was published in 1860, and which Gandhi claimed completely transformed his life (Gandhi 1993). Despite his thirst for justice, Ruskin was not a leveler, castigating the wealthy for their cruelty and indifference but legitimating class divisions as being necessary and inevitable nonetheless. In Ruskin's cosmology, social inequality is divinely ordained, and a basic prerequisite for the practice of charity and justice (Ruskin 1985). Like Luther before him, Ruskin felt that perfect equality among human beings is possible only in the kingdom of heaven, which to him, as to most Christians, meant the afterlife.

By contrast with Ruskin's work, Leo Tolstoy's book *The Kingdom of God Is Within You*, published in 1894, perhaps the first adumbration of Christianity as a religion of nonviolence, entailed a complete and total delegitimation of the clergy, promoting a "priesthood of all believers" more radical than Luther's, and a corresponding emphasis on the "inner light"—Erikson's "inner space"?—as the source of numinous experience and all moral authority. And on the other hand, Tolstoy's attempt to recapture the ethos of "primitive," preclerical Christianity enjoined a dramatic detachment from personal wealth and possessions, a communitarian communism that eschews all differences in status based on heredity or wealth and provides us with a more radical and perhaps more faithful embodiment of the prophetic outlook, which was also more influential on Gandhi in the long run (Tolstoy 1985).

Having said that, I know very well that Gandhi's politics often seemed to be a patchwork of baffling inconsistencies—socialist but conservative, nationalist but universalist, secular but religious, and so on (Orwell 1949). Apart from several sustained and unifying themes, such as abolishing caste, promoting self-sufficiency and self-rule, and so on, his ideological leanings are profoundly obscure. I am simply suggesting that the source of some of these disparate "voices" or positions lay in Gandhi's inability to sort out his divided allegiances to Ruskin and Tolstoy, and their essentially *religious* visions of human community, with the pragmatics of governing a vast and fractious secular state bent on modernization and overthrowing colonial rule.

Moreover, and more importantly, for now, though I emphasize the prophetic element in Gandhi, I do not deny that Gandhi was also a saintly sort of person. In many ways he was, and Erikson's characterization of him repeatedly attests to that fact. But for heuristic purposes it is useful to differentiate between the prophetic and the saintly styles of religious leadership, because one of the distinguishing hallmarks of Gandhi's career was that *he combined them* in what was (briefly) a stunningly effective synthesis. India has had her share of saints over the centuries, but no prophets until Gandhi arrived. Had he not blended his prophetic attitudes and agenda with traditional modes of Indian saintliness, he would never have achieved anything—not in India, anyway. Say what you like about psychology, psychoanalysis, libido (or the lack of it), you simply cannot understand Gandhi's life and character without taking these facts into account. And strangely enough, despite some illuminating reflections on *homo religiosis*, Erikson never really got to the bottom of this.

GANDHI, FREUD, AND ERIKSON

Finally, two of Erikson's critics, Arjun Appadurai and Lawrence Friedman, have criticized Erikson for attempting to effect a conceptual integration of psychoanalysis and Satyagraha (Wulff 1997; Friedman 1999). I share some of their misgivings. Admittedly, as Erikson points out, psychoanalysis and Satyagraha do converge impressively to the extent that they both enjoin the patient cultivation of a nonviolent mode of relatedness to others, in which truths that have been deliberately avoided or obscured are gradually brought to light: a process which, ideally, will give the analysand or former adversary the courage to embrace the truth and to change himself accordingly. Fair enough. But as Friedman points out, there is something silly, self-serving, and faintly colonial minded in the attempt to collapse Gandhi's ideas into a Western frame of reference. You cannot substitute Erikson's advocacy for planned parenthood and the conscious celebration of loving sexual reciprocity for Gandhian celibacy or brahmacharya, as Erikson did, and still call your approach Satyagraha. And when he reckoned the Israeli army and even Huey Newton as embodiments of Gandhian principles—just who did he think was he kidding, anyway?

Still, though he flattered himself by posing as Gandhi's emissary to the West, as Friedman complains, Erikson had a genuine and heartfelt interest in promoting the spread of nonviolence, and his critique of Gandhi's oversights in this arena does have merit. Gandhi enjoined his followers to refrain

completely from sexual intercourse unless they were doing so with the express intention of having children, and warned them against the vigorous enjoyment of the act even in such circumstances. Erikson was repulsed by
such language, and found it tinged with hatred and intolerance—the very
passions Gandhi strove to extinguish in his followers. Erikson had an unusually deep and sympathetic understanding of the motives that may prompt
a vow of celibacy, but he refused to endorse the idea that the enjoyment of
sexual intercourse is vile or inimical to our ethical and spiritual welfare. Indeed, Erikson countered with the objection that if the effort to be virtuous
requires that we do violence to ourselves, the long-term effects of such efforts will eventually disfigure our relations to others. You don't have be
Freudian to see the merit of this argument. Experience indicates that while
a small percentage of people may thrive in a state of celibacy, for the vast
majority of human beings the routine condemnation and ruthless suppression of sexual needs and feelings prompts a restless search for furtive, clandestine, or substitutive gratifications, and/or the inappropriate sexualization
of ideas, interests, activities, and relationships that robs us of clarity and objectivity. These developments, in turn, prompt all kinds of deceptive and
self-deceptive maneuvers, all manner of dishonesty, secrecy, pious pretense,
and outright fraud that can only generate more injury and conflict in the long
run. Whether we like it or not, Freud was quite right about this. So with all
due respect to Tolstoy, Gandhi, and others who embrace and enjoin celibacy
on others, you cannot preach celibacy and/or aversion to sex as the sine qua
non of virtue or spiritual development without violating deep human instincts and harming the long-term prospects for nonviolence in the process.

Another of Erikson's objections regards Gandhi's views on the "bestial"
sources of violence in humans, an attitude which, oddly enough, he actually
shared with Freud. Reporters once asked Gandhi to give a message to the
English people. He replied that the time for resolving conflicts of interest by
force, as animals do, is past; that dignified human beings should not debase
themselves in this way. And in a similar vein, while reflecting on the scope
and enormity of human violence in *Civilization and Its Discontents*, Freud
cited Hobbes's dictum "homo homini lupus," and challenged anyone to deny
the truth of this assertion in light of historical experience.

Though he called himself a Freudian, as it happens, Erikson did challenge
the truth of this assertion, though not on the grounds of historical reflection
but on those of patient naturalistic observation carried out by ethologists like
Julian Huxley, Konrad Lorenz, and Nikolaas Tinbergen. Freud was quite
wrong about the roots of human aggression, because the guiding metaphor
behind Hobbes's dictum is misleading. Wolves do not prey on their own kind,
and even the more skilled or formidable predators—tigers, orcas, pythons,

bald eagles, and the like—very seldom kill members of their own species. As Erikson pointed out, only humans lack the built-in, instinctive constraints that other animals have that promote the ritualization of aggression and preclude mass slaughter. The scale, scope, and viciousness of human violence is unparalleled in the animal kingdom, rendering the pronouncements of both Freud and Gandhi on this score a gratuitous slur on other, less complex species. Worse still, this way of thinking about human violence clouds our judgment and compromises our realism about our own kind. If we see violence as a distinctively *human* phenomenon, rather than an expression of some generic animal tendencies, we must look to distinctively human traits or attributes to get to the roots of the problem.

6

Evolution and Conscience in Darwin, Freud, and Erikson

INSTINCT, ADAPTATION, AND PROGRESS

In a paper entitled "One of the Difficulties of Psycho-analysis" (Freud 1917), Freud famously compared his "discovery" of the unconscious with Copernicus's discovery of heliocentric astronomy and Darwin's theory of natural selection, which injured the collective narcissism of the human species, depriving us of a sense of centrality in the cosmos. Comparisons between Copernicus and Freud have not multiplied much in the interim, but comparisons between Charles Darwin (1809–1882) and Sigmund Freud certainly have. Recently, for example, Robert Wright dwelt at length on the parallels and differences between them in *The Moral Animal* (Wright 1994), while *Darwin's Worms*, by Adam Phillips, puts their intellectual kinship in a striking new light (Phillips 2001).

Viewing Darwin and Freud through psychohistorical lenses, Erikson noted that Darwin and Freud experienced abnormally prolonged "psychosocial moratoriums" in their mid- to late twenties, when their professional and marital status hung in the balance. Shortly after their respective marriages, while their ideas were "gestating," they were both plagued by diffuse bodily and mental complaints that goaded them into deeper reflection and creativity — Henri Ellenberger's "creative illness" (Ellenberger 1970). And as their respective crises ripened, Darwin and Freud were both driven to conclusions repugnant to prevailing common sense, conclusions that stressed the "lower," instinctual side of human nature and called into question our sense of distinctiveness in the animal kingdom. Both anticipated (and subsequently encountered) fierce cultural resistance, and both bore up bravely to the antipathy they engendered. For as Erikson put it,

> [A] creative man has no choice. He may come across his supreme task almost accidentally. But once the issue is joined, his task proves to be at the same time intimately related to his most stubborn conflicts, to his superior selective perception, and to the stubbornness of his one-way will: he must court sickness, failure or insanity, in order to test the alternative whether the established world will crush him, or whether he will disestablish a sector of this world's outworn fundaments and make a place for a new one. (1958b, 46)

Oddly enough, Erikson's first reflections on Darwin and Freud appear in *Young Man Luther*. The point Erikson was making there is that an identity crisis is simultaneously a crisis of conscience and of self-confidence, one whose resolution obligates the deeply creative individual to shake and reshape the prevailing "world image" even if—like Darwin, apparently—they are temperamentally averse to doing so. But the other recurrent theme in Erikson's scattered reflections on Darwin and Freud is the subject of conscience. In "Human Strength and the Cycle of Generations," first published in 1960, Erikson remarked that

> both Darwin and Freud have given us the means to reevaluate conscience itself, which was seen by Darwin as "by far the most important . . . of all the differences between man and the lower animals" yet solely devoted to "the welfare of the tribe—not that of the species, nor that of an individual member of the tribe." And it was Freud who revealed the instinctual crudeness and tribal cruelty in so much of man's morality (1964b, 144).

Was Freud some sort of Darwinian, then, or following in Darwin's footsteps? Yes and no. As Wright points out in *The Moral Animal*, there are deep similarities between the Freudian and the Darwinian (and neo-Darwinian) perspectives on human behavior and motivation. Like Freud, Darwin thought that the real causes of our behavior frequently reside outside of conscious awareness, and that consciousness mistakes and misconstrues them in deference to conventional prejudices and pieties, making them seem more rational, disinterested, or uniquely personal than they actually are. In short, when instinct intervenes, the contents of consciousness seldom mirror existential actualities, and most of the motives and reasons we adduce for our behavior are post hoc rationalizations for doing what nature bids us to do anyway.

Thus far, then, Darwin and Freud agree. But there are striking differences as well. To begin with, Darwin was *not* studying disturbed or deranged behavior. On the contrary, he was studying *normal* human behavior, which is the product of prepersonal and prehistorical processes of natural selection. That being so, Darwin simply supposed that in the normal course of events, an individual's upbringing and education does not equip them to experience, identify, and interpret their own motives and feelings in a dispassionate, scientific way. Unlike Freud, Darwin did not posit a mental "apparatus" that disguises and distorts our motives, rendering them opaque, that is, an "intrapsychic censor." He was not what Jaspers called an "unmasking psychologist," even if many neo-Darwinians—like Wright—make use of him as if he were.

Secondly, unlike Freud, Darwin was demonstrably more concerned with the *communicative* function of feelings, and the way in which the physiological arousal that accompanies strong emotion elicits complementary behavioral repertoires in other animals. Like Lorenz, Tinbergen, and other twentieth-century ethologists who followed in his footsteps, Darwin was chiefly interested in the *signaling* function of emotions, that is, in their ability to inform and activate other organisms in adaptive ways. It never occurred to him to ponder the infantile or childhood templates, that is, the *ontogenetic* basis, for adult emotional experience or expression. Similarly, for ethologists, the communicative function of an emotional display and its role in catalyzing alterations in the behavior of other animals in the present moment *is* its cause (Lorenz 1965; Tinbergen 1953, 1954). Further explanations are superfluous. By contrast, Freudians often treat the current cues and the situational constraints that elicit or accompany strong emotions as "surface," that is, as relatively superficial, focusing on antecedent causes or experiences, which filter the experience and the expression of the instincts through historically sedimented layers of symbolization reaching back to infancy in a uniquely personal way (Rapaport 1950; Schachtel 1959).

Despite far-reaching differences on their ideas about affect, Freud and Darwin both gave some credence to the ideas of Jean Baptiste Lamarck (1744–1829) on the inheritance of acquired characteristics, and the "biogenetic law" codified by Ernest Haeckel (1834–1919), which states that ontogeny recapitulates phylogeny. But for Darwin, as it turns out, these ideas were ancillary and ultimately expendable (Gould 1977). For Freud they were utterly indispensable. To see why, one must first grasp the analogies Freud made repeatedly between neurotic symptoms and religious beliefs and rituals. According to Freud, the whole structure and evolution of religious beliefs and rituals, like those of obsessional neurosis, are underscored by a primal ambivalence—an intractable inner conflict between love and hate, rebellion and remorse, repudiation and identification, all cathected to the paternal imago, and all striving for ultimate resolution in the domain of the imaginary. We acquire these dispositions (via Lamarckian mechanisms) from our prehistoric forbears and because our ontogenetic development, which propels children willy-nilly into Oedipal desire, recapitulates an earlier phase of species history in which the "sons" collectively rebelled against a dominant father for access to the women of the tribe (Freud 1913).

Though he alluded to it respectfully when the occasion required, Erikson basically ignored Freud's "archaic inheritance." Moreover, he was careful to distinguish between rituals that serve to express or maintain a neurotic equilibrium (à la Freud) and those that spring from a basic human need for what he termed *ritualization*. Like the rituals observed by ethologists, which govern sexual selection and mating, hierarchy, territoriality, and the deferral of aggression, human rituals (of the non-neurotic variety) serve to express emotion and to elicit complementary repertoires of emotion and behavior from other participants. Even prior to culturally coded rituals of this kind, said Erikson, the human infant possesses the ability to elicit powerful and complex responses from human adults by its spontaneous cries and gestures (Erikson 1966b).

Though he seldom said so explicitly, then, Erikson's approach to ritual was more consonant with contemporary biological theory than Freud's, whose phylogenetic fantasies elicited incredulity and derision in various quarters (Sulloway 1979). Indeed, Erikson derived the form and content of basic human rituals from a revised *ontogenetic* perspective that rendered phylogenetic tendencies or traits a completely peripheral issue. So while Freud claimed to trace the roots of ritual back to the totem meal and guilt toward the "primal father," according to Erikson, the first and in some sense primary human ritual occurs when a mother greets her child in the morning—a ritual rooted in ongoing evolutionary necessity rather than a prehistoric past. In addressing her child repeatedly and lovingly by name, ministering to its needs, and so on, the mother confers on the newborn a sense of growing mutual recognition and affirmation that is integral to the infant's later identity formation and to the emergent sense of the numinous, or "hallowed presence" (Erikson 1966a). Moreover, Erikson insisted, each successive phase of the epigenetic cycle has its own distinctive form of ritualization. The need for mutual recognition and affirmation between the different generations plays some role in all of them, but especially in infancy, adolescence, and middle age.

Unfortunately, these subtle but important differences between Darwin and Freud, on the one hand, and Freud and Erikson, on the other, are often lost sight of because of their frequent but decidedly disparate uses of the term *adaptation*. But like the term *ego* in psychoanalysis, the term *adaptation* is apt to mean different things depending on the context and the user. Fortunately, there is enough convergence and redundancy among most theorists to give an intelligible account of this idea to lay people, because however it is described or deployed by post-Freudian theorists, the concept of adaptation in classical psychoanalysis is always linked with correlative notions about the ego and the ego's ostensible role in taming, transforming, or deflecting (active and passive) instincts in deference to the constraints and demands of reality.

Since they presuppose the existence of entities, processes, and constraints that exist independently of the ego's will and wishes, and which the ego must master or accommodate to in some fashion—usually at some cost—it follows that despite their respective auras of ambiguity, the concepts of "ego" and "adaptation" tacitly presuppose a *realist* epistemology that is plainly at variance with the recent constructivist, hermeneutic, Lacanian, and postmodern versions of psychoanalysis. And so, not surprisingly, ego psychology is often attacked by representatives of these schools as outdated, conformist, or somehow irrelevant to what Freud and psychoanalysis are "really" going on about. To this again I reply, "yes and no."

Like British anthropologist Desmond Morris, author of *The Naked Ape*, Freud believed that human beings are "the sexist apes on the planet," that is, that we are endowed by nature with a vast surplus of sexual energy above and beyond what we actually require for mere reproduction (Morris 1967). By Freud's reckoning, our innate sexiness issues inevitably in neurotic conflict or, at the very least, acute distress, when the promptings of nature conflict with the requirements of civilized life. By the same token, however, Freud also maintained that the secondary transformation of surplus sexual energies, by means of reaction-formation, sublimation, and so on, are what render science, art, and civilization itself possible, turning a potential liability, in evolutionary terms, into a competitive advantage (Freud 1905).

Nevertheless, said Freud, from earliest infancy until our last dying gasp, adaptation to reality, and the consequent renunciation of free sexual expression, is a hardship borne by us reluctantly, turning most of us into secret "enemies of civilization" in the deepest recesses of our minds (Freud 1930). Even so, such renunciation is indispensable to avert a return to "a state of nature," and is mediated by the growth of the ego at the expense of the id, or instincts (Freud 1923). On balance, then, Freud valued adaptation as indispensable but emphasized that it comes at a very high price to the individual and to society at large.

Anna Freud changed the emphasis of her father's theories without substantially altering their content. In *The Ego and the Mechanisms of Defense* (Freud 1966), she laid the groundwork for an ego psychology that stresses the adaptive functions of "defense mechanisms" that had hitherto been regarded exclusively as psychopathological processes, emphasizing the ego's attempts to gain active mastery over the instincts and external circumstances that frustrate the organism or provoke internal conflict. Meanwhile, Anna Freud's contemporary (and erstwhile rival) Heinz Hartmann developed a concept of adaptation that is relatively cheap, in terms of human suffering, and therefore more consonant with mainstream American prejudices. Hartmann posited the existence of a pool of "desexualized libido" that is readily available to the nascent ego to perform its cognitive/adaptive functions, stressing that the ego performs optimally within a "conflict-free sphere." Hartmann also suggested that the achievement of mastery of the environment is intrinsically rewarding, and not a substitute for sexual pleasure (Hartmann 1951). And while he did not deny it outright, Hartmann downplayed the tragic conflict between the promptings of nature and the requirements of civilization that Freud said governs our individual and collective destinies (Hartmann 1960).

Americans warmed to Hartmann's ideas because they do not readily embrace a tragic view of life. And if you pause to think about it, that is one reason why Hartmann and Erikson were charged by Lacan and his followers with abetting the Americanization of psychoanalysis. Nowadays, in some circles, the term *Americanization* is often a synonym for trivialization, and despite the effrontery and ethnocentrism of this characterization, it carried a lot of weight during the last quarter of the twentieth century. Depending on the background and agenda of the user, this term may have referred to (1) the transformation of psychoanalysis from a marginal, subversive discourse into a mainstream one, (2) the replacement of the goal of deepening self-knowledge with a therapeutic program of mere normalization, (3) a heightened valorization of the ego's (rational) functions, and a corresponding minimization of the role of libidinal frustration and conflict with the environment, (4) the tendency to minimize the etiological and/or ontological centrality of the Oedipus complex, and a correspondingly greater emphasis on pre-Oedipal dynamics, (5) the replacement of a conflict model with a deficiency model of psychopathology, or (6) all of the above. (Ironically, those accused of abetting this sinister conspiracy are almost always Europeans, a fact conveniently forgotten by most critics.)

But these mean-spirited attacks miss the heart of the matter. For unless you happened to be a convinced Freudian already, Hartmann's notion of "desexualized libido" is either a baffling non sequitur or a perfect contradiction in terms. Even if we credit the notion of "desexualized libido" with some sense, in deference to Freudian thinking about the taming of instincts, the idea that there is a fund of psychic energy conveniently available to the ego—*without* heroic struggles with the id—is not a momentous theoretical breakthrough, but a strikingly self-evident assertion from the commonsense point of view. And on the other hand, as Hartmann's Freudian critics remarked early on, the notion that the ego ever develops a "conflict-free sphere of operations" is really at variance with the whole spirit of Freudian thought. Either way, much of Hartmann's work just sounds silly nowadays.

Still, by insisting that the ego is probably present at birth, or shortly thereafter, and in stressing the intrinsic rewards attendant on mature accomplishment, Hartmann did furnish a partial corrective to the oversights and excesses of the earlier Freudian perspective. Hartmann's work stimulated further research and theorizing by David Rapaport (Rapaport 1951), Robert White (White 1959), and, of course, Erik Erikson. Like Hartmann and White, Erikson suggested that the developing person derives considerable (nonsexual) satisfaction in the achievement of mastery, and that the promptings of nature and the various forms of culture are generally consonant, rather than at odds with one another, as Freud contended.

CONFORMITY, CONSCIENCE, AND PSEUDOSPECIATION

However, because of his wide interests in ethology, cultural anthropology, and history, Erikson introduced some important caveats into the theory of adaptation. According to Erikson, culture *ought* to aid the growing individual to mature successfully, but it can also fail the young person, and often does, especially if society attempts to impose greater uniformity than is necessary or desirable. In his own words:

> An attempt to construct a ground plan of human strength, however, could be accused of neglecting diversities, of contributing to the fetish of deadly norms, and thus to the undermining of the individual as a hero or rebel, an ascetic or a mere person of singularity. Yet the life process will always lead to more diversity than we can comfortably manage with our insights, our cures and our aspirations. And so will man's reaction to the diversity of conditions. In the processes of socio-genetic change we can ascribe a long-range meaning to the idiosyncratic individualist and to the deviant as well as to the obedient conformist. True adaptation, in fact, is maintained with the help of loyal rebels who refuse to adjust to "conditions" and cultivate an indignation in the service of a to-be-restored wholeness without which psychosocial evolution and all of its institutions would be doomed. (1964, 156)

So by Erikson's reckoning, adaptation is often achieved at the expense of wholeness, but "true adaptation" gives rebels and eccentrics a wide berth. Evidently, Erikson's concept of "adaptation" embraces the "loyal rebel" equally with the "obedient conformist," allowing the likes of Darwin and Freud to rub shoulders with Caspar Milquetoast and Adolf Eichmann. Is this good science?

Well, perhaps—but don't bet on it. A moment's reflection suggests that there is a liberal agenda behind this line of argument. Like John Stuart Mill,

Erikson enjoins tolerance of diversity and dissenting voices, and goes on to draw an implicit analogy between diversity of opinions and lifestyles and spontaneous mutation in the gene pool when he speaks of sociogenetic change. Whether we share Erikson's liberal leanings or not, the fact remains that the very idea of "sociogenetic progress" rests on an analogy and a tenuous linkage between biogenetic and sociocultural processes. This pseudo-Darwinian notion of "progress" flies in the face of contemporary Darwinism, which construes cultural evolution—such as it is—as a process that proceeds *independent of* (if not actually at odds with) natural selection.

However flawed in conception, the idea of sociogenetic progress is loosely compatible with another, somewhat Hegelian thread in Erikson's thought. As he grew older, Erikson often likened the psychoanalyst's mentality to that of the historian. Indeed, he cited R. G. Collingwood. who stated: "History is the life of the mind itself which is not mind except so far as it both lives in the historical process and knows itself as so living." "These words," said Erikson, "have always impressed me as applicable to the core of the psychoanalytic method" (Friedman 1999, 459).

The Hegelian derivation of Collingwood's approach to history is well known. And on reflection, this is not the first time Hegelian modes of reasoning surfaced in Erikson's work. The chapter "On American Identity" in *Childhood and Society* (1950) elucidates the historical vicissitudes of American motherhood and the gradual transformations of Puritan culture in an exquisitely dialectical fashion. Whether he derived his method from an actual study of Hegel is unknown, and in a certain sense, beside the point here. But there is also an unmistakably Hegelian ring to Erikson's concept of pseudospeciation, which is his term for a peculiar (though pervasive) deformation of conscience in adulthood. Like Darwin, Erikson was aware that guilt feelings and a sense of ethical obligation normally extend to the members of one's own tribe or reference group, and no further. In other words, according to Erikson, human beings have a pronounced tendency to dehumanize members of other cultures as a pretext for hatred and aggression. Despite the fundamental unity of the human species, said Erikson, the fragmentation of humanity into separate and mutually antagonistic enclaves is the result of pseudospeciation, which he described as

> man's deep seated conviction that some providence has made his tribe or caste and, yes, his religion naturally superior to others. This . . . seems to be part of a psychosocial evolution by which he has developed into pseudospecies. This fact is, of course, rooted in the tribal life and based on all the evolutionary peculiarities which brought about man. Among these is his prolonged childhood during which the new-born, "naturally" born to be the most "generalist" animal of all and adaptable to widely differing environments, becomes specialized as a mem-

ber of a human group with its complex interplay of an "inner world" and a social environment. He becomes indoctrinated, then, with the conviction that his
"species" alone was planned by an all-wise deity, created in a special cosmic
event, and appointed by history to guard the only genuine version of humanity
under the leadership of elect elites and leaders. (1968, 298–99)

That is the bad news. Fortunately, thought Erikson, there is a countervail-
ing tendency at work in our species that attempts to overcome our conviction
of our own natural superiority, our hatred and mistrust of the other, by promoting the development of more inclusive, encompassing identities in which
tribal, religious, linguistic, and/or national differences are *aufgehoben*—
absorbed, but not erased—in a more complexly differentiated totality. In the
same spirit, Hegel's philosophy of history relied confidently on "objective
spirit" to ultimately overcome (without entirely abolishing) all consciousness
of particularity, and impart a universalistic esprit de corps that embraces the
whole human family (Avineri 1974). The only question, thought Erikson, is
whether newer, more inclusive identities that mitigate and contain human destructiveness and pseudospeciation can emerge in time to avert a planetary
conflagration wrought by intraspecies conflict.

Of course, sober reflection on the future of our species was not unprecedented in the psychoanalytic literature. In *Civilization and Its Discontents*,
Freud had posed the question whether a resurgence of Eros—i.e., sublimated
libido, rather than raw sexual energy—could bind humanity together in a
peaceful world community and avert the ravages of the death instinct, which
threatened to engulf the entire species (Freud 1930). The difference between
Freud's way of posing this issue and Erikson's is that Erikson's hinged on the
vagaries of personal and collective identity, and the development of conscience *beyond* the Oedipal stage, while Freud's hinged on the economics of
the libido and conflicts between different groups of instincts.

Leaving cataclysm and war aside, Erikson said that there is another catastrophic scenario that could eventually annihilate our species: the steady and
irreversible degradation of the environment. Erikson explained the steady de-
pletion and "filthification" of our planet's precious natural resources as the result of a *collective crisis of generativity*, that is, a deficit or deformation of human conscience, rather than any lack of scientific knowledge. If Erikson was
correct, then the Bush administration's long-standing refusal to ratify the Ky-
oto Accords, its decision to disable the Environmental Protection Agency, and
to raise "acceptable" levels of mercury, lead, and other pollutants in the air
and water in deference to the demands of industry have little to do with a
paucity of information or scientific research. No matter how they are ration-
alized in economic terms, they are the result of shortsightedness and greed,
and are acceptable to the American electorate only because, on the whole, we

don't *care* enough to hold our elected officials accountable for these egregious offenses. The fact that our children's children may inherit a world that cannot sustain human life scarcely enters the minds of most elected representatives—many of whom now argue that the world is going to end soon anyway, so why bother saving it?

Before saying anything more on environmental and policy issues, we should probably address ourselves to elucidating Erikson's concept of conscience in more detail. But before we do, we must begin with a very basic question: What is conscience, anyway?

Conscience can express itself in myriad ways, but at a bare minimum, most of us recognize two modes of conscience that shape our attitudes and behavior, that "speak" to us or through us, as it were, compelling us to "listen" and to shape our conduct accordingly. *Negative conscience*, "bad conscience," or guilt feelings, as they are called, proscribe or punish thoughts, feelings, and behavior that, rightly or wrongly, we abhor. And if our conscience fails to deter us from thinking, feeling, and acting in certain ways, an entity or "voice" within us demands atonement, causing severe self-reproaches, lowered self-esteem, and internal division and discord. So, for negative conscience the proscription, deterrence, and punishment of our "baser" impulses—"Thou shalt not . . ."—is at the heart of the matter.

In contrast to negative conscience, *positive conscience* expresses itself in an urgent press to act in accordance with ideals of decency, humanity, and courage. In such instances, it is not what we do or wish to do that torments us; on the contrary, it is what we do *not* do, that is, our failure to translate our ideals into actuality, that calls forth feelings of shame, rendering it difficult to live comfortably inside our own skin. Conversely, to the extent that we act on our ethical ideals, we reap the rewards of a "good conscience"—a sense of inner harmony and vitality that adds depth and intensity to all aspects of life, sensuous pleasure included. Though seldom differentiated in everyday discourse, positive and negative conscience are experienced firsthand by any reasonably mature and intact adult who, almost by definition, has lively internal commerce with them both. The question then becomes how to account for them.

The first two theorists to examine conscience in an evolutionary perspective were Charles Darwin and Friedrich Nietzsche. Much of what we've termed *positive conscience* was subsumed by Darwin under the heading of love and altruism, topics to which he devoted far more time and attention in *On the Origin of Species* than most readings actually acknowledge (Miller 2004). But Darwin also saw an important evolutionary role for negative conscience, which proscribes and punishes antisocial behavior through the arousal of guilt feelings, which he thought to be a salutary (and uniquely human) feature.

Friedrich Nietzsche (1844–1900) took a very different view. In *The Genealogy of Morals: An Attack* (1887) and again in *Twilight of the Idols* (1888), Nietzsche heaped scorn on any trait resembling pity or disinterested concern for humanity at large. Moreover, he argued that guilt or "bad conscience" is nothing but a morbid deformation of the human spirit that arose in the last two millennia, due to the triumph of Christian slave morality over the noble ethos of pagan antiquity. Unlike Darwin, Nietzsche said that guilt does *not* serve an adaptive function, but is an unnatural imposition on the unfettered expression of instinctual impulses that actually retards or even *reverses* the whole evolutionary process (Burston 2003). These stark contrasts on the subject of conscience were only part of a deeper and more encompassing difference in perspective on human affairs. For, like Freud somewhat later, Darwin and Nietzsche were both atheists. But Darwin was a passionate and relentless critic of slavery, while Nietzsche thought that slavery for the many was indispensable for the freedom of the few. Nietzsche's elitist and antinomian conjectures would be irrelevant to our concerns were it not that he argued, long before Freud, that guilt is really "aggression turned inwards"—a vivid anticipation of Freud's theories of depression and the superego (Burston and Frie 2006).

In any case, despite disparate appraisals of the role of conscience in human evolution, Darwin and Nietzsche's reflections on guilt insured that the elucidation of conscience became a high priority among all biologically oriented twentieth-century psychologists, Freud among them. Freud seldom if ever cited Darwin or Nietzsche directly on this issue. Without wishing to diminish Freud's originality, the fact remains that Darwin and Nietzsche must be reckoned as powerful background influences in this regard. That being so, how did Freud himself account for conscience, and what evolutionary role did he attribute to it?

Freud explained positive conscience in terms of an idealized and exalted internal representation of parental figures (or their surrogates) that inspires ethical idealism, and/or a painful awareness of falling short of one's ideal. He called it the "ego ideal" (Freud 1921). As Freud pointed out, the ideational content of these normative ideals and the strivings for self-improvement engendered by the perceived disparity between the real self and the ego ideal are a derivative expression of the individual's "narcissism," albeit in a life- and growth-enhancing rather than a regressive or antisocial form. By sharp contrast, negative conscience is the domain of the superego, which derives its energy from the death instinct, whose modus operandi—aggression turned inward—is more unconscious and more impersonal, since it embodies and inherits fears and prohibitions that predate the individual's relation to his or her actual parents, or is phylogenetic in origin.

That was the prevailing wisdom in Erikson's day. This being so, it is instructive to note that while Erikson was training as an analyst, Freud slowly merged the ego ideal and the superego into a single entity, demoting the former to an aspect or attribute of the latter, more encompassing psychic "agency." What prompted this ill-advised theoretical move? One reason may have been a desire to contain the bewildering profusion of hypothetical entities comprising the psychoanalytic theory of the mind. After all, when he abridged his theory of conscience, Freud was trying to accommodate the newly minted "death instinct" into his evolving system. This required multiple additions to and excisions from his previous theories of gender, perversions, and so on, and the cumulative result was that the whole edifice of analytic theory became even more baroque than was previously the case. In view of circumstances, Freud probably felt it prudent to cut corners wherever possible.

Another motive for seeking a singular source of conscience so late in the game was a (partly unconscious) bias in Freud's thinking that had been (largely) latent until then. Negative conscience figures prominently in depression, obsessional neuroses, masochism, and other types of psychopathology, and was therefore subject to much careful scrutiny and deliberate conjecture. By contrast, positive conscience does not deal with proscription or punishment, but propels the individual toward acts of charity, courage, sacrifice, and solidarity. While sometimes a source of suffering and dissatisfaction, perhaps, it is seldom a source of psychopathological disturbance—by Freud's reckoning, anyway.

Unfortunately, then, when Freud collapsed the ego ideal into the superego, incentives to reflect on positive conscience in orthodox analytic circles diminished appreciably, leaving it to revisionists to explore. For example, Alfred Adler was extremely interested in positive conscience and defined psychopathology principally by its absence. He termed it *Gemeinschaftsgefuhl*, which is usually translated as "social feeling." More recently, Heinz Kohut attributed the development of positive conscience (in the form of mature empathy and wisdom) to the development of the individual's "narcissism" (Kohut 1971, 1977)—a baffling terminological juxtaposition, if ever there was one. Admittedly, in deriving the individual's empathy, ethical ideals, and so on from his "narcissism," Kohut was drawing on precedent. Freud himself did likewise. But the contrast between these two terms for positive conscience—*social feeling* versus *positive narcissism*—gives one pause. After all, in practical terms, how do modifications to the individual's narcissism (self-love) lead to the efflorescence of social feeling? It also prompts the question: Which term for positive conscience would Erikson have endorsed?

Obviously, there is no way of knowing for sure. What we do know with certainty is that whichever term he chose, he would have hastened to add that the full flowering of positive conscience does not occur until middle age. And while it may indeed germinate as a modification to the individual's narcissism, the positive conscience of the mature, "generative" adult emphatically *transcends* narcissism, involving a threefold process of decentration (in the Piagetian sense) rooted in the emergent ability

1. to envisage the consequences of attitudes and actions for society in the future, and beyond the individual's own life span, and not just for the individual or his family in the present; and
2. to play a responsive and responsible role in the nexus of generations by judicious attention to cultural conservation and innovation. Ideally, said Erikson, these developments give rise to a third, more radical form of decentration alluded too several times already; namely,
3. the ability to overcome *pseudospeciation*, which derives from the effort to see beyond the parochial perspectives of one's own culture, and to define oneself principally in terms of a panhuman identity, and not to privilege one's own group over others, or to pit them against one another in an adversarial fashion.

Unfortunately, Erikson's first reflections on the development of conscience in adulthood were somewhat opaque, leaving a careful reader puzzled. For example, he quoted Luther, who said: "Conscience is that inner ground where we and God have to learn to live together like man and wife." Erikson's interpretation of this maxim is: "Psychologically speaking, it is where the ego meets the superego, where our self can either live in wedded harmony with a positive conscience or is estranged from a negative one" (1958b, 195). This is solid literary prose, perhaps, but on reflection it is strikingly short on specifics. According to this account, conscience is located at some indeterminate place where ego and superego "meet," rather being situated squarely in the superego. But this begs the question: Did Erikson regard the superego as the source of both positive and negative conscience, as the later Freud evidently did? After all, there is no mention of the ego ideal in this connection. Possibly so, and possibly not, because in addition to the preceding, Erikson said that Luther was "liberated" from the Oedipal superego and achieved a "higher," more positive—and, incidentally, more maternal—conscience, yet was unable or unwilling to spell out more clearly where (or what) this "higher conscience" was, and what it really consisted in. The cumulative effect was thought provoking but fuzzy in the extreme.

Meanwhile, various publications after 1958 attest to Erikson's deepening conviction that the Freudian superego, with its characteristic emphasis on guilt and prohibition, is merely a *preliminary* stage in the development of a mature and predominantly positive conscience, and that his thinking on this score was inspired by evolutionary and ethological theory. For example, in "Human Strength and the Cycle of Generations," first published in 1960, Erikson gave a resounding endorsement to these remarks by Julian Huxley:

> The peculiar difficulties which surround our individual moral adjustment are seen to be largely due to our evolutionary history. Like our prolonged helplessness in infancy, our tendency to hernia and sinusitis, our troubles in learning to walk upright, they are a consequence of our having developed from a simian ancestry. Once we realize that the primitive superego is merely a makeshift developmental mechanism, no more intended to be the permanent central support of our morality than is our embryonic notochord intended to be a permanent central support of our bodily frame, we shall not take its dictates so seriously (have they not often been interpreted as the authentic Voice of God?), and shall regard its supercession by some more rational and less cruel mechanism as the central problem confronting every human individual. (Erikson 1964b, 145)

Having quoted him at length, Erikson noted that Huxley's prescription for surpassing the inflexible, all-or-nothing quality of the childish superego is completely consonant with the therapeutic goals of psychoanalysis, which aims to replace morbid, debilitating guilt with an as-yet-unspecified "mechanism" that is more rational and less cruel. But is it a *different* mechanism, or a more complex, mature, tolerant, and evenly modulated form of the Oedipal superego Erikson had in mind? Huxley's metaphor of the notochord and spinal column, which Erikson deployed suggestively here, clearly implies that *it is actually the same entity* at a later phase of development. But what sorts of transformations would the shift from a predominantly negative (punitive) to a predominantly positive (prosocial) conscience entail?

Though he never clarified precisely how this transformation takes place, Erikson did outline some intermediate steps between the emergence of the "primitive," that is, the Oedipal superego, and the "higher conscience." He distinguished between the *morality* of the superego, based on the childish fear of punishment or disapproval, which fosters morality and vindictiveness in the adult, and the ethics of adulthood, which are not compulsive or inflexible, or based on censure and condemnation, but have a quality of disinterestedness based upon *positive* ideals that the individual strives to attain, and acquires in postadolescent development (Erikson, 1950, 1958b).

That being so, it is interesting to note that the first person to differentiate between morality and ethics in something like this spirit was actually Immanuel Kant, in *The Groundwork of the Metaphysics of Morals*, first published in 1797. Needless to say, Kant did not bring either an evolutionary or a developmental perspective to bear on these issues, though he did furnish us with good grounds for supposing that an ethical sensibility represents a more "mature," more courageous, and more authentic stance than a merely moral one. Kant said that "moral" behavior is "normal" inasmuch as it accords with custom, convention, and the law of the land. But for that very reason, Kant insisted, conventional morality it is not the expression of a genuine virtue, but rather a form of careful (if often unconscious) compliance with prevailing cultural expectations, based on the person's desire for external approval or the fear of censure and reprisal—in short, of what Kant called ethical *heteronomy*. However comfortable or ego-syntonic it may be, morality in this sense is really a form of slavish conformity. By contrast, said Kant, real ethical judgment and genuinely principled behavior is guided by autonomous or self-chosen criteria of merit. And as Kant describes its internal reasoning, the autonomous or self-legislating psyche is capable of disinterestedness only by virtue of considerable decentration, which Kant subsumes under the heading of "practical reason" (Kant 1964).

Unfortunately, Freud never understood Kant, and in *Civilization and Its Discontents* (1930), misconstrued the *categorical imperative* as the voice of the superego—a move that invalidates Kant's distinction between heteronomous and autonomous modes of moral reasoning. After all, and by his own admission, Freud's superego is essentially *heteronomous*. It is a vestige of our "archaic inheritance" and/or the internalization of norms and prohibitions that are initially imposed from without, and is internalized only due to threats of reprisal or the potential loss of love (Lasky 2002).

That being so, it is instructive to note that Erikson's emphasis on ego strength as the foundation of mature conscience and his differentiation between morality and ethics are closer to the Kantian spirit, though they still beg the question as to where conscience is "located"—in the ego, the ego ideal, or the superego. Or does it shuttle from one to another at some as-yet-undisclosed point in the epigenetic sequence?

Unfortunately, as we mull over Erikson's body of work, this little mystery never gets resolved—or even acknowledged in so many words. If pressed, Erikson might have replied that the answer to this question (in theory) is quite irrelevant (in practice), since the id, ego, and superego are not real entities, but merely heuristic fictions. If this is so, then questions couched in terms of spatial metaphors such as "location" are handy (and hopefully illuminating) figures of speech, and nothing more.

Does that settle the matter then? Almost, but not quite, because Erikson then went on to specify an important *intermediary* phase between morality and ethics: the *ideological* phase of adolescence (1956a). Whereas most of us use the term *ideology* to denote a belief system that distorts or obstructs our grasp of reality, promoting prejudice or partisanship, Erikson's use of the term was never pejorative. On the contrary, he used it synonymously with what Erich Fromm termed *a framework of orientation and devotion*. Erikson emphasized that the search for an ideological orientation is integral to any adolescent identity crisis, adding sagely that the adolescent's need for the vigorous *repudiation* of certain people can also be served in this way.

At this stage of development, ideology replaces or subsumes what little is left of the ego ideal in Erikson's terminology. Or perhaps another, more Freudian way of expressing it is that the ego ideal becomes somewhat *depersonalized* in adolescence, and translated into abstract principles, rather than uncritical admiration of this or that particular person. Either way, in addition to furnishing a positive focus and binding commitments that point them toward the future, a youthful ideology affords young people with an instrument of individuation and self-definition. And that is a good beginning. But in due course, said Erikson, an ideological insistence on abstract principles can cease to be a means to an end, and become an end in itself—in short, an *idol*. To avoid the dangers of sterility and rigidity, a postadolescent conscience can (and must) become less fixated on abstract principles and more focused on the contributing concretely to the welfare of others. To make this transition, teenagers and young adults need role models—older people who think, feel, and act in this way—if they are to become fully human themselves. Absent opportunities for *intergenerational identification* and the cultural provision of inspiring role models for middle and old age, the adolescent or young adult may get "stuck" in the disappointment and rebellion of adolescence, leading to cynicism, indifference, and insularity or authoritarian rigidity in adulthood.

Another possible outcome, however, is that instead of becoming genuinely ethical, people "stuck" at the ideological level tend to bifurcate and compartmentalize social reality and fail to develop the virtue of "judiciousness." People who lack this quality tend to become tedious or obnoxious moralizers of either a puritan or radical persuasion, whose apparent preoccupation with other people's ethics (or lack of them) covers up all kinds of internal "deals" they made with (and against) their own consciences. In *Childhood and Society*, for example, Erikson writes:

> Judiciousness in the widest sense is a frame of mind which is tolerant of differences, cautious and methodical in evaluation and judgment, circumspect in action and—in spite of all this apparent relativism—capable of faith and indignation. Its opposite is prejudice, an outlook characterized by prejudiced values and dogmatic divisions. . . . By thus relying on preconceived notions the prejudiced frame of mind . . . has the advantage of permitting the projection of everything that feels alien within one's own heart onto some vague external enemy outside. (1950, 416)

So while it eschews the arrogance and exclusivity of youth, perhaps, Erikson never meant to imply that the openness and flexibility of the judicious mind implies an absence of passion or indignation, and even assigns a special place to feelings like these in clinical work. For example, in "The Nature of Clinical Evidence," he says:

> I do not wish to make too much of this, but I would suggest in passing that some of us have, to our detriment, embraced an objectivity which can only be maintained with self-deception. If "psychoanalyzed" man learns to recognize the fact that even his previously repudiated or denied impulses may be "right" in their refusal to be submerged without a trace (the traces of his symptoms), so he may also learn that his strongest ethical judgments are right in being persistent even if modern life may not consider it intelligent or advantageous to feel strongly about such matters. Any psychotherapist, then, who throws out his ethical sentiments with his irrational moral anger, deprives himself of a principal tool of his clinical perception. For even as our sensuality sharpens our awareness of the orders of nature, so our indignation, admitted and scrutinized for flaws of sulkiness and self-indulgence, is, in fact, an important tool both of therapy and theory. It adds to the investigation of what, indeed, has happened to sick individuals a suggestion of where to look for those epidemiological factors that should and need not happen to anybody. But this means that we somehow harbor a model of man which could serve as a scientific basis for the postulation of an ethical relation of the generations to one another; and that we are committed to this whether or not we abrogate our partisanship in particular systems of morality. (1998, 267–68)

This is a remarkable statement. Not only does Erikson reproach some of Freud's followers with self-deception, he declares that the "ethical relation of the generations to one another" can have a genuinely scientific basis if—and only if—we do not silence our conscience in deference to a specious ideal of "objectivity." This assertion flatly contradicts the ethical relativism entailed in the "value neutrality" espoused by many of his generation—and, above all, by Heinz Hartmann. Then as now, an analyst's "subjective" responses to a patient's communications were apt to be lumped indiscriminately under the heading of "countertransference"—a weasel word that can mean almost anything depending on the context and the user. That being so, it is instructive to note that Erikson ranks indignation—properly scrutinized, of course—as an indispensable aid to the identification and remediation of the various modes of "missed mutuality" that have derailed a patient's existence. And implicit in all of this, he says, is a tacit "model of man," that is, of basic human nature, which must guide the development of theory and therapy.

So, though he did not to make too much of it—in truth, not nearly *enough*—Erikson quietly underscored the need for clinicians to have an ethical backbone to guide their inquiry into human development. Why? Because in the final analysis, the ongoing dance of the generations, their reciprocal recognition and affirmation, is as integral to Erikson's perspective on mental health as the dialectic of *Eros* and *Thanatos* was to more orthodox contemporaries like Karl Menninger and Norman O. Brown. Another way of framing this issue is that Erikson's notion of life cycle development entails a normative and *prescriptive* dimension that *transcends* cultural relativism. Indeed, in conversation with Richard Evans, Erikson said that "insofar as every human being is born as an organism, there are certain aspects of his development which remain universal, no matter where he grows up. The culture can only aggravate or play down, and in that way make the stages more or less intense, or more or less prolonged. But what emerges is pretty much tied to what is fundamental" (Evans 1967, 23).

In short, despite Erikson's intense and longstanding associations with Alfred Kroeber, Ruth Benedict, and Margaret Mead, and the cultural relativism entailed in their brand of cultural anthropology, his epigenetic perspective on the development of conscience presupposes a biological foundation for the relationship between generations that culture builds upon—or else violates, at great cost to its members. But strangely enough, he never acknowledged or addressed the implications of his differences with Hartmann or the followers of anthropologist Franz Boas on ethical relativism explicitly, and in print.

FAMILY, TRADITION, AND THE CYCLE OF GENERATIONS

Having said that, however, the core intuition that underlies Erikson's perspective on mental health is sound. Basically, he maintained that ego strength or mental health—and, by implication, the unfolding of conscience—is contingent on the reciprocal recognition and affirmation of individuals in different phases of the life cycle. This led Erikson to view the development of conscience in ways that some of his contemporaries and critics regarded as repressive or tradition-bound, and curiously at odds with his oft-stated liberalism. Thus, for example, in "Human Strength and the Cycle of Generations," Erikson said:

> It is not always understood that one of the main rationales for marital and family loyalty is the imperative need for inner unity in the child's conscience at the very time when he can and must envisage goals beyond the family. For the voices and images of those adults who are now internalized must not contradict each other too flagrantly. They contribute to the child's most intense conscience development—a development which separates, once and for all, play and fantasy from that future which is irreversible.

. . . Conscience accepts such irreversibility as internal and private, and it is all the more important that it incorporate the ethical example of a family purposefully united in familial and economic pursuits. This alone gives the child the inner freedom to move on—to whatever school setting his culture has ready for him. (1964b, 121)

Of course, one could cavil with the assertion that familial commitments are inherently "irreversible," and that "a family purposefully united in familial and economic pursuits" is indispensable for the growth of conscience in children. There are many instances where divorce is vastly preferable to staying together, and where it is precisely the *absence* of honesty and unanimity among parents which prompts a premature quickening of conscience, as Erikson himself observed in his remarks on "Dora" (Erikson 1964d). But remember, these reflections on "family solidarity" were made in 1960, before the Left and the emerging feminist and gay liberation movements launched an all-out assault on the family for curbing sexual freedom, stigmatizing sexual minorities, and reproducing patriarchal social norms. These scathing critiques of family life promoted the utopian belief that children will develop into more sociable, intact adults who are less cowed by authority in non-familial settings, where they would presumably be free from patriarchal-authoritarian conditioning and/or the subtle but deep emotional complications that arise in an Oedipally constellated family situation (Deleuze and Guatari 1977; Poster 1980).

In those heady, remarkable times, many intelligent people and well-intentioned people questioned the necessity of the family, and it was quite natural for someone like Paul Roazen to interpret Erikson's underlying agenda as culturally conservative. Indeed it was, given the temper of the times. But how would *contemporary* conservatives greet Erikson's ideas, if they were aware of them? Since the Reagan era, the culture wars in America have become so stark and envenomed that most American conservatives would welcome Erikson's emphasis on family solidarity, but treat his avid environmentalism and his plea for embracing diversity and the "loyal rebels who refuse to adjust to conditions" as grounds for suspicion, if not outright dismissal.

While his theorizing was family centered, Erikson lacked the harsh, punitive, and judgmental quality that disfigures the American conservative movement today. In the current climate of discussion, attributing the decline of the two-parent nuclear family to the impact of feminism, gay liberation, and so on, merely provides right-wing zealots with a handy scapegoat and a plausible excuse for punishing and humiliating "deviants" of one sort or another, and cleverly averts attention from the fact that despite all their "family values" rhetoric, all the Right has to offer are punitive policies and prescriptions.

They offer little or nothing by way of tangible support and incentives to nourish and sustain the ties that bind. Indeed, it is the right wing's idolatry of "free markets" and their steady erosion of government oversight and regulation that erode family solidarity at a practical, grassroots level. As a result, day care for toddlers is often shockingly unsafe and inhumane, and the average day-care worker in the United States earns as much as a parking lot attendant—and, significantly, gets just as much training. In a society where two incomes—and, by implication, two or more jobs—are virtually indispensable for a family's survival, most adults work so hard that they lack the peace and presence of mind and, indeed, the very time it takes to cultivate warm family ties. Long hours, low pay, minimal family leaves, inadequate or nonexistent health insurance, and a host of hidden penalties if familial obligations intrude on incessant productivity—this is what "free market" enthusiasts have to show on behalf of their "family-centered" ethos (Hewlett 1998; Olfman 2005).

If Erikson were alive today, he would vigorously deplore this state of affairs. Moreover, he would also call attention to other threats to family solidarity and intergenerational identification that are now looming on the horizon and threaten to engulf the twenty-first century. To put these emerging threats into historical perspective, let's briefly retrace our steps and have another look at the notions of instinct and developmental stages, and the role of tradition in the development of human culture.

Darwin, Freud, and their contemporaries still believed that most animal behavior is governed by "instinct," or by hereditarily "hardwired" behavioral repertoires that are triggered by specific environmental stimuli. Since Freud's day, however, ethology informs us that much behavior that was formerly deemed instinctive is in fact learned. Without sensitive and attentive instruction from their elders at critical developmental periods, herons and geese forget their ancestral migration routes, wolves forget how to hunt, and chimpanzees forget how to mate and rear their young. In short, once again, other animals are a lot more like us than we previously imagined, albeit in ways that are opposite to the way that Darwin and Freud sometimes had us believe.

Though animals resemble us much more than we thought, however, there is still one crucial difference between them and ourselves. Much as individual specimens differ in size and strength, cunning or courage, members of other animal species learn a single, specific template for crucial survival tasks like seasonal migration, evading predators, finding food, and mating and rearing their young. Granted, in many instances, the template is not entirely instinctive, in the narrow or old-fashioned sense of the term, but for all animals, regardless of their individual characteristics, there is one—and only one—way to be a competent male or female specimen, and to transmit the skills and knowledge needed to perpetuate the life of the species to their young.

For human beings, this is simply not the case. Different cultures generate a multitude of responses to basic questions like: How do I acquire food? cope with scarcity? greet my neighbor? confront or evade an enemy? find and woo a mate? raise my young? Not only is there no single hereditary pattern to follow, but the "basic" repertoire of skills and attitudes required to address these needs and contingencies varies widely according to custom, history, climate, geography, and overall level of technological development.

Despite this built-in indeterminacy, for most of human history tradition and prevailing cultural consensus provided our kind with authoritative and uncontroversial answers to basic existential questions like these. In preindustrial settings, these cultural patterns or templates functioned analogously to animal instincts by canceling the indeterminacy of the human brain, providing attitudes and action schemas regulating mating behavior, food production, the resolution of internal conflicts, or the conduct of war with neighboring groups. But here again, to minimize indeterminacy, one basic pattern tended to prevail. As a result, members of different tribes or of different social strata followed (for the most part) in their mothers' and fathers' footsteps unreflectively and without complaint.

The unmistakable advantage to this mode of social adaptation is that it entails a very low degree of identity confusion. People tend to know who they are, what to expect, and what is expected of them in turn. Unfortunately, however, in these cultural settings, class and caste divisions define one's identity to a large extent, while male and female gender roles have an "essentialist" cast that many find repressive nowadays. So the disadvantage here is that in the process of canceling out indeterminacy, tradition also *narrows the scope of human possibilities* to a finite set of alternatives—namely, becoming a slave, an artisan, a warrior, or a priest, if male; or a wife, a courtesan, or or a maiden aunt, if female—though in truth, there was usually much more elasticity and room for individual differences in these milieus than many of us imagine.

This relatively stable state of affairs changed drastically in the wake of the industrial revolution. The global reach of capitalism displaced large populations and provided powerful incentives for immigration, bringing disparate cultural sensibilities into close and frequent contact with one another. Moreover, the nature and power of the market is such that it eroded the influence of *all* traditional mores to a very considerable degree. In bygone eras, tradition modulated the pace of technological change and the changes in social and political structures that inevitably follow. Nowadays, however, technological change drives the market, and the market is such a fickle and amoral entity that looking to precedent, to the experiences and perspectives of our elders, yields less and less of the "competitive edge" young people need to thrive.

In such circumstances, the idea that tradition—*any* tradition—can provide clear-cut and authoritative answers to basic questions of how to live seems quaint or faintly ridiculous to many people—a fact that is amply reflected in the tenor of modern philosophy and the role played by the concept of chance or contingency in the pre- and postindustrial worlds. Under feudalism, for example, Arab and Christian philosophers who denied the existence of natural law, and who construed the universe as an essentially chaotic place, staked their audacious claims on God's omnipotence. Presumably, it was his will alone that imparted a certain regularity to the rhythms and processes of nature, enabling it to unfold in predictable patterns. It is only in the nineteenth and twentieth centuries that atheists like Nietzsche and Sartre coupled their insistence on the radical contingency of human existence with the equally emphatic declaration that God is dead, and that we create ourselves entirely through our own individual actions and decisions. Such thinking was not popular—or perhaps even possible—in the preindustrial era. But the Industrial Revolution and the rise of modern markets introduced an unprecedented level of structured indeterminacy in human affairs, which catalyzed a corresponding decline in the power of tradition.

The advantage to this relatively new state of affairs is that modernity opens up new opportunities for the critique or deconstruction of many ethnocentric and sexist prejudices from days gone by, and, with it, new possibilities for exploration and self-expression. These are not to be lightly dismissed. But by the same token, the ceaseless clash of cultural perspectives, and the decline of tradition generally, promotes identity confusion and uprootedness, and creates the climate for the fundamentalist backlashes of *extreme* traditionalists and fundamentalists that are currently fomenting conflicts all around the world. With rare exceptions, fundamentalists—Christian, Jewish, Muslim, or Hindu—seek to "cure" the experienced or incipient chaos of a market-driven society by reintroducing or imposing idealized or distorted versions of preindustrial norms and identities on the population at large, and do not shrink from using coercion and deception (in various forms) to achieve these ends.

TECHNOLOGY, IDENTITY, AND
THE DECLINE OF INTERGENERATIONAL TIES

As if all this were not bad enough already, we are deepening our present malaise by tinkering with the biological building blocks of the human life cycle—sometimes deliberately (Ho 2000), sometimes inadvertently. For example, powerful industrial pollutants known as *pseudo-estrogens* are now so pervasive that they are causing many girls to start puberty at the age of seven or eight, robbing them of much of their childhood. As if this biological assault on childhood were not bad enough, we also promote or permit the precocious sexualization of our children to an alarming degree. We sit them in front of electronic baby-sitters called televisions, where they suck up all kinds of trash that exploits and trivializes sexual signifiers for hours at a time. The bland acquiescence of the cultural mainstream in this sad, peculiar state of affairs is mind-boggling. Thanks to our inadvertence and numb indifference, culture and environment collude to abbreviate, if not annul, childhood, especially for girls. No one asks if seven- or eight-year-old brains were designed to cope with early estrogen saturation, and what the cognitive and emotional consequences of such neurophysiological transformations might be (Olfman 2005).

And at the other end of the life cycle, we are trying to *extend* the human life span by postponing old age indefinitely, as people peddling human growth hormone (and kindred interventions) argue that we can all live well into our hundreds. Hardly anyone stops to ask if we were meant to live that long, or what developmental and psychological consequences of such drastic alterations in the life cycle are likely to ensue (Fukuyama 2002).

How an abbreviated childhood and a long-postponed senescence will affect family life over a series of generations is still uncertain. But new and developing technologies pose other, more menacing threats to our collective mental health in the twenty-first century, and Erikson would have opposed them as well. I say this somewhat reluctantly because, though he did not believe in technological panaceas, neither was Erikson opposed to new technologies, at least in principle. In "Identity and Uprootedness in Our Time," for example, Erikson stated: "There is no reason to insist that a technological world, as such, need weaken inner resources of adaptation, which may, in fact, be replenished by the good will and ingenuity of a communicating species" (Erikson, 1964c, 103–4).

Or again, in the same essay: "[W]hy should not man, a locomotor being, equipped with an inventive brain as well as a sensitive conscience, create a mechanical world reasonably well fitted to his striving for a cultural and technological identity? Why should he not be at home (as much as it is his lot to be at home in any technology) managing whatever energies he can extract from nature to create whatever synthetic products he can fuse into a new style?" (107).

Clearly, Erikson was no Luddite. Nevertheless, his optimism seems misplaced today, when intact families, communities, and the possession of "a sensitive conscience" cannot be taken for granted, and must *not* be assumed to guide the development and deployment of new technologies by our inventive minds. And were he alive, Erikson would no doubt agree. In his absence, one thinker who *has* drawn attention to this problem is Francis Fukuyama. Though he does not speak in terms of an epigenetic sequence, of intergenerational identification, and so on, his recent book *Our Posthuman Future: Consequences of the Biotechnology Revolution* is extremely pertinent to these issues (Fukuyama, 2002). Fukuyama defines human nature, or our "human essence," in terms of characteristics that have evolved through natural selection, and warns that we are courting self-extinction if we industrialize human reproduction and try to extend the human life span indefinitely. That being so, Fukuyama calls for legislation to regulate and/or halt the research and development of any and all techniques that could hasten their social and commercial ascendancy.

On a purely philosophical plane, there are some problems with Fukuyama's stance that warrant brief discussion. As Erich Fromm points out, the notion of a generic, universal human nature that transcends or in some sense *precedes* cultural and historical contingencies—which Erikson embraces and transforms, in his characteristic style—first emerged in connection with Enlightenment rationalism (Fromm 1994). So when Ludwig Feuerbach first coined the term the *human essence* in the mid-nineteenth century, it referred to an as yet largely unrealized potential for a kind of rational sociability that is intimately linked to "sensuousness." Reason, by this account, is a distinctively human trait, not found elsewhere in the animal kingdom, as it was for Descartes—and Aristotle, for that matter. But unlike the Cartesian mind, Feuerbachian "reason" promotes and celebrates sensuousness, rather opposing itself to it. Indeed, Feuerbach defined the whole task of philosophy as the demystification and eventual liberation of the human essence—sensuous, sociable, and rational—from the asceticism and otherworldliness of Platonism and conventional Christian piety.

Among other things, perhaps, Marx's theory of alienation was an attempt to specify the political and economic conditions that would make the realization of Feuerbachian reason a widespread social reality. And until he junked or attenuated the idea in *Das Kapital*, Karl Marx defined the human essence in terms of nonalienated labor, defined as free, purposive activity, and planned interventions into the natural order that engender a distinctively human world, one that is not governed by natural laws, and therefore leaves a great deal of room for indeterminism and the exercise of human freedom—a freedom not found elsewhere in the animal kingdom, where determinism, instinct, and necessity prevail. The concept of alienation that Marx developed—then abandoned or attenuated, for the most part—was predicated on the idea that we are profoundly estranged from our human essence, and that human history is a process of the loss and recovery of that "essence" through "revolutionary social praxis" (Avineri 1976).

Though also a child of the Enlightenment, Freud did not define the human essence in terms of an inherent rationality or sociability that any amount of deliberate *praxis* is likely to redeem or revive. Instead, he defined it in terms of a tragic and intractable conflict at the heart of human existence. And unlike Marx, who dwelt on the vicissitudes of labor, Freud focused on sexuality, or, more specifically, the prodigious *surplus* of sexual energy with which our species is endowed. By Freud's account, our efforts to adapt to a hostile or indifferent world engender cultural constraints on the exercise of our impulses that, via sublimation, create science and art, affording us (1) greater leverage against nature, (2) a steady source of pleasure and distraction from reality, and (3) intractable and sometimes unbearable inner conflicts in the vast majority of people. By Freud's account, then, self-estrangement is inherent in the whole civilizing process, in the very creation of a human society, and cannot possibly be transcended completely.

By contrast with Marx and Freud, Sartre flatly denied that there is such a thing as a human essence that precedes our individual existences. According to Sartre, our only essential characteristic is that we have no essence (Sartre 1956). As a result, we determine our own character and fate through individual choice and decision. Unlike Marx and Freud, who acknowledged that we are born into and inherit structures of consciousness that are culturally and historically predetermined, Sartre insisted that human existence is founded in radical contingency, and, correlatively, in radical freedom to become whoever and whatever we decide to be. The only other attribute that Sartre accorded our species, besides a lack of "essence," is that we are "doomed to freedom," that is, unable *not* to choose who we are.

Reviewing these descriptions of the "human essence" in historical sequence always engenders ambivalence and dismay. Though each one is profoundly illuminating, making large claims about the nature of human nature (or "existence"), none of them is entirely adequate or persuasive on its own, and efforts to integrate them invariably lapse into syncretism or incoherence. Having said that, however, it is also instructive to note that with the partial exception of Freud, most of Fukuyama's predecessors described the human essence in terms of a more or less *radical break with* the natural order— saying that being human confers qualities, possibilities, and/or dilemmas of one sort or another on us that are peculiar to our species, and ours alone. Therefore, defining the human essence in terms of evolutionary and/or genetically inherited characteristics, as both Erikson and Fukuyama do, is a shift away from most modern (and, of course, postmodern) philosophy.

Fortunately, in addition to his emphasis on epigenesis, intergenerational identification, and so on, Erikson added another dimension to his theory of human nature that takes technology, alienation, and our rupture with nature into account. Nor was it appended as mere afterthought, but as a conscious corrective to the one-sidedness emphasis on sexuality in psychoanalytic discourse. For example, in "The Problem of Ego Identity" (1956a), Erikson reflected thoughtfully on the inextricable intertwining of identity and the sense of competence or "workmanship" in childhood and adolescence, and the role "work paralysis" plays in psychopathology. And two years later, in *Young Man Luther* (1958b), he said:

> [T]he most neglected problem in psychoanalysis is the problem of work, in theory as well as in practice: as if the dialectic of the history of ideas had ordered a system of psychological thought which would as resolutely ignore the way in which the individual and his group makes a living as Marxism ignores introspective psychology and makes a man's economic position the fulcrum of his acts and thoughts. Decades of case histories have omitted the work histories of the patients or have treated their occupation as a seemingly irrelevant area of life in which the data could be disguised with the greatest impunity. Yet, therapeutic experiments with the work life of hospitalized young patients indicate that patients in a climate of self-help, of planful work, and of communal association can display an adaptive resourcefulness which seemed absent only because our theories and beliefs decreed that it be absent. (17)

In "The Problem of Ego Identity" and *Young Man Luther*, Erikson's focus was on epigenetic issues and the case history method and/or its application to historical research. Meanwhile, however, in "Identity and Uprootedness in Our Time" (1964c), his emphasis shifted from the elucidation of individual conflicts and their potential remediation toward the cultural or collective transformations wrought by humankind's own tool-making abilities—in short, from ideographic research techniques toward an explicit philosophical anthropology.

In any case, Erikson's position here is a thoughtful compromise between Marx and Freud. According to Erikson, human beings are uniquely endowed with a capacity to invent tools and, by implication, to shape and reconfigure their relationships to nature and to one another. Indeed, all human cultures are profoundly shaped by the kinds of tools they characteristically employ, generating new possibilities for human development and new modes of estrangement from nature at one and the same time. All of this accords with Marx's vision of human history. However, Erikson also asserts that there never was a time when human beings did not invent tools, and were therefore *not* estranged from nature to some degree. And since an element of distancing, exploitation, and estrangement from nature is inherent in the tool-making/culture-building process, there is no reason to anticipate a time when alienation can be definitively abolished or overcome. In words strangely suited to our present reflections, Erikson said:

[S]omewhere between the exploitation of nature and the self-exploitation of
mercantile and mechanized man a gigantic transformation has taken place which
was first the subject of Marx's passionate attention: it is the creation of middle
men between man and nature. And it dawns on us that the *technological* world
of today is about to create kinds of alienation too strange to be imagined. All
this, however, must not becloud the universality of the problem of technical estrangement which started with the creation of tools and the development of a
self-conscious brain at the beginning of mankind. (1964c, 104–5)

Fair enough. Let us abjure any utopian hopes of overcoming alienation
once and for all. But by the same token, remember Erikson's prediction that
the world is "about to create kinds of alienation too strange to be imagined."
While he certainly spoke the truth, Erikson did not anticipate the kind of tool-
making culture Fukuyama anticipates, where we can dispense with natural selection completely, and, by implication, modify, disrupt, and perhaps destroy
those distinctively human characteristics that emerged as a consequence (Ho
2000).

To put the matter in a slightly different way, let us begin by acknowledging that humans are capable of various forms of sexual satisfaction. However,
until now, natural selection has shaped our behavior so that the vast majority
of our kind are primarily interested in heterosexual activities and choices.
(Contrary to the claims of many fashionable theorists, ideology and socialization alone will not do the job.) However, as recent technological advances
make plain, we are not chained to this state of affairs indefinitely. For better
and worse, we are the *only* species capable of driving a wedge, as it were, between sex and reproduction—of becoming middlemen, as Erikson put it, between ourselves and nature. Whether this development is the expression of
some underlying essence, or merely one trait that will *become* our defining attribute through our collective choices scarcely matters in the long run. What
does matter is that this distinctive ability, which we are deepening through
stem cell and cloning research, efforts to revive and replenish mitochondria,
and so forth, makes us the only species capable of stepping completely outside the evolutionary framework of natural selection that has governed the
destiny of *all* species on this planet until now.

Of course, not all technological interventions into reproductive biology are
bad. Liberating the pursuit of sexual pleasure from the exigencies of unwanted childbirth and/or domestic servitude of one sort or another has been
extremely important for many women. Indeed, were it not for the fact that
family planning is still unavailable to large numbers of women who want and
need it, we might describe advances in contraception as one of the triumphs
of the twentieth century (Porter 1997). But inviting new technologies into the
sexual and reproductive arena has had other, more sinister side effects. For

example, nowadays divorce lawyers tell us that male use of cyberporn is a factor in the estrangement of more than half the couples seeking divorce today. Arguably, you could interpret the use of cyberporn as more of a symptom of a preexisting marital estrangement than an underlying cause. But this a sterile, chicken-and-egg way of framing the issue. It is abundantly clear to most mental health professionals that the use of cyberporn creates and intensifies desires, expectations, and modes of behavior that are completely at variance with the attitudes required to sustain a steady, committed, monogamous union.

So, unless present trends abate, technological advances and the galloping commercialization of sex will soon render it possible to sever the primordial connection between sex and childbirth altogether. Not everyone deplores this possibility, of course. As early as 1970, Shulamith Firestone argued that the technological rupture between sex and reproduction will be deeply liberating for women (Firestone 1970), and others on the Left, like Donna Haraway, have since followed suit (Haraway 1991). Pondering their blighted visions of the future, we realize that any attempt to accord primacy to work and tool-making, to our conflicted sexuality, or to anything else about the human condition as "essentially" human will become completely moot in the twenty-first century, especially if we pursue the merger of flesh with machines that many are heralding as the next step in human evolution. Researchers who work at the interface between artificial intelligence and the new reproductive technologies now predict that computers will soon be sentient, and human intelligence will soon be "upgraded," augmented, and enhanced by all kinds of artificial implants and prostheses—and eventually "downloaded" into biomechanical cyborgs that are virtually immortal (Brooks 2001; Kurzweil 1999). Needless to say, none of them pauses to reflect upon what effect this will have on our collective mental health, or whether or not these posthuman entities will even have a conscience. If Erikson is right, and the possession of vibrant mental health and an intact conscience depend on a carefully nurtured cultural balance between the needs and abilities of the generations, annulling the natural human life cycle in this way will be nothing short of disastrous.

Though few people are aware of it, we are treading on a very slippery slope, and the thoughtless, giddy excitement and profound horror that grip many science watchers nowadays reflect the fact that events "on the ground" are rapidly outpacing public awareness and society's ability to regulate technology in the public interest.

Despite the raging controversies surrounding stem cell research in Congress, the conditions for a free and democratic debate on these issues in the culture at large do not yet exist. Though each and every human being—alive and unborn—has a stake in this debate, only a small fraction of the population can discuss this issue knowledgeably, and if we act too quickly on our newly acquired knowledge, future generations—who will be the most affected by these developments—will not be consulted or free to refuse them. Technological developments move at such blinding speed nowadays (Kurzweil 1999) that the vast majority of people haven't the faintest idea of what they entail or portend for the future, and cannot engage in a lucid, rational, or democratic discussion about their potential uses and abuses. And for every successful experiment that gets reported by the scientific community and the world at large, there are probably several conducted in a clandestine manner to avoid public scrutiny. So to suggest, as Erikson did, that the goodwill and ingenuity of a "communicating species" can easily offset the potential pitfalls of galloping technological developments is to be a Pollyanna, at least at this point in our history.

So, we have entered an era when technological innovations may bring about an irrevocable rupture between sex and reproduction, and a corresponding decline in the kind of family solidarity Erikson deemed necessary to consolidating the development of conscience. So if we still hope to avert the worst, where do we draw the line? At present, those actively engaged in the debates around biotechnology all draw the line a little differently, depending on circumstances and their own personal convictions. But if Erikson were alive today, he would join geneticist Mae-Wan Ho in her call for a complete moratorium on experiments of this nature, and an end to the obscene practice of granting patents on new life forms—a policy that dates to the "conservative" Reagan era (Ho 2000). He would also agree with Fukuyama that tinkering with the human genome is taking things *much* too far. Why?

Like our animal cousins, we humans are the products of natural selection, which entails the gradual "selection" of adaptive traits wrought by random and spontaneous mutations, rather than individuals transmitting specific traits to their offspring through purposive interventions into our own genetic structure. The way *natural* selection works, we are not capable of transmitting personal choices or adaptations by genetic means, only by education or example—in short, by cultural means. What will happen to our culture and the harmonious unfolding of conscience if childhood is truncating and the human life span is extended indefinitely, if sex and reproduction are completely and irrevocably sundered and genetic material—human or otherwise—becomes a commodity that is alienable and manipulated at will, like other raw materials?

From an Eriksonian perspective, developments like these alter the nature and quality of the human life cycle and therefore threaten to upset a delicate balance that is built into the structure of the psyche, jeopardizing our collective mental health. Admittedly, once we've tinkered extensively with our own gene pool, the newer breeds of human being may be superior to us in strength, intelligence, or longevity. They may even be moral, in that they defer to authority and convention, if we are lucky. (If not, of course, we can drug them.) But from a genuinely ethical standpoint, successive generations of factory-bred humans will be utterly vacuous.

Another way of framing this problem, perhaps, is that the deliberate manipulation of the human genome promises to turn Lamarck's discredited theory of the inheritance of acquired characteristics into a palpable social reality. If we choose which traits we transmit—or refuse to transmit—to our offspring, we are irreversibly altering the biological basis of human reality and eroding our kinship with the rest of the animal kingdom. In view of what we now know about heritability of human traits, Sartre's vision of radical freedom and total responsibility for oneself was probably little more than a Scotch-inflected amphetamine dream. But the element of biologically based indeterminism and contingency that, until now, ruled over our individual births and gave us the freedom to make something of ourselves—within limits—will suddenly become subject to individual whim and caprice, obscure and irrational (racist and sexist) prejudices. Indeed, this process has already begun. Only yesterday, the tabloids screamed about a deaf lesbian couple who tried to ensure that their in vitro offspring was born deaf as well. Bizarre choices like these will increase steadily as these technologies proliferate, but they will not dominate the landscape. More "sensible" or fashionable ones will be the norm, for example, "Let's augment our family with a blond, blue-eyed boy—possibly from a surrogate, but preferably from a synthetic womb, if they are online next year."

Meanwhile, the argument that the burgeoning markets in human genetic material, stem cells, and the new techniques developed for their future use or exploitation will be used strictly to fight disease is blind to the possibilities for depravity and self-estrangement at work here. Why? Because since the dawn of recorded history, human societies have had (open or clandestine) markets in human flesh—flesh for rent and flesh for sale. Only now, if the transhumanists have their way, it will be "designer flesh," built to our prior specifications. And the market, as we know, is an inherently amoral mechanism. So in all likelihood, the newer, evolving forms of slavery and prostitution—scarcely imaginable at present and instigated in the name of curing disease and of choice, personal freedom, building better babies, and so on—are going to become so routine that they will be regulated by contract law, if only because they will be so lucrative. And so for that very reason, the newer forms of alienation that await our kind will be more subtle and pervasive than they are now, and inscribed, enforced, and legitimated by the powerful technocratic elites that own and manage the emerging means of reproduction.

To conclude, despite a debatable philosophical rationale, Fukuyama is quite right to call for more extensive and effective regulation of the biotech industry. I, for one, do not blame him. The sad fact of the matter is that the vast majority of human beings are presently too ill informed or too apathetic to join in a vigorous and meaningful debate on these issues. If Erikson were alive today, he would join Mae-Wan Ho and Francis Fukuyama in calling for the broadest possible moratorium on research into the modification of mitochondria, stem cells, cloning, and so on, until the next generation, whose future is at stake, has been thoroughly educated in the scientific dimensions and ethical ambiguities of these emerging technologies, and had a chance to reflect and to debate them at length, with a view to understanding how best to deploy them in the public interest rather than for the sake of a few greedy and power hungry corporations. Anything less would not be genuinely democratic.

Is this a callous trivialization of the agony and privation suffered by the many millions of people who have incurable diseases? Not at all. There are other effective ways to address these problems, including (but certainly not limited to) the provision of universal health care, genuinely safe hospitals, and cleaning up our toxic environment. Even if other efforts to conquer disease were unavailing in the short term, the fact remains that if Erikson's understanding of the intricate interplay of developmental processes is correct, the human species is now standing on a fateful, historic threshold, and the interests of those who are ill today have to be balanced against the mental health of future generations, whose humanity may be deeply, irrevocably compromised if we do not proceed with extreme caution.

As Bertrand Russell frequently observed, no amount of new scientific knowledge and technique can substitute for a pervasive lack of wisdom or the judgment to discern how best to use the knowledge we already have to promote the common good. Knowledge proliferates at blinding speed now, but if things unfold in their present pattern, wisdom will not survive (much less flourish) in the headlong competition among scientists and venture capitalists to get there first, patent the process, corner the market, and get their share of glory. Wisdom will drown in the relentless "spin" that mammoth multinationals put on these issues—unless people on all sides of the political spectrum organize and speak up.

Meanwhile analysts and other mental health professionals should start to debate whether, or to what extent, Erikson's epigenetic perspective is a valid way of understanding the biological bases of mental health, and what the future portends if we sever the primordial tie between sex and reproduction completely. We know that Erikson's developmental schema was far from perfect. All such schemas are flawed, finally, and therefore destined to be superseded by newer ones. But despite all of his errors, omissions, and in-consistencies; his occasionally maddening elusiveness, and so on, Erikson still has something vitally important to say to us—and hopefully, indeed, to future generations. Let us hope that our children's children still comprehend his message when we have all returned to dust.

The Historicity of Dreams—
Freud, Fliess, and Jung

THE CLASH OF INTERPRETATIONS

When Erikson started to write psychohistory in the 1950s, the history of psychoanalysis was still in its infancy. Ernest Jones's three-volume biography of Freud, the first volume of which appeared in 1953, was not complete until 1957, and from then until 1970 the history of psychoanalysis was a meager field dominated by the Freudian faithful, or those with some sectarian axe to grind. Fortunately, three memorable volumes—*The Discovery of the Unconscious* (Ellenberger 1970), *Freud and His Followers* (Roazen 1971), and *The Freud/Jung Letters* (McGuire 1974)—changed things irrevocably, exploding many myths and misconceptions and putting the development of analytic theory and practice into a whole new historical perspective. These books set a new standard for scholarly rigor, and since then we have been deluged with hitherto-unpublished letters, diaries, recently released archival material, and newly published testimony from the friends, family members, and patients of prominent pioneers in the history of the discipline. Though analysts are still active in this field of scholarship, the influx of seasoned historians, philosophers, and independent scholars now ensures that many old sectarian squabbles are being reappraised in light of a deeper, more diverse body of knowledge than the average analyst previously possessed.

In light of what follows, it is important to emphasize that most of Erikson's contributions to the history of psychoanalysis *preceded* the sea change that occurred in the 1970s, and are couched as psychohistorical reflections on Freud, Fliess, and Jung. As he examined their lives and relationships, Erikson was elucidating the processes of identity formation, the need for intimacy, and the crises of generativity that engendered their respective needs and conflicts, their startling creativity, and their impact on subsequent generations.

Many professional historians are wary of this approach because it presupposes a theory of mind and human development that it also seeks to prove. My view is that reading the history of psychoanalysis through psychohistorical lenses brings important ideas and information to light or, in some instances, renders existing information more readily intelligible. In others, Erikson's protective stance toward Freud, and his reluctance or inability to follow through consistently and take his fertile ideas and observations to their logical conclusion, diminished both the accuracy and importance of Erikson's reflections. This trend is particularly evident in Erikson's use of Freud's dreams as "data"—something most scholars in this field tend to avoid. Dream interpretation is legitimate in the clinical arena, but using it for purposes of historical research is risky, because one and the same dream can be subject to disparate interpretations depending on how the interpreter situates himself in relation to Freud and his theories. Fortunately, patient reflection on the clash of interpretations concerning Freud's dreams yields robust and often unexpected dividends, becoming a new source of historical insight in its own right. That being so, as this chapter unfolds we will be commenting on commentaries about Freud's commentaries on his own dreams—a kind of meta-meta-commentary—so readers who are anxious to follow the thread of argument closely are strongly advised to read the primary sources first, these being Freud's *The Interpretation of Dreams* (1900), Freud's letters to Wilhelm Fliess (Masson 1986), and the complete correspondence between Freud and C. G. Jung (McGuire, 1974).

FREUD, FRIENDSHIP, AND THE FEAR OF DEATH

Erikson never wrote a full-length psychobiography of Freud, so his ideas have to be inferred from a variety of sources. The composite portrait that emerges is quite instructive, and there is no need to track down every fugitive reference to Freud in Erikson's work to discern its main outlines effectively. Though scattered, the material is abundant, and sometimes little fragments speak volumes. For example, the passage in "The Nature of Clinical Evidence," cited in chapter 1, in which Erikson exempts Freud from the lamentable tendency to reify his theoretical constructs that he observes in Freud's followers. He said:

> Freud was sovereignly aware of this danger, but was always willing to learn by
> giving a mode of thought free reign to see to what useful model it might lead.

He also had the courage, the authority, and the inner consistency to reverse such a direction when it became useless. Generations of clinical practitioners cannot be expected to be equally detached or authoritative. (1998, 271)

Let us grant that Freud's theoretical constructions often had the tentative, playful quality Erikson describes, and that he regarded them primarily as heuristic devices rather than ontological truths. Even so, the first thing that strikes one on rereading this passage is the phrase "sovereignly aware." Evidently it was not enough to state that Freud was aware of the danger of reification. Erikson had to imply, albeit obliquely, that if Freud reversed course or dropped a particular line of inquiry, he was entitled to behave with impunity because he was imbued with an aura of majesty, like a king or head of state.

This ambiguous turn of phrase may have endeared Erikson to Freud's worshipful admirers, but it alerts us to the idealizing attitude that both permits and obliges him to overlook Freud's tendency to reckless speculation by treating the latter as mere playful curiosity leavened with judicious detachment. And though Erikson neglects to say so here, if subsequent analysts lacked Freud's "detachment" and "authority"—the attributes of "sovereign awareness"—this is partly because Freud seldom granted his subjects the right to treat his ideas in the same tentative, playful spirit. And if he did, on occasion, his approval was quickly revoked if he did not like the direction in which their conjectures were going (e.g., Tausk, Rank, Ferenczi).

Apart from "detachment" and "authority," the chief characteristic of sovereignty is power or potency, and in this regard, thankfully, Erikson was more balanced and realistic. For example, Erikson points out that Freud's prodigious epistolary outpourings (to Fliess and Jung alike) were conducted in a cultural climate that no longer exists, and we should not judge the volume, content, or the style of his letters according to contemporary conventions. Nevertheless, Erikson also conceded that Freud's letter writing was somewhat unusual and often motivated by an acute and sometimes demanding *neediness* that is quite contrary to the image conveyed by the phrase "sovereign awareness." As Erikson points out, at one point in their correspondence, Freud apologized for burdening Fliess with his "death deliria," his feverish premonitions of a premature death—which even Freud thought extravagant, judging from his choice of words. Moreover, Freud fainted twice in Jung's presence—(in Bremen in 1909, and in Munich in 1912)—as his hopes for a smooth succession were dashed. And again, as Erikson observes, in German the term *Ohnmacht*—with which these fainting episodes were designated by both parties in their correspondence—means "to faint," or, alternatively, a state of "powerlessness" or "impotence," suggesting the existence of feelings of helplessness in Freud that render any notion of "sovereignty" on his part faintly ludicrous (Erikson 1980).

While a morbid fear of death could perhaps stem from other sources, Erikson's characterization of Freud during his friendship with Fliess is congruent with his reflections on other men of this "type," including Luther, Kierkegaard, Darwin, James, Shaw, and Gandhi. Taken together, these portraits make an impressive case for the existence of a developmental anomaly in highly creative but conflicted men, in whom the need to prolong youth in order to find their true "voice" combines with a certain precocity that complicates their psychological profiles enormously. In a manner of speaking, they are somewhat immature and yet vastly ahead of their time.

In any case, the fact is that in his relationships with his two closest male friends, Fliess and Jung, Freud was often powerless to govern his fears or feelings, or to avert the disastrous, demoralizing, and completely irrevocable rupture that occurred between them. Why? According to Erikson, Freud's deep and unresolved fear of a premature death strongly colored both relationships. And the fear of a premature death, by his reckoning, is a developmental anomaly common among creative men whose adolescent identity crisis is deeper and more prolonged than usual. A prolonged or intensified adolescent crisis, said Erikson, delays someone's ability to grapple with the issues of *intimacy versus isolation* that ideally characterize young adulthood. And sure enough, when his correspondence with Fliess began, Freud was in his early thirties and had just married after a long and turbulent courtship. Moreover, Erikson adds, in addition to a prolonged adolescence, Freud was suffering from a premature crisis of *generativity*. In short, though not yet middle-aged, Freud acted as if he were, becoming deeply preoccupied with his legacy and gift to posterity, and mourning the fact that he would not be recognized in his own lifetime.

And what of Freud and Jung, specifically? Given his friendship with Joseph Wheelwright in San Francisco, Erikson might be expected to treat Jung with more respect than most analysts of his generation, and make Freud shoulder some of the blame for their deep and wrenching mutual disenchantment. And indeed, he did. In "Themes of Adulthood in the Freud/Jung Correspondence" (1980), Erikson suggested that when his correspondence with Jung commenced in 1906, Freud was experiencing an age-appropriate generativity crisis—though significantly, Jung was now the same age that Freud was when he began writing to Fliess. Moreover, Freud *still* suffered from the fear of an early death, and used Jung inappropriately to overcome it. Indeed, Erikson even said that Freud was in the grips of a "Laius complex," which parallels the Oedipus complex. As proof, he cites the fact that he often referred to Jung as his "Joshua"—an oblique reminder of Freud's early and intense identification with Moses, who died before he reached the Promised Land (Yershalmi 1991). At first Jung was flattered, and colluded enthusiastically with Freud's dynastic ambitions, adopting a filial mode of address. But his ultimate refusal to shoulder the burden of succession hurt Freud deeply. Once the sympathy engendered by their initial misalliance was completely shattered, and their irreconcilable differences were clearly and articulately expressed, Jung ceased being filial toward Freud, and in the end, said Erikson, turned the tables, addressing Freud as if *he* were a child.

Since Erikson published his reflections on Freud's correspondence in 1980, much new material has become public. Aldo Carotenuto's *A Secret Symmetry*, published in 1982, disclosed the existence of romantic intrigues between Jung and Sabina Spielrein, a former patient of his who later trained as a Freudian analyst (Carotenuto 1982). Then, in 1986, Jeffrey Masson published *The Complete Letters of Sigmund Freud to Wilhelm Fliess* (Masson 1986). These books unleashed a whole new phase of Freud scholarship, which Erikson was now too old to assimilate or respond to. In fairness to Erikson, when he first wrote about Freud and Fliess (Erikson 1954) a full, annotated edition of Freud's letters to Fliess did not yet exist. The expurgated version edited by Marie Bonaparte, Anna Freud, and Ernst Kris, published in 1954, was all he had to work with.

But even if we take this fact into account and acknowledge the ways in which he was insightful about Freud's behavior, there were aspects of the Freud/Fliess relationship that eluded Erikson, or that he simply preferred to ignore (in print, at least). As Erikson knew very well, for example, after a lengthy and turbulent courtship Freud was deeply disappointed with marriage, and, more specifically, with his wife, Martha. Freud had hoped to engage her interest in his evolving theories, but she was actually quite appalled by his ideas, forcing Freud to turn to Fliess and his sister-in-law Minna for a sympathetic audience. So though Erikson was too tactful to say so bluntly, Freud's prompt disillusionment with marriage contributed mightily to his oft-stated longing for "intimacy" with a male coworker and his breathless anticipation of his yearly "congresses" with Fliess.

Apart from a clamoring desire for intimacy fuelled by marital discord, another factor that deepened Freud's isolation and eventual estrangement from Fliess was a measure of dishonesty and self-deception that Erikson never addressed. This trait is evidenced, among other things, in many dreams and textual references to Fliess in *The Interpretation of Dreams* (Freud 1900). But in order to get them all into proper perspective, we must first review some basic facts about Freudian dream interpretation and Erikson's revisionist approach.

MEN, WOMEN, AND PROFESSIONAL IDENTITY

Whether as a therapist or as a psychohistorian, Erikson always approached dreams as historical artifacts. In so doing, of course, he was following Freud, for whom dream interpretation invariably has a retrospective or "archeological" cast. In *The Interpretation of Dreams*, Freud stipulated that the "manifest dream" (or dream narrative) uses recent experiences and current conflicts, called *day residues*, as a screen or disguise for the "latent dream thoughts," which, when finally brought to light, attest to unresolved infantile wishes and conflicts that are strikingly at variance with the dreamer's conscious attitudes, desires, and ethical standards. While it frequently refers to people and situations in the dreamer's current life, the process of dream production—the "dream work," as Freud called it—supposedly disguises timeless, "prehistoric" impulses, and the residues of infantile wishes with images of people or external events that serve primarily as props to represent and/or disguise our unremembered past (Freud 1900).

In addition to the standard "archeological" decoding apparatus stipulated by Freud, Erikson's approach to dream interpretation had a strong *prospective* dimension, as we shall see. The past, while omnipresent, is not privileged, not deemed "deeper," more "authentic," or even more "repressed" than the present, nor does it determine—much less "overdetermine"—our future in any straightforwardly deterministic way. Remember that for Erikson, the main function of ego identity is to furnish a bridge between past, present, and future, lending coherence to human experience. And ego identity is not passively accepted, but actively forged through choice and decision.

The first installment in Erikson's commentary on the Freud/Fliess relationship is "On the Dream Specimen of Psychoanalysis" (1954), in which Erikson reanalyzed "the dream of Irma's injection"—or, more simply, "the Irma dream." He began by echoing Freud's own conviction that this, the first dream to be "exhaustively analyzed," should be commemorated as "an historic document," as well as studied by all students in the field. However, as Adolf Grünbaum very cogently points out, Freud's associations to the Irma dream fail to furnish the infantile determinants that presumably engender the latent dream thoughts. Considering the fact that this is deemed to be *the* dream specimen for aspiring analysts to study and emulate, says Grünbaum, this is a stark and disturbing omission (Grünbaum 1984).

Furthermore, notes Grünbaum, this odd state of affairs obligated Erikson to *manufacture* some infantile determinants by interpreting some remarks of Freud's in light of associations culled from a *different* dream specimen, and then patching them together with some of Erikson's own associations. Though Grünbaum does not say so in quite so many words, it is clear enough from context that giving a dream interpreter license to interpret one dream in light of associations culled from another one, which are then interspersed with the interpreter's own associations, encourages of all kinds of specious and arbitrary inferences and makes a mockery of methodological rigor (Grünbaum 1984, chap. 5).

While all of this is true, however, Grünbaum is nonetheless profoundly mistaken in his insistence that Erikson's interpretation is an "orthodox" one, and that Erikson himself was an "orthodox" analyst. For while invoking "urethral eroticism" and an early childhood memory of Freud's as background determinants of the Irma dream, Erikson's gloss on "the specimen dream" still puts Freud's present-day professional preoccupations on center stage. This aspect of his paper—in which Freud's relationship to the analytic vocation is problematized through a strange interlude with an alternately resistant and compliant patient—is not at all orthodox, and has considerable merit, notwithstanding this paper's muddled beginning.

To render this discussion more concrete, recall that in Freud's dream he was in a great hall receiving guests with Martha when his patient Irma appeared, looking gravely ill. Freud took Irma aside and quietly reproached her for not accepting his "solution"—presumably, his interpretation of the meaning of her complaints. Nevertheless, Freud was so disturbed by Irma's physical appearance that he feared he had overlooked some organic condition. To rule out this possibility, he checked her throat, found several anomalies, and called Dr. Leopold, Dr. M., and Dr. O. ("Otto," i.e., Fliess) to examine her chest and shoulders as well. Dr. M. confirmed that there was something organically wrong with her but offered an idiotic diagnosis, and Freud concluded by saying that Irma's infection was due to an injection from Dr. O., who used what is usually translated as "unclean syringe."

Ever on the alert for linguistic ambiguity, Erikson noted that an unclean syringe—or *Spritze*, in German—also means "dirty little squirter," which, in German as well as English, is an unmistakable phallic metaphor. Erikson also noted Freud's fear that he might be held accountable for Irma's sudden decline and reckoned a "dirty little squirter" in Otto's place. That seems clear from context. But now things get really interesting, for in addition to identifying with the community of (male) doctors, Freud identifies somewhat with his (female) patient, who has been violated in some fashion. Commenting on "Dr. Leopold's" examination of Irma, Erikson says:

> At this point something happened which is lost in the double meaning of the manifest words, in the German original as well as the translation. When the dreamer says that he can "feel" the infiltrated portion of skin on the (patient's) left shoulder, he means to convey (as Freud states in his associations) that he can

feel it on his own body: one of those fusions of a dreamer with a member of his dream population which is always of central importance, if not the very center and nodal point of the dream. The dreamer, while becoming again a doctor in the consenting community of doctors, thus at the same time turns into his and their patient. (Wallerstein and Goldberger, 1998, 149)

So by Erikson's reckoning, Freud "becomes his own patient" by laying himself open to examination by the scientific community. Indeed, on this reading, the peremptory medical examination Freud and his colleagues conduct on Irma presages his imminent self-analysis and the "birth" of a whole new discipline through dream interpretation. In his own words: "The Irma dream . . . anticipates Freud's self-inspection and with it the inspection of a vastly aggrandized Fliess. We must try to visualize the historical fact that here a man divines an entirely new instrument with unknown qualities for an entirely new focus of investigation" (163).

Did Freud's Irma dream actually anticipate his self-analysis, as Erikson claimed, or was it contemporaneous with it? That is a matter for specialists to resolve. Either way, however, if Erikson's is right, current conflicts and concerns, issues of identity and concern for the future, evoked Freud's dream imagery far more than any infantile determinants that happened to get dredged up along the way. Though scarcely orthodox, in view of what we know now, this is *not* a far-fetched interpretation. Moreover, it vindicates Erikson's contention that dreams are often field reports or oblique commentaries about an ongoing *identity in the making* (Erikson 1998). Many more dreams of this type could be furnished to buttress this contention.

But while Erikson was busy expanding on this important theme, he neglected to note that Freud's brief moment of "fusion" with his patient, that is, his ability to feel *her* injury on his own body, which Freud himself calls attention to, suggests that he also felt "violated" by Fliess in some fashion. If we bracket the dream and turn to actual historical events, we now know that Freud underwent precisely the same nasal operation as Irma—whose real name was Emma Eckstein. Fliess himself had recommended this procedure as a way to curb her vigorous masturbation and claimed that it had other salutary effects that would benefit Freud (Sulloway 1991). However, as fate would have it, when Fliess performed this procedure on Eckstein, he inadvertently left some surgical gauze embedded in her nasal tissues, which promptly became infected, causing a series of near-fatal hemorrhages. The resulting postoperative infections (and subsequent surgical procedures to correct them) nearly killed her and left her permanently disfigured.

In fairness to Erikson, remember that it was not until Max Schur published "Some Additional 'Day Residues' of 'The Specimen Dream of

Psychoanalysis'"—a decade after he wrote "The Dream Specimen of Psychoanalysis"—that the whole sordid story was made public (Schur 1966). And it was not until 1985, when the unexpurgated letters of Freud to Fliess were finally published, that we knew of Freud's initial response to his patient's prolonged postsurgical ordeal, which was to blame the victim for her own suffering and to express unshakable trust in the competence of his male friend and colleague (Masson 1985). Surely, said Freud in his letters to Fliess, Eckstein's hysterical *malice* was responsible for this dreadful turn of events, and/or her inability to recover promptly from the ill effects of Fliess's surgical blunder.

Erikson was not aware of it, perhaps, but Freud's characterization of poor Emma Eckstein here was so vile, and his feverish assurances to Fliess so perverse and irrational under the circumstances, that they are scarcely believable today. But they shed a great deal of light on the Irma dream. Why? If Erikson was right, and Freud's ability to "feel" the effects of Fliess's "dirty little squirter" *on his own body* is in fact the nodal point of the dream, then it is safe to conclude that Freud's epistolary condemnations of poor Emma Eckstein— which provided his detractor Jeffrey Masson with such potent ammunition— were really deeply defensive in character and, in a certain sense, thoroughly insincere. Though he was repressing it to the best of his ability, if this dream is any indication, Freud was much more identified with his patient's perspective than he was *consciously* aware of, or than his perfectly bizarre letters to Fliess would suggest. Either that, or Freud really was the base hypocrite and flaming misogynist that Masson, editor of the Freud/Fliess letters, made him out to be (Masson 1985). At the very least, one would have to conclude that if he *really* meant what he said about Eckstein to Fliess, his unconscious furnished him with what Jung called a *compensatory dream*, or one that depicts our current situation and conflicts in a more genuine and realistic light than our conscious, waking ego is willing or able to acknowledge.

Another interesting angle that Erikson neglected to exploit is that Freud claimed that the motive for the Irma dream was a childish wish for *revenge* against Fliess. On closer inspection, however, the dream really augurs the breakdown of *basic trust*. Freud had been far too gullible and trusting, and was on the verge of repenting his credulous faith in Fliess's insight and ability. Oddly enough, Erikson's remarks merely *hint* at this issue obliquely. But clearly, in the wake of the Eckstein episode, some searching self-analysis was in order!

Erikson's second reinterpretation of Freud's dreams, entitled "Psychological Reality and Historical Actuality" (1964d) was similar to "On the Dream Specimen of Psychoanalysis" (1954). Once again, Erikson deployed a hermeneutic strategy that includes but transcends the reductive, past-centered "archeological" approach of Freud. Present-day professional preoccupations are intricately intertwined with infantile motifs, though in Erikson's view the latter are not privileged as the true source or meaning of the dream narrative. And all this is quite plausible, to be sure. But before addressing this issue, let us review the dream itself. In *The Interpretation of Dreams*, Freud said:

> I went into the kitchen in search of some pudding. Three women were standing in it; one of them was hostess of the inn and twisting something about in her hand, as though she was making Knödel (dumplings). She answered that I must wait till she was ready. (These were not definite words spoken). I felt impatient and went off with a sense of injury. I put on an overcoat. But the first I tried on was too long for me. I took it off, rather surprised to find it was trimmed with fur. A second one that I put on had a long stripe with a Turkish design set into it. A stranger with a long face and a short, pointed beard came up and tried to prevent my putting it on, saying that it was his. I showed him then that it was embroidered all over with a Turkish pattern. He asked: "What have Turkish (designs, stripes . . .) to do with you?" But then we became quite friendly with each other. (1900, 295–96)

Before we explore Erikson's interpretation of this dream, it is vital to note that Erich Fromm tackled it first in *Sigmund Freud's Mission: An Analysis of His Personality and Influence*, written in 1959. In chapter 2, entitled "His Relationship to His Mother: Self Confidence and Insecurity," Fromm wrote:

> In this dream we recognize the wish to be fed by Mother. (That the "hostess," or perhaps all three women, represent Mother becomes quite clear from Freud's associations to the dream.) The specific element in the dream is the impatience of the dreamer. When he was told that he must wait till she was ready, he went off "with a sense of injury." And what does he do then? He puts on a fur trimmed coat which is too long for him—then another one which belongs to somebody else. We see in this dream the typical reaction of the mother-favored boy; he insists on being fed by Mother ("feeding" to be understood symbolically as "being cared for, loved, protected, admired, etc."). He is impatient and furious if he is not "fed" immediately, since he feels he has a right to immediate and complete attention. In his anger her walks out and usurps the role of the big man-father (symbolized by the coat which is too long and belongs to a stranger). (11–12)

Fromm remarked that this dream attests to the truth of Ernest Jones's claim that Freud had "extremely strong motives for concealing some important phase of his development—perhaps even from himself. I would venture to surmise it was his deep love for his mother" (cited in Fromm 1959, 12). Though severely critical of Jones, for the most part, Fromm endorsed this interpretation and Jones's corollary assertion that Freud's remarkable self-confidence was rooted in his sense of being his mother's pride and joy in infancy and early childhood. However, something went awry, said Fromm, because Freud's enduring fears of starvation, of poverty, and of travel, which he frequently confided to Fliess, for example, attest to lingering maternal fixation as well.

Much of *Sigmund Freud's Mission* buttressed Fromm's unflattering characterization of Freud as a middle-aged mama's boy. For example, in chapter 3, entitled "His Relationship to Women: Love," Fromm construed Freud's avowed loss of interest in sex after forty as a sign of a weak and inhibited libido, which he explained, in good orthodox fashion, by an overabundance of fixated oral libido. And in chapter 4, "His Dependence on Men," Fromm said that Freud's vaulting intellectual ambition and repeated emotional and intellectual reliance on male friends represented so many reaction formations against underlying wishes for dependency, and the shame and self-loathing prompted by the intensity of these wishes for maternal comfort and support. To support this interpretation, Fromm noted that Freud's associations to the Dream of the Three Fates led him to recall the great happiness he enjoyed as a student of neurology under Ernst Brucke, and to cite Goethe's *Faust*, part 1, where Mephistopheles tempts Faust by saying, "Thus, at the breasts of Wisdom clinging; Thou'lt find each day a greater rapture bringing."

According to Fromm, Freud turned to the pursuit of scientific knowledge as a way of *escaping from women*, and from his deeply repressed fears of dependence and disappointment. In due course, however, as he became more successful, these unresolved issues plagued his professional life, because Fliess, Joseph Breuer, and Jung were unsuitable mother substitutes, and because the demanding character of Freud's unconscious oral strivings rendered mutual ambivalence and misunderstanding between them all inevitable in the long run. According to Fromm, Freud's unresolved oral dependency did not merely interfere with his personal life. It warped his judgment as well. Summing up in *Sigmund Freud's Mission*, Fromm remarked:

[C]onsidering the intensity of his own attachment to his own mother, and the fact that he tended to repress it, it is understandable that he interpreted one of the most powerful strivings in man, the craving for the care, protection, all enveloping love and affirmation of Mother, as the more limited wish of the little boy to satisfy his instinctual needs through mother. He discovered one of the most fundamental strivings in man, the wish to remain attached to mother, and that is to the womb, to nature, to pre-individualistic, pre-conscious existence — and at the same time negated this discovery by restricting it to the small sector of instinctual desires. His own attachment to Mother was the basis of his discovery and his resistance to seeing his attachment was the basis for the limitation and distortion of this very discovery. (1959, 15)

To grasp what Erikson's agenda was, it is important to remember that his interpretation of the Dream of the Three Fates first appeared two years after *Sigmund Freud's Mission*. Erikson had read Fromm's book, no doubt, and couched his interpretation as an oblique corrective to (or dismissal of) Fromm's less reverent and traditional approach. Though Erikson did not mention Fromm by name here, in reality he was scolding Fromm for his roguish impertinence—a move designed to soothe his own conscience and to placate his more orthodox colleagues. Reading these two interpretations side by side, it is apparent that Fromm tried to identify Freud's psychopathology, using his own techniques and ideas against him, as it were, while Erikson disclaimed any intention of indulging in "the sport of newly interpreting what might be presumed to have been unconscious to Freud himself" (1964d, 178). Instead, he used Freud's dream to illustrate the way in which midlife crises and the exigencies of bodily need can briefly rekindle the conflicts of infancy, and the accompanying symbols and conflicts relating to food, mouth, and skin, the issue of basic trust versus mistrust, the first vital virtue of hope, and the sense of cosmic order.

So, to summarize this curious juxtaposition of perspectives, Fromm, the forthright revisionist and member of Freud's loyal opposition, said that though Freud was a genius and possessed of remarkable courage in some ways, he lacked insight into his own difficulties—and then used Freud's psychosexual schemata to justify this position. Erikson, the crypto-revisionist, defended a more orthodox and more flattering view of Freud as a vibrantly healthy specimen, while harvesting Freud's dreams and associations for corroborating testimony to support his *own* theory of psychosocial development, which constitutes a significant departure from Freud's. As a result, Erikson's interpretation of the dream's first segment was more sympathetic and thorough than Fromm's. Fromm ignored the dream's "day residues," or the actual circumstances of the dreamer on the day preceding the dream in question. This enabled him to declare bluntly that Freud's oneiric search for food represented a deep-seated fear of starvation and neglect, while Erikson quite rightly reminded us that on that particular night Freud went to bed without his supper, after a long and tiring journey. Moreover, Erikson insisted that "an orality aroused by actual and acute alimentary disappointment is different from the orality of a pathologically regressed dreamer to whom all the frustrations of the day turn into insults on the oral level" (1964d, 179).

Having specified the conditions of acute oral frustration that elicited the dream, however, Erikson nevertheless conceded that the tone of the first part of the dream is one of "demanding receptivity." Moreover, he pointed out that Freud's unyielding hostess is denoted by the German word *Wirtin*, which connotes a "food-and-drink dispensing, all maternal and yet on occasion romantic woman." She offers to feed Freud eventually, provided he can tolerate a delay. And whereas Fromm construed Freud's sense of injury as characteristic of an overindulged mama's boy, Erikson insisted it betokened an attitude of "basic mistrust" provoked by a transient crisis of orality kindled by the day's events, as evidenced by Freud's free associations, which touched on the manifold expressions of "oral" psychopathology, namely, *delusion, addiction, and depression.*

In the course of reviewing Freud's free associations, Erikson also dwelt perceptively on an episode that occurred when Freud was six. As Freud recalled in connection with his frustrating *Wirtin*, his mother once attempted to prove the truth of the biblical account of creation by rubbing her hands together, "just as she did when making dumplings," and showing the astonished boy the "dirt" created by the resulting friction. She then admonished little Sigmund that this "proved" that we are made from the earth. Evidently, this demonstration created a deep and lasting impression on the young lad, and Freud attempted to capture the astonishment and dismay he felt then by citing Shakespeare: "thou owest nature a death." In fact, said Erikson, the quote *should* read "thou owest God a death," and by substituting nature, a maternal figure, for God, a paternal one, Freud was unconsciously confirming the primacy of the maternal imago at this first stage of life's journey—according to Erikson, anyway.

In the second part of the dream, notes Erikson, maternal symbols vanish, and Freud engages a solitary male figure. Conflicts with a man, presumably a father figure, now displace conflicts with women as the dream's central drama. But curiously, notes Erikson, the men Freud recalls in connection with his bearded accuser all have names associated with food—such as *Knödel* (dumplings) and *Fleischl* (meat). And when his associations form a bridge (*Brucke*) to the Institute of Physiology, he recalls how happy he was there, and recalls Mephistopheles' attempts to entice Faust with the rapture he will experience while "clinging to the breasts of Wisdom," that is, devoting himself exclusively to plumbing the secrets of nature.

So despite dwelling thoughtfully on day residues and putting a brave face on things generally, in some ways Erikson's observations about the dream's first part actually *corroborate* Fromm's contention that Freud harbored unresolved oral issues. After all, Freud's relationship to the bearded paternal figure—if that is what he is—are inextricably intertwined with references to meat and dumplings, "clinging to the breasts of nature," and the like: all maternal signifiers, all pointing backward, as it were, to the dream's first segment, implying that conflicts with the *Wirtin* were deferred or displaced, not genuinely transcended. But this was *not* how Erikson read the dream. Instead, he claimed that Freud's dream was a kind of cautionary tale about the dangers of dependency and distrust and the virtues of more autonomous modes of relatedness. In his own words:

> [T]he dreamer's associations warn of incautious intake and, in fact, addiction. As so often in Freud's dreams, he remembers cocaine, which he once helped introduce into local anesthesia, before its addictive qualities were known. But one thing was known: "cocaine takes hunger away." It is, of course, the very function of basic mistrust, which orality also bestows on every human being, to prevent the all too trustful incorporation of bad substances. But the danger of too much mistrust is the inhibition of the wish to take. Thus, the dreamer feels that *the dream warns him to take what one can even if it involves doing a small wrong*. The second part of the dream, then, emphasizes, the turn from dependence to self-help, from women to men, from perishable substances to eternal substances, and ends with a friendly affiliation with a man with a pointed beard—a paternal teacher figure.
>
> In summary, a hungry sleeper—and we should add, one who loves good food—abandons himself to the frustrations of the earliest stage of life when hunger was first experienced, and to the anger over unreliable women and whatever is too perishable, too dangerous or too mortal to be relied upon. It should be pointed out again that this is not an "oral" dream in a regressed, dependent, hopeless or foolishly hopeful sense. It successfully graduates from orality to turn resolutely away from the mother and to transfer all trust to more autonomous situations . . . the dreamer returns to his earliest dealings with (and subsequent reiterations of) one of life's major themes, and he thinks himself forward again, through a number of stages, convincing himself that each mournful loss and each frightening graduation brings with it an increased autonomy and an enhanced ability to find in adult actuality the resources of competence and tradition. (1964d, 184; emphasis added)

So, far from expressing abiding character traits, Erikson claimed that the Dream of the Three Fates reflected a *temporary* regression provoked by the exigencies of travel, which are promptly reversed in a more autonomous, father-centered direction in the dream's second phase. Which of these interpretations is true—or, at any rate, nearer the truth? At this point, any judgment is premature. The dream itself is still somewhat opaque, and further interpretation will demonstrate that neither Fromm's nor Erikson's interpretation is entirely correct—or without merit, either.

Meanwhile, we have demonstrated that dream interpretations never occur in a vacuum. An interpreter is not a neutral observer. Fromm interpreted Freud's dream as evidence of latent psychopathology to justify his evolving critique of Freud's theory and technique, while Erikson found such interpretive efforts distasteful and misguided. But Erikson attempted to extract a thread of coherence from Freud's dreams to justify his own theory of development, albeit at the expense of idealizing Freud. The biographical roots of his tendency to idealize Freud are clearly hinted when he suggests that the second part of the dream suggests an "investiture theme." In his own words: "[T]he dreamer turns from the women who have disappointed him to a man with whom he becomes quite friendly. The associations, as we will see, picture father figures who gave young Freud more substantial hope primarily by taking the intelligent boy into their community of learning" (1964d, 182).

Well, up to a point, perhaps. But if you pause to reflect for a moment, Erikson is probably reconstructing Freud's past by analogy with his own. For unlike Erikson, who was a dutiful and deferential student, Freud's relations with his various *Doktor-Vaters* were mostly quite ambivalent. Besides, it is a single man, not a community of scholars, that Freud actually turns to in his slumber, and in making one man represent the whole medical profession on Freud's behalf, Erikson is indulging in a blatant conjecture. And contrary to the attitude that Erikson attributes to him, that man does not seem particularly *welcoming*. Instead, he accuses Freud of appropriating something that is not rightfully his.

Finally, though he noted the prevalence of maternal signifiers quite clearly, Erikson's interpretation completely disregards an important theme that crops up repeatedly in Freud's associations to the dream, namely the subject of plagiarism. For the name *Knödel*, which prompts Freud's association to dumplings, is also reminiscent of a certain Herr Knodl, whom one of his teachers at the Institute of Physiology was going to sue for plagiarism. On closer inspection, this associative material renders Erikson's investiture interpretation somewhat tenuous, at best. The real issue between Freud and his antagonist is the theft of intellectual property, not one of induction into a scientific society, as we shall see presently.

RIVALRY, PLAGIARISM, AND OEDIPAL EVASIVENESS

To get this issue into perspective, let us backtrack a little more. As Ernest Jones pointed out, in the summer of 1900, during a congress at Achensee, Freud and Fliess got entangled in what soon became a bitter priority dispute over the theory of bisexuality. Fliess had related his theory of bisexuality to Freud in their Breslau congress three years earlier, and yet on this more recent occasion Freud discussed the same theory of bisexuality—with minor modifications—as if it were entirely his own. Fliess was alarmed and offended, and it took Freud an entire week to recall their Breslau talks and to apologize for his tactless bout of amnesia.

Meanwhile, judging from his letters, Freud felt that Fliess's angry out-
burst at Achensee and subsequent reproaches on this score were entirely
overwrought. But were they really? For the moment, let us ignore the partisan portrayals that still circulate in analytic circles, which depict Fliess as
paranoid and attribute his angry accusations to repressed homosexual desire. For now, simply note that there are numerous references to Fliess and
to bisexuality in *The Interpretation of Dreams*, and that *not a single one of
them actually acknowledges Fliess as the originator of that theory*, which
Freud had already woven deeply into the fabric of his book. Indeed, in
chapter 6, section C, Freud reports a dream in which he personally deliv-
ers a recently completed book on bisexuality to his friend Fliess (Freud,
1900, 445). To someone unaware of the historical background, or the vast
majority of his readers, Freud's report of *this dream gives the distinct impression that he gave Fliess the idea about bisexuality and neuroses,
rather than the other way around*. These oversights are too cunning to be
purely accidental.

Indeed, though they broached the subject in private as early as 1897, it was
not until *The Psychopathology of Everyday Life*, published in 1901, that
Freud actually acknowledged Fliess's priority on the theory of bisexuality in
print (Masson 1986, 460). Having done the right thing, finally, Freud then had
the audacity to propose in a letter dated September 19, 1901, that Fliess and
he should *coauthor* a book on bisexuality. Not surprisingly, Fliess declined,
and their correspondence ground to a halt in 1902, only to resume two years
later when Freud invited Fliess to contribute something to a new journal on
sexology that some younger associates of his were trying to establish. Fliess
demurred after talking with their mutual friend Oscar Rie, who told Fliess that
a former patient of Freud's named Hermann Swoboda had transmitted the
substance of some unpublished ideas of Fliess's on left-handedness and fem-
ininity in males to Otto Weininger, who then published them in a book entitled *Sex and Character* (1903). Weininger's book, which caused a huge sen-
sation, dwelt at great length on the theory of bisexuality without citing either
Freud or Fliess as sources. Indeed, though he credited Swoboda somewhat,
Weininger had the audacity to claim that the theory of bisexuality was actually his own (Kerr 1993).

Fliess was enraged by this turn of events, and blamed Freud, since it was
an indiscreet conversation that Freud had with Swoboda (some time previously) that facilitated this blatant misappropriation of his ideas. For his part,
Freud was quite embarrassed by and angry at Swoboda, but pleaded innocent
to the end. In his final letter to Fliess, dated July 27, 1904, he said: "Throughout my life I have scattered suggestions freely without asking what will come
of them. I can without feeling diminished admit that I have learned this or that

from others. But I have never appropriated something belonging to others as my own (Masson 1985, 467).

So, if we take these contextual and background items into account, the bearded accuser in Freud's Dream of the Three Fates can be none other than Wilhelm Fliess. Just track the various associative networks, and the places where they converge and overlap. The dream's references to dumplings, or *Knödel*, remind Freud of one of his university teachers who, as Freud recalled, associated the name Knodl with a person whom he litigated for plagiarizing his ideas. And Freud's recollection of his teacher's rage was preceded by an association to Pelagie, one of three women who drove a character in a novel he recently read to madness. Moreover, in a very telling gesture, Freud himself noted the phonemic resemblance between the name Pelagie and the word *plagiarism* in *The Interpretation of Dreams*. Summarizing the nodal points of his associative digressions midway through his analysis of this dream, Freud also juxtaposed the theme of madness—and, by implication, Pelagie—with a drug that stills hunger, namely, cocaine. Indirectly, this implicates Fliess as well. Though Erikson was not aware of it at the time, evidently, Freud had been using cocaine off and on since 1882, and as late as June 12, 1895, confided to Fliess that he "needs a lot of cocaine" to keep his spirits up, and his professional work on track (Masson 1985, 132). Indeed, it wasn't until October 26, 1896, approximately fourteen years after he started using it, that Freud reported in a letter that the cocaine brush "has been completely put aside" (201). So Erikson's normalizing agenda notwithstanding, the dreams' oblique references to the theme of addiction probably address Freud's *current* conflicts, and not merely the temporary evocation of infantile ones due to a transient arousal of genuine hunger pangs.

So, to sum up, neither Fromm nor Erikson discerned that the Dream of the Three Fates, like the Irma dream, is principally about Freud's relationship with Wilhelm Fliess. To dispel any lingering doubts on this score, consider Freud's free associations. The face of Freud's bearded accuser reminded him of a shopkeeper named Popovic, who introduced himself with some embarrassment, because his Slavic name alludes to the German word for "bottom," and, by implication, to the bodily location of the excremental functions. Freud's associations then led him to reflect on the many times his own name was used in punning references to sexual functions, and this was followed by the recollection of a questionable witticism of Herder's, to the effect that Goethe's unusual name indicated his descent from God (*Gott*), or perhaps the Goths, or perhaps from mere dirt or excrement (*vom kote*).

In other words, associations to the memory of the merchant Popovic brought to mind instances when Freud's own name was made fun of in connection with sexual activities, and then an episode of one famous man who

dragged the name of his equally famous friend through the mud, metaphorically speaking. Perhaps Freud feared that as a result of their priority dispute—
which finally burst into flames in the Weininger affair—Fliess would sue him
(e.g., the reference to Knodl), or expose and discredit him among his professional colleagues. After all, though Erikson failed to mention this, *Freud himself acknowledged that the bearded accuser's charge was similar to being reproached for plagiarism.*

So, as indicated earlier, theft, rather than investiture, is the issue here. And
unlike the Eckstein affair, which was covered up by the Freudian faithful until 1966, Freud's priority dispute with Fliess was well known in analytic circles all along. Even Fromm had some perceptive commentary on the Freud/
Fliess affair in chapter 4 of *Sigmund Freud's Mission* (1959). How could
Erikson miss this—unless he was strongly motivated to? So, in conclusion,
we are confronted with a very strange and disquieting state of affairs. In keeping with their dogmatic prescriptions about the source and meaning of
dreams, Freud and his followers have always interpreted the Dream of the
Three Fates in purely Oedipal terms (Grinstein 1980). Since dreams *cannot*
refer to contemporaneous events, this argument goes, the dream's references
to misappropriation and theft, and the two references (in Freud's associations)
to missed opportunities for sexual pleasure in infancy and childhood, *must* refer to forgotten events in the distant past.

Though he did not dispute the validity of this retrospective approach, Erikson broke with convention by showing how the dreamwork symbolizes the
adaptive thrust of ego development as it progresses through successive psychosexual stages, turning a helpless nursling into a competent professional
man. Well, all right, give the man some credit. Though it is not particularly
germane in this instance, Erikson's contention that dreams often have a
prospective dimension and symbolize adaptive as well as irrational strivings is
well taken. But Erikson ignored Freud's copious associations on the theme of
plagiarism, which he knew implicated Fliess in some fashion. And when Freud
said to Fliess: "I can without feeling diminished admit that I have learned this
or that from others. But I have never appropriated something belonging to others as my own," he was not merely being defensive. He was lying, both to himself and to Fliess. And this was not an isolated occurrence. Freud had great difficulty owning up to his debts to numerous thinkers, including (but not limited
to) Johann Friedrich Herbart, Gustav Fechner, Arthur Schopenhauer, Friedrich
Nietzsche, Eduard von Hartmann, and others who dwelt upon the vagaries of
unconscious mental processes before he did. Though he sometimes acknowledged them in a cursory fashion, he seldom gave them their due and often employed a subtle rhetorical sleight of hand to obscure, minimize, or deny the
original source of a particular train of thought and present it as his own.

Fromm was inclined to explain Freud's galloping estrangement from Fliess as a result of unresolved oral needs, yet credits him with unwavering courage and a rare degree of intellectual honesty that precludes sham and pretense. But it is difficult to explain recurrent episodes of plagiarism in Freud as the result of a mere defense. A kind of programmatic dishonesty (in the service of self-aggrandizement) is plainly in evidence here. In the Dream of the Three Fates, Freud said, his "unconscious" counseled him: "One should never neglect an opportunity, but always take what one can, even when it involves doing a small wrong [*sic*]." In light of the preceding, this cryptic counsel suddenly becomes quite intelligible. Orthodox Freudians also ignore the plagiarism issue and echo Freud's contention that this suggestive remark really referred to regrets Freud harbored over missed opportunities for oral (and/or sexual) gratification with his mother (Grinstein 1980). Well, perhaps. There is no way to verify or disprove this contention altogether. But when read in light of his actual historical words and deeds, one cannot dispel the impression that this Oedipally focused interpretive strategy averts our attention from contemporaneous *ethical* issues which crop up repeatedly in Freud's relations to others, living and dead. Paul Lippmann zeroed in on this curious state of affairs in *Nocturnes: On Listening to Dreams*. In his own words:

> Erikson's creative teleology about the underlying purpose of the Irma dream—it was dreamt in order to become analysed as the "specimen dream" . . . , and thus give birth to psychoanalysis, takes us further in this inquiry into dreams and disguise. . . . Certainly the Irma dream . . . shows a great deal more than it knows, while it also hides itself in dream, associations, and in interpretation. Freud took up this dream, looked deeply into it . . . and created a whole psychology from its study. But as for the dream itself and its deeper meanings . . . , as much was revealed as was concealed. . . . Freud's theory . . . provided an elaborate disguise for the facts behind the dream. . . . Hidden and disguised in our specimen dream is not a single set of principles, but rather the whole messy human drama of love and betrayal, trust and dishonor, a secret confession of the worst aspects of our method of treatment, and a need to hide our guiltiness about our failures—all to be discovered as the century unfolded. (2000, 78)

Truer words were never spoken. Nevertheless, to play devil's advocate, the fact that it operated in the service of misdirection, evasion, and/or self-deception does not automatically invalidate the Oedipal interpretation Freud gave to his dream. But it does provoke considerable skepticism—or it ought to, anyway. After all, one must doubt the value of an interpretive method that supposedly augments self-knowledge while abetting or purposefully overlooking bad behavior. If it avoids dealing with dishonesty today, or explains it all as the belated enactment of some ancient rivalry or childhood injustice, how much of the knowledge yielded by this method is really genuine, and how much is specious or contrived for the occasion? And how on earth can we know for sure?

In *Erik Erikson: The Power and Limits of a Vision* (Roazen 1976), Paul Roazen called attention to Erikson's first characterization of Fliess as "clearly paranoid" in 1954, which shifted to being merely "somewhat paranoid" in 1968. In Roazen's estimation, this is evidence of Erikson's slippery and evasive style of writing, and his unwillingness to own up to his own exaggerations and mistakes (203). Perhaps this is so. But whatever his motives, Erikson's refusal to engage the plagiarism issue spared him from severe disappointment in Freud. Whether Fliess was unbalanced or not, as Freudians frequently allege, the fact remains that he had *reason* to be deeply mistrustful, at least where Freud was concerned.

INNER, OUTER, AND IN-BETWEEN

Freud's theories of dream interpretation were originally intended to shed light on patients' irrational thoughts and feelings, and how their unconscious or "psychic reality" warped their judgment, in keeping with fears, fantasies, and wishes from early childhood that colored all their contemporary attitudes, activities, and relationships. As we have just seen, this insistence on the infantile derivation of neurotic conflicts is sometimes very useful. At times, however, it totally obscures the importance of real-life, contemporaneous relationships as a source of inner conflict.

As noted in chapter 2, Erikson always questioned the distinction drawn by Anna Freud and Heinz Hartmann between the patient's "inner" and "outer" worlds, and their characteristic emphasis on addressing the inner world of fantasies and defenses to the manifest neglect or exclusion of the patient's "real" or outer world. According to Erikson, the real world inevitably registers in our dreams, fantasies, and symptoms. To treat "psychic reality" or a dream scenario as a closed-off, self-encapsulated realm of purely infantile or self-referential images and processes that are essentially disengaged from commerce with the present-day outer world, as some analysts do, totally misrepresents the nature of the psyche. Because he paid close attention to the "manifest dream," the patient's current problems and preoccupations, and the intricate interconnections between dreams, play productions, and waking, day-to-day experience, Erikson was often reproached for superficiality by more orthodox colleagues like Kurt Eissler, Robert Waelder, or even Heinz Kohut. This approach, it was frequently alleged, lacked depth—as if "depth" was merely a function of how early or how repressed a particular conflict or item of experience is, or of how estranged it was from contemporary actualities.

Meanwhile, in Erikson's own estimation, Anna Freud and Heinz Hartmann were creating a false dichotomy, while Freud himself was innocent of reifying the psyche in this way. Though he never codified it explicitly as a principle of interpretation, said Erikson, the intricate interconnection between the inner and outer worlds is always faithfully reflected in Freud's clinical formulations. In his own mind, at least, by asserting the inextricable interconnectedness between our inner and outer worlds, Erikson was remaining true to the Professor, while Anna and Heinz—both ego psychologists—were the real revisionists. The question then becomes: Did Erikson's conviction have merit, or was it merely a useful delusion that buttressed his sense of kinship and fidelity to Freud?

As his early case histories attest, as a young man Freud was more attentive to social, environmental, and/or class-related problems and pressures and their impact on his patients' lives. With the passage of time, however, Freud began making very strong claims about the priority of the inner over the outer world, and, by implication, of the past over the present. But while this trend became more pronounced with the passage of time, there are still plenty of instances early in Freud's career where inner or psychic reality is accorded dominance. Take the Irma dream, for example. While an Oedipal interpretation (in keeping with Freud's own commentary) makes a certain amount of sense, it also diverts attention from his enveloping social context, and urgent conflicts regarding issues of honesty, intellectual integrity, and the vicissitudes of friendship—conflicts which are no less complicated or profound for being contemporaneous, or even acutely conscious, for that matter. If it is alleged that the Oedipal interpretation is "truer" or "deeper," or that Freud's conflicts with Fliess are mere repetitions of older, infantile issues, then clearly the outer world has been devalued, and the inner world, and, by implication, the past, has been invested with an inflated significance.

For an earlier (and more drastic) example of this tendency to inflate psychic reality, take Freud's deranged letters to Fliess in the wake of Eckstein's botched surgery, which attributed an almost supernatural power to his patient's ostensible desire to prolong and intensify her own suffering in the service of frustrating her physicians by robbing them of a "cure." Here the overvaluation of the patient's (real or alleged) inner world leads in a direction that is unsound, scientifically. Moreover, in view of the Hippocratic oath, which Fliess violated through gross negligence, it is *ethically reprehensible* to even talk in this way, even in defense of a very dear friend. And, in due course, Freud recognized this—though this dawning awareness registered in

his actions, attitudes, and, above all, his dreams, and not in an explicit re-
traction of his words—at least as far as we know. If anything, the Irma dream
suggests that after an interval of reflection, Freud recoiled from his initial interpretation of this tragic mishap, only to take up *another* evasive maneuver
in his relationship to Fliess, this one designed to spare *himself* embarrassment.

So if we judge by his letters and celebrated self-analysis, rather than Erikson's excessive Freudian piety, Sigmund Freud sometimes acknowledged the
seamless interconnectedness of the inner and outer worlds. But as often as
not, he also promoted the questionable inner/outer dichotomy that was later
embraced and espoused by Anna Freud and Heinz Hartmann—and, in a different and much more extreme fashion, by Melanie Klein and her followers.
This is another instructive reminder that Erikson's sense of fidelity to Freud,
however integral to his own sense of identity, was colored by strong tendencies toward idealization. But if we are going to be fair all around, this fact
must not deter us from appreciating Erikson's approach to dream interpretation, which was rooted in a deeper appreciation of the real historicity of the
psyche than Freud's narrowly "archeological" approach.

8

Erikson's Erasure

IRRELEVANCE AND THE ACADEMY

Years ago, Gore Vidal coined the memorable phrase "United States of Amnesia" to satirize Americans' propensity to forget their own history. As Vidal observed, dire conflicts, vexing issues, and compelling personalities that once dominated the cultural landscape have had a curious way of slipping insensibly into some dim recess of the collective psyche, as a result of which our history often repeats itself—as tragedy or as farce, depending on circumstances or one's point of view. It is much the same with psychoanalysis. As Paul Roazen recently complained, despite many efforts to keep his ideas alive, Erikson, once a towering figure, is all but forgotten in psychoanalytic circles (Roazen 2002). And so this brief concluding chapter asks: What are the cultural forces that contribute to Erikson's posthumous neglect, and what trends or issues might help to consolidate his weakening grip on posterity?

Because of the explosive generational conflicts that gripped America in the 1960s and 1970s, Erikson's popularity *outside* the analytic profession hinged primarily on his approach to adolescence. In 1965, for example, Edgar Z. Friedenberg—a political scientist, not an analyst—declared that no one understood adolescence as deeply or empathically as Erikson (Friedenberg 1965), and in the decade that followed a chorus of voices from the mental health professions echoed this appraisal enthusiastically. Within the mental health professions proper, Erikson was equally famous for his writings on infancy, childhood, and play therapy—a fact borne out by numerous publications from that era, and by his long, fruitful association with Benjamin Spock and Fred Rogers at the Arsenal Family and Children's Center and the Western Psychiatric Institute and Clinic in Pittsburgh.

Despite all the fanfare in America, however, Erikson's ideas made little headway in Europe, where psychoanalysis became popular only after 1968, but where American psychoanalysis was regarded warily at best, even though its leading theorists were all transplanted Europeans. But even here, since 1975 Erikson's ideas have become steadily less relevant to clinical and public discourse. One reason for this diminution, of course, is that the influence of psychoanalysis as a whole on American culture has declined dramatically. Indeed, the same is true, to a lesser extent, elsewhere in the English-speaking world. Admittedly, in the United States, there are pockets of stubborn resistance in the fields of English and comparative literature, film studies, cultural studies, and so on. And if the vagaries of fashion were less capricious they might have insured Erikson a strong, stable, and sympathetic audience, today and for the foreseeable future. After all, no one in the Anglo-American world pushed psychoanalysis in the direction of history and the human sciences more than Erikson, as the spectacular (if regrettably short-lived) success of the psychohistory movement during the 1970s indicates (Runyan 1988).

But contrary to expectation, this did not come to pass. For whether in defiance of prevailing attitudes or in compliance with prevailing fashions, English-speaking academics who embrace psychoanalysis generally favor Europeans like Jurgen Habermas, Paul Ricouer, Jacques Lacan, and their followers, and see it principally as a method of cultural critique, or even an instrument of ideological "subversion," rather than as a practical technique to address human suffering. They treat ego psychology—with which Erikson is still associated, unfortunately—with frank suspicion, if not outright derision, and, in view of their language-based approach to psychoanalysis, show no sympathy or interest in Erikson's attempts to overhaul the biological underpinnings of psychoanalytic theory, which they perceive, perversely enough, as somehow inimical to what Freud was *really* going on about.

Meanwhile, outside of the academy psychoanalysis has suffered serious (and perhaps irreversible) setbacks as a treatment modality. Not only is it time consuming and expensive, but many cogent doubts about its theoretical underpinnings and therapeutic efficacy have been raised both in and out of analytic circles (e.g., Grünbaum 1984; Sulloway 1991), and it has been pilloried in the popular press (Gray 1993). And as if all this were not bad enough, Erikson's personal reputation was tarnished in the *Atlantic Monthly* (Erikson Bloland 1999). In an article detailing her father's emotional vulnerabilities and blind spots and his avid (if seldom obvious) pursuit of fame, Sue Erikson Bloland, herself an analyst, cited several analytic theorists, including Heinz Kohut, Ernest Becker, and W. R. D. Fairbairn, to explain the psychological basis of her father's shortcomings. And in all fairness to Erikson Bloland, there is no reason *not* to cite these gentlemen. Kohut, Becker, and Fairbairn all had important and illuminating things to say.

Nevertheless, when describing her father's unrequited yearning for his own father, and its impact on his life and work, Erikson Bloland did not mention, much less make use of, her father's ideas, nor did she bother to address her father's contribution to psychoanalysis and the mental health field in general. This striking omission merely ratifies the prevailing consensus: Erikson's ideas are no longer "a climate of opinion," as they were from 1960 to 1975; they are no longer relevant, period. Quite the contrary, the impression one gets from reading her article is that Erikson's ideas are completely passé, even when considering his *own* life history.

Another, more menacing and deep-seated threat to Erikson's credibility nowadays is that his theory of human development, and the epigenetic principle on which it rests, are based on premises that are widely deemed suspect, if not downright reprehensible in many quarters. After all, Erikson assumed the existence of a basic, biological substrate to our humanity, arguing that normative or ethical conclusions can (and must) be drawn from the study of the human life cycle, both for clinical work and cultural critique. Nowadays, however, large numbers of people are convinced that this way of thinking is either obsolete, repressive, or both. There are several reasons for this.

CHILDHOOD IN AMERICA: THEN AND NOW

To begin with, despite the formidable challenges and uncertainties of his own early upbringing, Erikson generally assumed the existence of stable, intact nuclear families—ones in which the father works and the mother manages the household affairs. Erikson wrote at a time when the divorce rate was much lower than it is today, when women were just entering the workforce in numbers. This was a world of typewriters and rotary telephones; in which home computers, the Internet, and cell phones were still figments of futurists' imaginations. It was also a world in which most gay and lesbian adults still remained "in the closet" and seldom dreamed of parenting or adopting children, much less getting married.

Moreover, in 1975, when his reputation was at its height, having a high school diploma still meant something in this country. The average person did not yet need a BA to get entry-level positions in many branches of commerce and industry, and the average time a teenager spent in school before launching a career was much less than it is today. Day-care centers were still somewhat exotic and experimental undertakings, patronized chiefly by unconventional or "progressive" parents, rather than by all and sundry. The average age when secondary sex characteristics started to appear, signaling the onset of puberty, was later than it is today, especially for girls, who now frequently commence puberty as early as age nine. Not surprisingly, the age at which the average teenager became sexually active was also higher then—around nineteen or twenty, rather than thirteen or fourteen—or, in many cases, even younger. And while birth control pills were all the rage, AIDS was still unknown.

There is another important and instructive contrast between the seventies and today. In that era, many mainstream churches were poorly attended and faced a credibility crisis of unprecedented proportions. For those seeking spiritual illumination, there was no shortage of gurus, meditation teachers, or exotic cults available, and some—like Transcendental Meditation, Krishna Consciousness, Guru Maharaji, and EST—were big business, and their leaders made headlines in the popular press. Yet in most of this country, people who talked often and earnestly of their faith, and the pivotal role it plays in their lives, were often considered pushy, odd, or ill educated, especially in the universities. For the most part, in their turn, evangelical and fundamentalist Christians shunned "the world"—that is, the media and public schools—and were a fairly retiring and insular community.

Nowadays, by contrast, evangelical Christians are organized, outspoken, and steadily growing in numbers and influence. Evangelists and their followers are frequently in the news, while cults are falling on hard times, and, mercifully, in some cases disappearing entirely. In the intervening decades, mainstream churches have enjoyed a modest resurgence in terms of attendance, but the increasing polarization between their liberal and conservative wings threatens to fragment many of them completely. Meanwhile, instead of being considered pushy, odd, or ill educated, people who speak often and earnestly of their faith are now considered normal in most parts of the country, and seek to ban the teaching of evolutionary theory in favor of creationism or "intelligent design" and to reintroduce prayer into public schools.

In short, in the quarter century since Erikson's reputation peaked, the world has changed drastically. Nowadays, whether they marry or not, women usually work outside the home, and often defer childbearing until their late thirties or early forties. Day-care centers are ubiquitous, and there are as many single-parent households as there are intact nuclear families. In addition, gay couples frequently have custody or adopt, and lesbian couples have children through in vitro fertilization. The average American household boasts four television sets, and the average teenager watches more than four hours of television a day. And a new screen technology, the home computer, monopolizes more and more of our time, becoming the primary mode of sociability for many children, teenagers, and adults, who actually prefer "chatting" online to face-to-face encounters. Meanwhile, almost 11 million American children and adolescents are on antidepressant medications, and another 5.5 million are on Ritalin or other stimulants. And 40 percent of all children who take psychotropic medication of some sort actually take two or more medications concurrently (Olfman 2005).

One could go on at greater length, but why bother? The conclusion is inescapable. The "average expectable environment" that confronts and envelops infants, adolescents, and teenagers today is vastly different from that of Weimar Germany, where Erikson grew up, or the Cold War era, when he wrote his most influential work. As a result of these cultural transformations, the onset, duration, and texture of childhood and adolescence has changed drastically, and critics like the late Neil Postman argue that the media and mass culture have drastically abridged childhood, and may even annul it entirely in the twenty-first century (Postman 1982). As if to hasten the fulfillment of Postman's prediction, federal laws that were ostensibly designed to promote early literacy now effectively ban play in our nation's nurseries (Olfman 2003). The experience of aging has changed dramatically, too—quantitatively, due to increased longevity, and qualitatively, due to the dramatic increase in the prevalence and incidence of cancer, diabetes, and chronic illness, and the skyrocketing costs of drugs and medical services.

HUMAN NATURE, HUMAN NEEDS, AND TECHNOLOGICAL CHANGE

Whatever else he did, Erikson could not foresee the future, nor could he anticipate the profound social changes that have relativized our understanding of the human life cycle. He worked with what he knew, what he saw, and what was ready to hand. Inevitably, as a result, many doubt that *any* of his ideas still apply. So if Erikson seems irrelevant today, it is because the world has changed, even if human nature has not. But even framing things in this way provokes strong objections because of the vexing controversies about the nature of "human nature" in contemporary discourse. Admittedly, these controversies rage for a very good reason. Even if we define human nature very broadly, as the ground of possibility for certain kinds of prototypical experiences and relationships or as a set of built-in constraints that limit what we can experience, endure, and so on, we are left with the question: How do we disentangle what is "natural" in human behavior from cultural artifact? The human sciences have wrestled with this question for over a century, and while only cynics deem these efforts fruitless, the fact remains that there is no single, clear-cut, and unambiguous formula for doing this kind of thing effectively.

And yet there is a curious and potentially instructive dimension to this seemingly perennial problem that warrants closer attention. Recall that in the 1940s, in defiance of orthodox Freudianism, Erikson revised Freud's psychosexual schemata in *Childhood and Society* (1950). And remember, please, that his efforts were influential in the Cold War era because they occurred at a time when the rate of technological change was still much *slower* than it is today. Another way of putting this is that theories like Erikson's still had time to "sink in" and take hold of the public imagination before they became obsolete. But that would soon change. As Erikson's friend and former graduate assistant Kenneth Keniston pointed out:

> A man born in the beginning of this [twentieth] century has seen in his lifetime changes in the quality of life which no one in his youth could have anticipated or prepared him for. Changes that once took centuries . . . now take less than a generation. Technological changes that were the science fiction of our parents are the commonplaces of their children. . . .
>
> The human capacity to assimilate to such innovations is limited. Men can of course adjust to rapid change—that is, make an accommodation to it and go on living—but truly to assimilate it involves retaining some sense of connection with the past, understanding the relationship of one's position to one's origins and one's destination, maintaining a sense of control over one's life in a comprehensible universe undergoing intelligible transformations. This assimilation becomes increasingly difficult in times like our own. Whatever is radically different from the present inevitably tends to lose its relevance. (1974, 251–52)

What was true in 1974 is doubly true today. If recent experience is any indication, then the rate of social change, driven by technological innovation, is accelerating with each passing decade, and if present trends persist, the world that confronts the average adolescent in 2025 will be even more unlike our present world than the Vietnam era, when I grew up, is from today (Kurzweil 1999). As a result, anyone who tries to update Erikson's stages in the same way that Erikson updated Freud a half century ago (Maccoby 2002) is likely to meet the following objection: *Why bother to revise a theory that will be obsolete in less than a quarter of a century?*

Before we reply to this objection, please note the historic correlation between the rate of techno-social change and the belief in a basic human nature. In simple terms, the correlation can be stated as follows: The slower the rate of techno-social change, the greater the prevalence of the belief in a universal human nature. As the rate of techno-social change increases, belief in "human nature" tends to recede. In itself, this correlation proves nothing, perhaps, beyond the fact that belief in the existence (or nonexistence) of human nature is, in part, a social artifact—a point we return to further below. The critics have a point. Contemporary objections to Erikson's psychosocial stages are based on experience. We cannot foresee the future, so the argument goes, so why bother to revise developmental timetables, add or subtract stages, or redefine their specific conflicts and characteristics? Who knows what will stand the test of time?

Other, more sweeping objections to Erikson's life cycle theory arise from the postmodern, poststructural, and constructivist camps in the mental health and cultural studies arenas. They do not merely question the wisdom of revising developmental schemata on prudential grounds. They deny the existence of anything remotely resembling universal human nature in the first place, and deem the attempt to grasp and describe universal developmental stages, conflicts, or characteristics as flawed in principle. By their account, any theory that posits the existence of universal human experiences, conflicts, and needs is merely a covert attempt to legislate a particular set of norms, and, with it, of power relations, in order to valorize a particular historical moment, freezing it arbitrarily in time. In short, it is a covert power play, however much it is dressed in the language of humanism or disinterested concern for human welfare.

This critique has merit, up to a point. But it ignores the fact that the ardent *disbelief* in the existence of human nature, which prides itself on being emancipated and avant garde, is also a social artifact whose evident inability to grasp its own ideological roots and ramifications exerts the same pressure to sustain the uncritical acceptance of its basic premises as any other ideological belief system. It is also profoundly injudicious in its relentless (and clearly partisan) emphasis on the *negative* consequences of belief in human nature, and ignoring *the other* rhetorical uses to which theories of human nature are put. After all, if you reflect for a moment, it is difficult to impossible to justify a theory of universal human rights, or of fundamental human needs, without invoking some notion of human nature, however tacit and inarticulate it may be. Indeed, one could argue that in the final analysis, *all* efforts to elucidate or defend basic human rights or needs that do *not* affirm the existence of human nature lapse into complete incoherence, sooner or later.

Though anathema to many contemporary cultural theorists, historically speaking, theories of human nature have inspired movements for individual and collective emancipation at least as often as they have movements to repress them. And in instances where impending social or economic developments threaten human dignity and the quality of life, theories of human nature can challenge their legitimacy and help to limit or to mitigate the damage done in the process. Besides, the obvious facts that (1) it is difficult to impossible to discern the lines of cleavage between "nature" and "culture" in many instances, and (2) that theories that posit such a cleavage often serve a rhetorical function, do not warrant the conclusion that human nature does not exist, or that we should not persist, despite all difficulties, in our efforts to grasp it. Logically speaking, the latter conclusion simply does not follow from the former, however much we may want it to, to allay some inarticulate fear or satisfy some obscurely contrarian desire.

In any case, thanks to the explosion of structuralist, poststructuralist, and postmodern thought since Erikson was in vogue, we have developed a supple and sophisticated discourse on the vagaries of power and its historical shifts and transformations. But at the same time, our discourse on human needs— basic or generic human needs, and those that are more prominent at specific phases of the human life cycle—has become deeply impoverished. And the tragic upshot of the corrosive skepticism so fashionable nowadays is that it is utterly deaf to its own oversights and abuses. In fairness to Foucault and his followers, for example, every human society, every cultural system (without exception) is structured in terms of power differentials, modes of authority, and so on (Foucault 1977). But by the same token, every culture is a system that is designed to make provision for basic human needs. And if it does not make adequate provision for the needs of the majority, said Freud, it lacks legitimacy, or any compelling raison d'être (Freud 1930).

Of course, Freud attributed special significance to the role culture plays in affording or denying opportunities for sexual satisfaction—an importance Foucault deemed quite exaggerated, if not entirely false (Foucault 1978). But while Freud may have exaggerated the importance of sex somewhat, since Freud's day psychoanalysts like Erikson and Fromm addressed other fundamental human needs that go begging in contemporary discourse—that is, the needs for identity, a sense of cosmological coherence and of intergenerational identification, which Keniston eloquently called attention to. Without saying so in quite so many words, Keniston acknowledged that both these needs are implicated in the creation of a sense of identity. Why? Because "the closest link between social history and individual history is the individual's sense of relationship to his own personal history as embodied in his parents, his ancestors, and all they come to represent to him. This sense of relationship defines an individual's sense of self as surely as does his work or his children" (Keniston 1974, 254).

In this time of genocide and ethnic uprooting, clinical work with war refugees and victims of "ethnic cleansing" bears out the truth of this contention (Apfelbaum 2000; Papadopoulos 1997). No one doubts its applicability in cases like these. But despite Erikson's eloquent reflections on "uprootedness" in American culture, those of us who feel relatively safe from the threats of genocide and cultural displacement are reluctant to apply these insights to ourselves, and, despite mounting evidence, to address the role of technology in creating a culture characterized by extremes of poverty and excess and of disconnection and instability at all levels. Why? Because ceaseless technological innovation is precisely what drives and defines our culture. To acknowledge, much less emphasize, that this fact is a potent pathogenic factor in our culture is to risk immediate dismissal by thousands of intelligent and influential people—Left, Right, and center.

Nevertheless, and for that very reason, it is important to emphasize that our deepening inability to identify with the experiences, the values, and the perspectives of our elders renders us increasingly oblivious to the past, and skeptical of the relevance of their ideas to our circumstances. If one were to address this phenomenon in Freudian terminology, we could say that as technology advances with ever increasing speed, the past is increasingly decathected, or divested of emotional energy and significance. This does *not* mean, incidentally, that the past is increasingly "repressed." In fact, the opposite is true. In repression, certain psychic "contents" (or representations) are strongly cathected with emotional energy but denied access to consciousness because of an inner conflict. Indeed, if they were *not* deeply cathected, these items would not be repressed in the first place.

The process we are talking about here entails a different form of erasure, one that involves little or no internal conflict, because the narrative or symbolic representations of the past that meant so much to our forebears no longer have adaptive value. As a result, the past is experienced as irrelevant, rather than as something that is potentially disruptive to our emotional equilibrium. Rather than being a mere aberration, or the symptom of an individual's neurotic conflict, this attitude becomes a necessary adaptation to a rapidly changing world—one that is shared by the vast majority.

As if these developments were not deep and deleterious enough, the steady decline of literacy (Sanders 1995) and of attention spans in the average citizen (Postman 2002) poses an additional threat to intergenerational identification. The dwindling ability to read and to listen attentively, abetted by the colonization of our everyday rhythms, fantasies, and public spaces by television and other media, has led to a progressive impoverishment and flattening out of our critical faculties, our tolerance for complexity, and our ethical and aesthetic sensibilities. The flip side of this socially patterned defect is a pervasive anti-intellectualism outside of the academy, and a kind of airy fetishism of ideas within it. The impact of all this on American democracy is frighteningly apparent in recent years.

These reflections on contemporary culture provoke a rather startling conclusion. Erikson is one the few theorists who developed a theory that accounts brilliantly for his own erasure, his perceived irrelevance to the contemporary scene, though in truth his ideas and insights are as relevant now as they ever were. This is a rare accomplishment in the history of the human sciences. Unfortunately, however, we lose sight of this curious fact if we focus on the growing disparities between Erikson's account of the prototypical conflicts and challenges that beset us at various stages on life's way and those that confront contemporary children, youth, and adults. But we see this paradox very clearly indeed if we hang on to the basic principles and convictions regarding the dialectical interplay of the generations that underlies his best work.

So the question remains: Should we attempt to revise and update Erikson's developmental schemata the way he updated Freud's in *Childhood and Society*? I answer that question with a cautious yes—provided we are willing to revise some of the crucial coordinates of our thinking every decade or so. But for purposes of this study, I elected not to revise Erikson's schemata. Instead of defending, adding, or excising this or that specific stage from Erikson's theory, I thought it was prudent to first stand back and review some of the fundamental and overarching insights and principles that gave rise to this undertaking in the first place.

Meanwhile, those brave souls who revise and update Erikson in the interests of making him relevant to today should not harbor any illusions. The very processes that contribute to Erikson's perceived irrelevance in America today could engulf the entire analytic profession by the end of twenty-first century. Despite the depiction of Freud as some sort of radical in some quarters, psychoanalysis is really a product of bourgeois culture. It presupposes leisure, literacy, and opportunities for patient reflection, in a culture in which the value of cultivating self-knowledge is taken for granted. It also presupposes a flourishing middle class. Absent these conditions, psychoanalysis *must* decline as a treatment modality. It may lead a kind of feverish half-life in academia, as a branch or perspective within the human sciences. But in the relentless onslaught of new trends and technologies, that situation can only last so long.

This fact registers in a vivid and alarming way in the dramatic rise of psychopharmacology. Thanks in part to his personal efforts, when Erikson was alive and active, crises of childhood and adolescence were often viewed by psychologists, psychiatrists, and psychoanalysts as opportunities to explore the patient's familial history and broader social context, and to put the patient's interpersonal development back on track. In that dimly remembered long-ago time, psychotropic drugs were viewed as a treatment of last resort. In the brief interval of time since Erikson's death, drugs have become the treatment of choice, and the kinds of sensitive, discerning psychosocial evaluations of children and adolescents that Erikson did have become a thing of the past, giving way to behavioral checklists, brain scans, and all sorts of dubious—and hasty!—diagnostic procedures that leave the real roots of children's suffering unaddressed. Just look at the literature on child and adolescent psychiatry coming out of the Western Psychiatric Institute and Clinic, where Erikson worked during the 1950s, for example. There is lots of talk about genes, hormones, neural circuitry, and neurotransmitters, and next to nothing about basic trust or mistrust, industry and inferiority, identity crises, or even the faintest suggestion that a child's symptoms have a hidden meaning or that the disturbed child is trying to *communicate* something to the adults around it in some desperate, disjointed fashion (Burston 2006).

Nevertheless, it is abundantly clear (to all but the willfully obtuse) that the growing epidemic of child and adolescent psychopathology is attributable in large part to the fact that the basic developmental needs of children and adolescents are no longer being met in our society. And instead of addressing them as such, we seek individually calibrated chemical solutions to what are in fact systemic or cultural problems. Admittedly, psychotropic drugs may help normalize behavior and palliate the fears of parents, but there is something strikingly irrational in our efforts to foster the "adjustment" of individual children whose problems are symptomatic of a deeper cultural malaise. Indeed, when you scrutinize the current mental health scene closely, it may dawn on you that future historians will probably look back on our era as the time when the chemical colonization of childhood began in earnest. Whether they view this development as temporary or irreversible, with approval or with horror and indignation, remains to be seen, and depends in part on whether—or to what extent—we act now. In the meantime, the future of Erikson's beloved, beleaguered, and impossible profession in the United States looks very grim indeed.

Bibliography

Aichhorn, A. 1960. *Wayward youth*. New York: Meridian Books.

Albin, M., ed. 1980. *New directions in psychohistory: The Adelphia Papers in honor of Erik H. Erikson*. Toronto: D.C. Heath.

Apfelbaum, E. 2000. And now what, after such tribulations? Memory and dislocation in an era of uprooting. *American Psychologist* 55(9): 108–13.

Auden, W. H. 1960, June. Greatness finding itself. *Mid Century* 13: 9–18.

Avineri, S. 1974. *Hegel's theory of the modern state*. London: Cambridge University Press.

———. 1976. *The social and political thought of Karl Marx*. London: Cambridge University Press.

Berke, J. 1996. The wellsprings of fascism: Individual malice, group hatreds and the emergence of national narcissism. *Free Associations* 6(3): 334–50.

Blechner, M. 2001. *The dream frontier*. Hillsdale, NJ: Analytic Press.

Berman, M. 1970. *The politics of authenticity: Radical individualism and the emergence of modern society*. New York: MacMillan

———. 1975, March 30. "Review of *Life History and the Historical Moment*." *New York Review of Books*, 1–2.

Bronfenbrenner, U. 1988. Strengthening family systems. In E. F. Z. M. Frank, ed., *The parental leave crisis: Toward a national policy* (143–60). New Haven, CT: Yale University Press.

Brooks, R. 2001. The merger of flesh and machines. In J. Brockman, ed., *The next fifty years: Science in the first half of the twenty-first century* (183–93). New York: Vintage.

Brown, N. O. 1960. *Life against death: The psychoanalytical meaning of history*. New York: Vintage.

Browning, D. 1975. *Generative man: Psychoanalytic perspectives*. New York: Delta.

Brunner, J. 2001. *Freud and the politics of psychoanalysis*. New Brunswick, NJ: Transaction.

Buber, M. 1988. *Eclipse of God*. Atlantic Highlands, NJ: Humanities.

Burston, D. 1989. Freud, the father and the philosophy of history: Early dissident appraisals and their relevance to contemporary thought. In L. Spurling, ed., *Sigmund Freud: Critical appraisals* (3: 46–55). London: Routledge.

———. 1991. *The legacy of Erich Fromm.* Cambridge, MA: Harvard University Press.

———. 1994. Freud, the serpent and the sexual enlightenment of children. *International Forum of Psychoanalysis* 3: 205–19.

———. 1996. *The wing of madness: The life and work of R. D. Laing.* Cambridge, MA: Harvard University Press.

———. 2000. *The crucible of experience: R. D. Laing and the crisis of psychotherapy.* Cambridge, MA: Harvard University Press.

———. 2002a. Embracing the impossible profession. *Psychoanalytic Review* 89(1): 465–83.

———. 2002b. Rank, Otto (1884–1939). In E. Erwin, ed., *The Freud encyclopedia: Theory, therapy and culture* (461–62). London: Routledge.

———. 2003. Nietzsche, Scheler and social psychology. *Journal of the Society for Existential Analysis* 14(1): 2–13.

———. 2005a. "The Passion of the Christ" and the future of Christian-Jewish dialogue. In D. Burston and R. Denova, eds., *Passionate dialogues: Critical perspectives on Mel Gibson's "The Passion of the Christ"* (217–44). Pittsburgh, PA: Mise.

———. 2006. Diagnosis, drugs and bipolar disorder in children. In S. Olfman, ed., *Drugging our children* (121–39). Westport, CT: Praeger.

Burston, D., and R. Frie. 2006. *Psychotherapy as a human science.* Pittsburgh: Duquesne University Press.

Bush, M. L. 1967. *The history of Europe 1450–1660: Renaissance, reformation and the outer world.* London: Blandford.

Carotenuto, A. 1982. *A secret symmetry: Sabina Spielrein.* New York: Dell.

Coles, R. 1970. *Erik H. Erikson: The growth of his work.* Boston: Little, Brown.

———. 2000. Psychoanalysis: The American experience. In M. Roth, ed., *Freud: Conflict and culture* (140–51). New York: Vintage.

Crossan, J. D. 1996. *Who killed Jesus?* San Francisco: Harper Collins.

Deleuze, G., and F. Guatari. 1977. *Anti-Oedipus: Capitalism and schizophrenia.* New York: Viking.

Demos, J. 1976. Developmental perspectives on the history of childhood. In L. Rappoport and M. Kren, eds., *Varieties of Psychohistory* (180–92). New York: Springer.

Dickens, C. 1986. *A Christmas carol.* New York: Bantam Classics.

Dufresne, T., ed. 1997a. *Returns of the French Freud: Freud, Lacan and beyond.* London: Routledge.

———. 1997b. *Freud under analysis: Essays in honor of Paul Roazen.* Northvale, NJ: Jason Aronson.

Dupont, J. 1988. *The clinical diaries of Sandor Ferenczi.* Cambridge, MA: Harvard University Press.

Ellenberger, H. 1970. *The discovery of the unconscious.* New York: Basic Books.

Ellwood, R. 1999. *The politics of myth: A study of C. G. Jung, Mircea Eliade and Joseph Campbell.* Albany: State University of New York Press.

Erikson, E. 1950. *Childhood and society*. New York: Norton.

———. 1954. On the dream specimen of psychoanalysis. *Journal of the American Psychoanalytic Association* 2: 5–56.

———. 1956a. The problem of ego identity. *Journal of the American Psychoanalytic Association* 4: 56–121.

———. 1956b. The first psychoanalyst. *Yale Review* 46: 40–62.

———. 1958a. On the nature of clinical evidence. *Daedalus* 137(4): 65–87.

———. 1958b. *Young man Luther*. New York: Norton.

———. 1962. *The Golden Rule and the cycle of life*. Paper presented on May 4 at the George W. Gay Lecture on Medical Ethics, Harvard Medical School, Cambridge, MA.

———. 1964a. *Insight & responsibility*. New York: Norton.

———. 1964b. Human strength and the cycle of generations. In Erikson 1964a, 109–58.

———. 1964c. Identity and uprootedness in our time. In Erikson 1964a, 83–107.

———. 1964d. Psychological reality and historical actuality. In Erikson 1964a, 161–215.

———. 1964e. A memorandum on identity and Negro youth. *Journal of Social Issues* 20: 429–42.

———. 1966a. The Ontogeny of ritualization. In R. Lowenstein, L. Newman, M. Schur, and A. Solnit, eds. *Psychoanalysis—A general psychology: Essays in honor of Heinz Hartmann* (601–21). New York: International Universities Press.

———. 1966b. Words for Paul Tillich. *Harvard Divinity Bulletin* 30(2): 13–15.

———. 1968. *Identity, youth and crisis*. New York: Norton.

———. 1969. *Gandhi's truth: On the origins of militant nonviolence*. New York: Norton.

———. 1972. On protest and affirmation. *Harvard Medical Alumni Bulletin* 46(6): 30–32.

———. 1974. *Dimensions of a new identity: The Jefferson lectures*. New York: Norton.

———. 1975. "Identity crisis" in autobiographical perspective. In *Life history and the historical moment* (17–47). New York: Norton.

———. 1976. Reflections on Dr. Borg's life cycle. *Daedalus* 105: 1–31.

———. 1980. Themes of adulthood in the Freud-Jung correspondence. In N. J. Smelser, ed., *Themes of work and love in adulthood* (43–74). Cambridge, MA: Harvard University Press.

———. 1981. The Galilean sayings and the sense of "I." *Yale Review* 9(8). Reprinted in R. Wallerstein and L. Goldberger, *Ideas and identities: The life and work of Erik Erikson* (277–322). Madison, CT: International Universities Press, 1998.

———. 1982a. For Joseph Wheelwright—My Jungian friend. In Schlein 1987, 713–15.

———. 1982b. Psychoanalytic reflections on Einstein's centenary. In G. Holton and Y. Elkana, eds. *Albert Einstein: Historical and cultural perspectives* (151–73). Princeton, NJ: Princeton University Press.

———. 1998. The nature of clinical evidence. In R. G. Wallerstein, ed. *Ideas and identities: The life and work of Erik Erikson* (245–75). Madison, CT: International Universities Press.

Erikson, J. 1970. *St. Francis and his four ladies*. New York: Norton.

Erikson, K. 1973. *In search of common ground: Conversations with Erik H. Erikson and Huey Newton*. New York: Norton.

Erikson Bloland, S. 1999, November. Fame: The power and cost of a fantasy. *Atlantic Monthly*, 51–62.

Evans, R., ed. 1967. *Dialogue with Erik Erikson*. New York: Harper & Row.

Feinstein, H. 1983. Words & work: A dialectical analysis of value transmission between the generations of the family of William James. In Albin 1980, 131–42.

Firestone, S. 1970. *The dialectic of sex: The case for feminist revolution*. New York: William Morrow.

Foucault, M. 1977. *Discipline and punish: The birth of the prison*. Trans. A. Sheridan. Harmondsworth, UK: Penguin.

——. 1978. *The history of sexuality*. Trans. R. Hurley. Harmondsworth, UK: Penguin.

Freud, A. 1966. *The ego and the mechanisms of defense*. New York: International Universities Press.

Freud, S. 1900. *The interpretation of dreams*. Trans. J. Strachey. (1974 ed., vol. 4–5). London: Hogarth.

——. 1905. *Three essays on the theory of sexuality*. Trans. J. Strachey. (1974 ed., vol. 7). London: Hogarth.

——. 1907. The sexual enlightenment of children. Trans. J. Riviere. In M. Khan, ed., *Sigmund Freud: Collected papers* (2: 36–44). London: Hogarth.

——. 1908. On the sexual theories of children. Trans. J. Riviere. In M. Khan, ed., *Sigmund Freud: Collected papers* (2: 59–75). London: Hogarth.

——. 1910a. *Leonardo da Vinci and a memory of his childhood* (vol. 11). London: Hogarth.

——. 1910b. The antithetical sense of primal words. Trans. J. Riviere. In M. Khan, ed., *Sigmund Freud: Collected papers* (1971 ed., 4: 185–91). London: Hogarth.

——. 1911. Formulations regarding the two principles of mental functioning. Trans. J. Riviere. In M. Khan, ed., *Sigmund Freud: Collected papers* (1971 ed., 4: 13–21). London: Hogarth.

——. 1913. *Totem and taboo*. Trans. J. Strachey. (1974 ed., vol. 13). London: Hogarth.

——. 1917. One of the difficulties of psycho-analysis. Trans. J. Riviere. In M. Khan, ed., *Sigmund Freud: Collected papers* (1971 ed., 4: 347–56). London: Hogarth.

——. 1921. *Group psychology and the analysis of the ego*. Trans. J. Strachey. (1974 ed., vol. 18). London: Hogarth.

——. 1923. *The ego and the id*. London: Hogarth.

——. 1930. *Civilization and its discontents*. Trans. J. Strachey. (1974 ed., vol. 21). London: Hogarth.

——. 1932. *New introductory lectures on psychoanalysis*. Trans. J. Strachey. (1974 ed., vol. 22). London: Hogarth.

——. 1954. *The origins of psychoanalysis: Letters to Wilhelm Fliess*. Trans. James E. S. Mosbacher. New York: Basic Books.

Friedenberg, E. Z. 1965. *The dignity of youth and other atavisms: With a new essay of Erik Erikson*. Boston: Beacon.

Friedlander, A. 1968. *Leo Baeck: Teacher of Theresienstadt*. New York: Holt, Rinehart & Winston.

Friedman, L. J. 1999. *Identity's architect: A biography of Erik H. Erikson*. New York: Scribner.

Friedman, M. 1994. *The worlds of existentialism*. Atlantic Highlands, NJ: Humanities.

Fromm, E. 1941. *Escape from freedom*. New York: Holt, Rinehart & Winston.

———. 1947. *Man for himself: An inquiry into the psychology of ethics*. New York: Holt, Rinehart & Winston.

———. 1955. *The sane society*. New York: Holt, Rinehart & Winston.

———. 1959. *Sigmund Freud's mission: An analysis of his personality and influence*. New York: Harper & Row.

———. 1962. *Beyond the chains of illusion: My encounter with Marx and Freud*. New York: Simon & Schuster.

———. 1970. *The crisis of psychoanalysis: Essays on Marx, Freud and social psychology*. New York: Holt, Rinehart & Winston.

———. 1973. *The anatomy of human destructiveness*. New York: Holt, Rinehart & Winston.

———. 1994. A new humanism as a condition for one world. In R. Funk, ed., *On being human* (61–79). New York: Continuum.

Fromm, E., and M. Maccoby. 1970. *Social character and a Mexican village*. Englewood Cliffs, NJ: Prentice-Hall.

Fukuyama, F. 2002. *Our posthuman future: Consequences of the biotechnology revolution*. New York: Picador.

Fuller, P., ed. 1985. *Beyond psychoanalysis: Charles Rycroft*. Chicago: University of Chicago Press.

Gandhi, M. K. 1993. *Gandhi an autobiography: The story of my experiments with truth*. Boston: Beacon.

Gay, P. 1988. Psychoanalysis in history. *Poetics Today* 9(1): 239–47.

Gerth, H., and C. W. Mills, eds. 1946. *From Max Weber: Essays in sociology*. New York: Oxford University Press.

Golomb, J., W. Santaniello, and R. Lehrer, eds. 1999. *Nietzsche and depth psychology*. Albany: State University of New York Press.

Gould, S. J. 1977. *Ontogeny and phylogeny*. Cambridge, MA: Belknap Press of the Harvard University Press.

Gray, P. 1993. The assault on Freud. *Time*, November 29, 47–51.

Greeley, A. 1972. *Unsecular man: The persistence of religion*. New York: Schocken.

Green, V. H. H. 1964. *Martin Luther and the Reformation*. London: New English Library.

Grinstein, A. 1980. *Sigmund Freud's dreams*. New York: International Universities Press.

Grosskurth, P. 1986. *Melanie Klein: Her world and her work*. New York: Knopf.

Grünbaum, A. 1984. *The foundations of psychoanalysis: A philosophical critique*. Berkeley and Los Angeles: University of California Press.

———. 1998. A century of psychoanalysis: Critical retrospect and prospect. In Roth 2000, 183–95.

Haraway, D. J. 1991. *Simians, Cyborgs and women.* New York: Routledge.

Harnack, A. 1900. *Das Wesen des Christhenthums.* Leipzig: J. C. Hindrichs.

Hartmann, H. 1951. Ego psychology and the problem of adaptation. In D. Rapaport, ed., *Organization and pathology of thought* (362–96). New York: Columbia University Press.

———. 1960. *Psychoanalysis and moral values.* New York: International Universities Press.

Heschel, A. J. 1969a. *The prophets: An introduction* (vol. 1). New York: Harper & Row.

———. 1969b. *The prophets* (vol. 2). New York: Harper & Row.

Hewlett, S. A., and C. West. 1998. *The war against parents: What we can do for America's beleaguered moms and dads.* New York: Houghton Mifflin.

Ho, M.-W. 2000. *Genetic engineering: Dream or nightmare?* New York: Continuum.

Hogenson, G. 1983. *Jung's struggle with Freud.* South Bend, IN: Notre Dame University Press.

Homans, P. 1978. *Childhood & selfhood: Essays on tradition, religion and modernity in the psychology of Erik H. Erikson.* Lewisburg, PA: Bucknell University Press.

Horkheimer, M., and T. Adorno. 1941. Research project on antisemitism. *Studies in Philosophy and Social Science* 9: 124–43.

Janeway, E. 1971. *Man's world, woman's place.* New York: Morrow.

Jones, E. 1961. *The life and work of Sigmund Freud.* Ed. L. Trilling and S. Marcus. Harmondsworth, UK: Penguin.

Jung, C. G. 1959. *Aion: Researches into the phenomenology of the self.* Trans. R. F. C. Hull. Princeton, NJ: Princeton University Press.

Kant, I. 1964. *Groundwork of the metaphysics of morals.* New York: Harper Torchbooks.

Keniston, K. 1974. Psychological development and historical change. In Lifton and Olson 1974, 149–64.

Kerr, J. 1993. *A most dangerous method: The story of Freud, Jung and Sabina Spielrein.* New York: Knopf.

Kierkegaard, S. 1968. *Attack upon "Christendom."* Trans. W. Lowrie. Princeton, NJ: Princeton University Press.

Kirsner, D. 2000. *Unfree associations: Inside psychoanalytic institutes.* London: Process.

Knowles, R. 1985. *Human development and human possibility: Erik Erikson in light of Heidegger.* Lanham, MD: University Press of America.

Koestler, A. 1959. Mahatma Gandhi: A revaluation. *Times* (London), Oct. 5. Reprinted in *Bricks to Babel* (London: Picador, 1980), 595–19.

Kohut, H. 1971. *The analysis of the self: A systematic approach to the treatment of narcissistic personality disorders.* New York: International Universities Press.

———. 1977. *The restoration of the self.* New York: International Universities Press.

Kovel, J. 1974, March–April. Erik Erikson's psychohistory. *Social Policy* 4: 60–64.

Kren, G., and L. Rappoport, eds. 1976. *Varieties of psychohistory.* New York: Spring Publishing.

Kurzweil, R. 1999. *The age of spiritual machines.* New York: Penguin.

Lasky, R. 2002. Superego. In E. Erwin, ed., *The Freud encyclopedia* (551–52). New York: Routledge.

Levine, M. 2002. *A mind at a time*. New York: Simon & Schuster.

Lifton, R. 1961. *Thought reform and the psychology of totalism: A study of brainwashing in China*. New York: W.W. Norton.

Lifton, R., and E. Olson, eds. 1974. *Explorations in psychohistory: The Wellfleet Papers*. New York: Simon & Schuster.

Lippmann, P. 2000. *Nocturnes: On listening to dreams*. Hillsdale, NJ: Analytic.

Lorenz, K. 1965. *Evolution and modification of behavior*. Chicago: University of Chicago Press.

Maccoby, H. 1980. *Revolution in Judea: Jesus and the Jewish resistance*. New York: Taplinger.

Maccoby, M. 2002. Toward a science of social character. *International Forum of Psychoanalysis* 11: 33–34.

Mahoney, P. J. 1998. Freud's world of work. In M. Roth, ed. *Freud, conflict & culture: Essays on his life, work and legacy* (32–40). New York: Vintage.

Malcolm, J. 1983. *The impossible profession*. New York: Knopf.

Manuel, F. 1976. The use and abuse of psychology in history. In G. Kren and L. Rappaport, eds. *Varieties of phychohistory* (38–62). New York: Spring Publishing.

Marcuse, H. 1973. *Studies in critical philosophy*. Boston: Beacon.

Marius, R. 1999. *Martin Luther: The Christian between God & death*. Cambridge, MA: Belknap Press of the Harvard University Press.

Masson, J. M. 1985. *The assault on truth: Freud's suppression of the seduction theory*. New York: Penguin.

——, ed. 1986. *The complete letters of Sigmund Freud to Wilhelm Fliess*. Cambridge, MA: Harvard University Press.

Mazlish, B. 1974. The Mills: Father and son. In Lifton and Olson 1974, 136–48.

McGuire, W., ed. 1974. *The Freud/Jung letters: The correspondence between Sigmund Freud and C. G. Jung*. Princeton, NJ: Princeton University Press.

Miller, R. 2004. Darwin's lost theory and the crisis in Western education. In R. M. Eisler, ed., *Educating for a culture of peace* (42–55). Portsmouth, NH: Heinemann.

Morris, D. 1967. *The naked ape*. New York: McGraw-Hill.

Meyer, J., and B. Bauer. 2002. Ego psychology. In E. Erwin, ed., *The Freud encyclopedia: Theory, therapy and culture* (169–71). London: Routledge.

Neumann, E. 1963. *The great mother*. Princeton, NJ: Princeton University Press.

Nunberg, H., and E. Federn, eds. 1962. *Minutes of Vienna Psychoanalytic Society.* (vol. 1). New York: International Universities Press.

Olfman, S., ed. 2003. *All work and no play: How educational reforms and harming our preschoolers*. Westport, CT: Praeger.

——. 2005. *Childhood lost: How American culture is failing our children*. Westport, CT: Praeger.

——. 2006. *No child left different.* Westport, CT: Praeger.

Orwell, G. 1949. Reflections on Gandhi. In *A Collection of Essays*. New York: Doubleday Anchor.

Papadopoulos, R. 1997. Individual identity and collective narratives of conflict. *Harvest: Journal of Jungian Studies* 43(2): 7–26.

Perrin, N. 1967. *Rediscovering the teachings of Jesus*. London: SCM.

Phillips, A. 2001. *Darwin's worms: On life stories and death stories*. New York: Basic Books.

Pollack, R. 1997. *The creation of Dr. B: A biography of Bruno Bettelheim*. New York: Simon & Schuster.

Porter, R. 1988. *Gibbon*. London: Wiedenfield & Nicholson.

———. 1997. *The greatest benefit to mankind: A medical history of humanity*. New York: Norton.

Poster, M. 1980. *Critical theory of the family*. New York: Seabury.

Postman, N. 1982. *The disappearance of childhood*. New York: Vintage.

———. 2002. *Building a bridge to the eighteenth century*. New York: Knopf.

Rank, O. 1929. *The trauma of birth*. London: Routledge & Kegan Paul.

———. 1941. *Beyond psychology*. Philadelphia: E. Hauser.

Rapaport, D. 1950. *Emotions and memory*. New York: International Universities Press.

———. 1951. *Organization and pathology of thought*. New York: Columbia University Press.

Rappoport, L., and Kren, M. 1976. *Varieties of Psychohistory*. New York: Springer.

Reich, W. 1975. *Reich speaks of Freud*. Trans. T. Pol. Harmondsworth, UK: Penguin.

Riesman, D. 1950. The themes of work and play in the structure of Freud's thought. *Psychiatry* 13: 1–16.

Roazen, P. 1971. *Freud and his followers*. New York: Knopf.

———. 1976. *Erik H. Erikson: The power and limits of a vision*. New York: Free Press.

———. 1985. *Helene Deutsch: A psychoanalyst's life*. New York: Anchor.

———. 1986. *Brother animal: The story of Freud and Tausk*. New York: New York University Press.

———, ed. 1991. *Sexuality, war & schizophrenia: Victor Tausk's collected psychoanalytic papers*. Somerset, NJ: Transaction.

———. 2000a. What is wrong with French psychoanalysis? Observations on Lacan's First Seminar. In J. M. Rabate, ed., *Lacan in America*. New York: Other Press.

———. 2000b. *Oedipus in Britain: Edward Glover and the struggle over Klein*. New York: Other Press.

———. 2000c. *The historiographies of psychoanalysis*. New Brunswick, NJ: Transaction.

———. 2001. The exclusion of Erich Fromm from the IPA. *Contemporary Psychoanalysis* 37(1): 5–42.

———. 2002. *The trauma of Freud: Controversies in psychoanalysis*. New Brunswick, NJ: Transaction.

Rolland, R. 1926. *Mahatma Gandhi*. Trans. C. D. Groth. New York: Century.

———. 1929. *The life of Ramakrishna*. Calcutta: Vedanta Press.

Roth, M., ed. 2000. *Freud, conflict & culture: Essays on his life, work and legacy*, New York: Vintage.

Rubin, C. 2003, Spring. Artificial intelligence and human nature. *New Atlantis*, 88–100.

Ruether, R. 1975. *Faith and fratricide: The theological roots of anti-Semitism*. Eugene, OR: Wipf & Stock Publishers.

Runyan, W. M. 1982. *Life histories and psychobiography*. New York: Oxford University Press.

———, ed. 1988. *Psychology & historical interpretation*. New York: Oxford University Press.

Ruskin, J. 1985. *Unto this last and other essays*. Harmondsworth, UK: Penguin.

Rycroft, C. 1985a. On ablation of parental images, or the illusion of having created oneself. In P. Fuller, ed., *Psychoanalysis and beyond: Charles Rycroft* (214–32). Chicago: University of Chicago Press.

———. 1985b. Psychoanalysis and the literary imagination. In P. Fuller, ed., *Psychoanalysis and beyond: Charles Rycroft* (261–77). Chicago: University of Chicago Press.

———. 1991. On selfhood and self-awareness. In *Viewpoints*. London: Hogarth.

Sanders, B. 1995. *A is for Ox*. New York: Vintage.

Sandmel, S. 1978. *Judaism and Christian beginnings*. New York: Oxford University Press.

Santaniello, W. 1994. *Nietzsche, God and the Jews*. Albany: State University of New York Press.

Sartre, J. P. 1956. *Being and nothingness*. Trans. H. E. Barnes. New York: Philosophical Library.

Schachtel, E. 1959. *Metamorphosis: On the development of affect, perception, attention and memory*. New York: Basic Books.

Schlein, S., ed. 1987. *Erik H. Erikson: A way of looking at things: Selected papers*. New York: Norton.

Schneiderman, S. 1984. *Jacques Lacan: The death of an intellectual hero*. Cambridge, MA: Harvard University Press.

Schur, M. 1966. Some additional "day residues" to "the specimen dream" of psychoanalysis. In R. E. A. Loewnstein, ed., *Psychoanalysis—A general psychology*. New York: International Universities Press.

Schweitzer, A. 1911. *The psychiatric study of Jesus*. Trans. C. Joy. Boston: Beacon.

Segal, H. 1964. *Introduction to the work of Melanie Klein*. New York: Basic Books.

Shapiro, E., and Fromm, G. 1999. Erik Erikson's clinical theory. In B. J. Sadock and H. L. Kaplan, eds., *Comprehensive textbook of psychiatry* (1–30). New York: Williams & Wilkins.

Stepansky, P. 1999. *Freud, surgery & the surgeons*. Hillsdale, NJ: Analytic Press.

Strouse, J. 1974. *Women and analysis*. New York: Dell.

Sulloway, F. 1979. *Freud, biologist of the mind: Beyond the psychoanalytic legend*. New York: Basic Books.

———. 1991. Reassessing Freud's case histories: The social construction of psychoanalysis. *ISIS* 82(312): 245–75.

Swales, P. 2003. Freud, death and sexual pleasures: On the psychical mechanism of Dr. Sigm. Freud. *Arc de Cercle* 1(1): 5–75.

Tausk, V. 1919. On the Origin of the "Influencing Machine" in Schizophrenia. Reprinted in P. Roazen, ed., *Sexuality, war & schizophrenia: Victor Tausk's collected psychoanalytic papers* (Somerset, NJ: Transaction, 1991), 185–219.

Time. c. 1988. Retrospective: Psychology 1923–1988. Special issue: 66.

Tinbergen, N. 1953. *Social behavior in animals*. New York: Wiley.

———. 1954. The origin and evolution of courtship and threat display. In J. Huxley, A. C. Hardy, and E. B. Ford, eds., *Evolution as a process*. London: Allen & Unwin.

Tolstoy, L. 1985. *The kingdom of God is within you*. Lincoln: University of Nebraska Press.

Waelder, R. 1960. *Basic theory of psychoanalysis*. New York: International Universities Press.

Wallerstein, R., and L. Goldberger, eds. 1998. *Ideas and identities: The life and work of Erik Erikson*. Madison, CT: International Universities Press.

Weiner, H. 1966. Some thoughts on the concept of primary autonomous ego functions. In R. Loewnstein, L. Newman, M. Schur, and A. Solnit, eds., *Psychoanalysis—A general psychology: Essays in honor of Heinz Hartmann* (583–600). New York: International Universities Press.

White, R. 1959. Motivation reconsidered: The concept of competence. *Psychological Review* 66: 297–333.

Winnicott, D. W. 1989a. Erik Erikson: A review of *Childhood and Society* (1965). In C. Winnicott, ed., *Psychoanalytic Explorations* (493–94). Cambridge, MA: Harvard University Press.

———. 1989b. The mother-infant experience of reciprocity. In C. Winnicott, ed., *Psychoanalytic Explorations* (251–60). Cambridge, MA: Harvard University Press.

Wright, R. 1994. *The moral animal: Why we are the way we are*. New York: Vintage.

Wulff, D. A. 1997. *Psychology of religion: Classic and contemporary*. New York: Wiley.

Yankelovich, D., and W. Barrett. 1971. *Ego and instinct*. New York: Vintage.

Yershalmi, Y. H. 1991. *Freud's Moses: Judaism terminable and interminable*. New Haven, CT: Yale University Press.

Zimmer, H. 1968. The Indian world mother. In *The mystic vision: Papers from the Eranos Yearbooks, 6*. Princeton, NJ: Princeton University Press.

Index

213

About the Author

Daniel Burston was born in Israel, raised and educated in Toronto, and now lives in Pittsburgh, Pennsylvania, where he chairs the Department of Psychology at Duquesne University. He is married, with two children. Dr. Burston is the author of numerous books and articles on the history and theory of psychoanalysis, and the many points of convergence between psychology, philosophy, religion, and culture. His books and papers have been translated into Mandarin, Japanese, German, and Spanish.